Images of Australia

Gillian Whitlock has a PhD from Queen's University, Canada. She has edited *Eight Voices: Contemporary Australian Women's Writing* (UQP, 1989) and co-edited *Australian/Canadian Literatures in English* (Methuen, 1987). She is currently studying the writings of women travellers.

David Carter is a graduate of the University of Melbourne. He has edited *Outside the Book: Contemporary Essays on Literary Periodicals* (Local Consumption, 1991) and co-edited *Celebrating the Nation: A Study of Australia's Bicentenary* (Allen & Unwin, forthcoming). He is currently writing a biography of Judah Waten.

Both editors teach in the School of Australian and Comparative Studies at Griffith University.

Tracey Moffatt is an Aboriginal artist, born in Brisbane in 1960 and a graduate of the Queensland College of Art. She currently works as an independent filmmaker and photographer. The cover image, from her series "Something More" (1989), deals with clichés of Western cinema and other media which gloss over political issues of sexual and racial stereotyping.

Images of Australia

An Introductory Reader in Australian Studies

Edited by Gillian Whitlock
and David Carter

University of Queensland Press

First published 1992 by University of Queensland Press
Box 42, St Lucia, Queensland 4067 Australia
Reprinted 1993, 1994, 1996, 1999

Typeset by University of Queensland Press
Printed in Australia by McPherson's Printing Group, Victoria

Distributed in the USA and Canada by
International Specialized Book Services, Inc.,
5804 N.E. Hassalo Street, Portland, Oregon 97213–3640

Cataloguing in Publication Data
National Library of Australia

Images of Australia: an introductory reader in Australian studies.

Bibliography.

1. Australia — History. 2. Australia — Social life and customs.
3. Australia — Social conditions. I. Whitlock, Gillian Lea, 1953–   .
II. Carter, David, 1954–   .

994

ISBN 0 7022 2447 2

Contents

Introduction

Not long ago an historian writing on attempts to define Australia's national identity described his book as "the history of a national obsession". From a time even before the European invasion of the continent, in the myths of the Great South Land, right through to the latest Coca Cola television advertisements there have been attempts to capture "Australia" on paper — and on canvas or film, in statues or symbols, or in celebrations like the Bicentenary.

There are problems in defining the culture or society of Australia and what it means to be Australian. Our country, our nation, is far from being something we can take for granted. We might think of recent debates about Australia becoming a republic instead of a monarchy or controversies about changing the Australian flag. Or we might think of the vast number of different and often contradictory phrases which pop up from time to time in the media to describe Australia or parts of Australia: a multicultural nation, a British nation, an Aboriginal nation, an "American" nation, an Asian-Pacific nation, a sporting nation, a nation of slobs, a Christian society, a secular society, an egalitarian society, a racist or sexist society, the land of the outback, the land of suburbia, a workingman's paradise, a banana republic . . .

The predominant images of national identity may seem to be natural or inevitable products of "our" experience as a nation — those images which associate the Australian national character with mateship, the land or the beach for example. But things look rather more complicated when we start to consider questions about just who we mean when we use a phrase such as "*our* experience as a nation". Who is included and who excluded by the familiar images of national identity? Where do the images come from — who produces them? How have they changed over time? Do we have different, even contradictory images present together? What groups identify with what images?

The concept of national identity itself is relatively recent, a modern way of identifying and constructing communities. Australia is not alone in engaging in this process, for we will find versions of it in many societies across the globe. Tourism, to take one contemporary development, produces enormous incentives for regions and nations to come up with readily identifiable images of their distinctive qualities. Nevertheless, as a "new" — settler and immigrant — society in a land first occupied by another culture, Australia will arguably have an extreme case of "identity crisis". Although the source of images of national identity will often be found in the realm of myth and legend rather than in fact, such images nevertheless have real effects and consequences in government policy, in culture, and in the day to day lives of the nation's citizens.

This reader is not "yet another" attempt to define Australia, nor is it a collection of past attempts. It is, instead, a series of edited articles and narratives which contribute to debates about Australian identity. The selection targets a small number of key issues: definitions of the nation and national identity; Aboriginal identity; multiculturalism; women and national identity; the bush legend and suburbanism in Australian culture. These are some of the central issues around which writers, readers and researchers in the field of Australian studies have pursued the question of national identity — which is, in other terms, the question of the nature of Australian society and culture.

Although the articles gathered here were published originally over a period of time and in different contexts, a number of continuing influences and preoccupations emerge in the way later items refer back to earlier ones: Walter, Davison, Lake, Hirst and Glynn, for example, discuss Russel Ward; Reekie and Castles et al discuss Richard White; Hirst and Jefferis refer to Henry Lawson's famous story, "The Drover's Wife". The excerpts presented below have been internally edited for the present volume. Ellipses within paragraphs or asterisks between paragraphs indicate where the readings have been edited.

Part One, "Whose Australia?", takes the reader through what we might call the issues behind the issue — what are the correct, or at least the most useful ways of approaching the question of national identity? If we can never hope to define our national character once and for all, what can we gain nevertheless by studying the history of such definitions?

Parts Two to Four introduce readers to three important contemporary areas of controversy and change in notions of Australia and Australian character: Aboriginal assertions of their own identity, and the challenges to received versions of Australian history which this represents; the challenge of new ways of thinking of Australia as a multicultural rather than an "Anglo-Celtic" nation; and the rewriting of masculine versions of national identity by feminist writers and critics.

The final two parts focus on two areas of Australian experience which have been described, debated and "mythologised" perhaps more than any others — the bush and the suburbs. Some writers have argued that Australian values are essentially of the bush; others have argued that they are essentially products of the cities and suburbs; others again have argued that there's nothing "essentially" Australian to go looking for in the first place! Going back to Russel Ward's classic 1958 account of the "Australian legend", we then follow through a series of debates about the origins of legends of the bush and of different attitudes, sneering and celebratory, towards our cities and suburbs.

Each section of the reader has a short preface and a list which identifies selected further readings. Most readings also contain detailed references to useful books and articles.

Images of Australia: An Introductory Reader in Australian Studies has been designed as part of the national Open Learning Project. It may be augmented by the Study Guide, television programs, and Program Notes which comprise the Australian Studies Unit of this project, *Australian Studies: Images of Australia*. Nevertheless we believe that the collection of readings assembled here will stand alone, presenting a challenging body of writing and thinking around questions of national identity in Australia.

The editors would like to thank Tony Bennett, Mark Finnane, Bronwen Hammond, Kath Kerswell, Olwen Schubert and Jill Weber for their assistance.

Part One
Whose Australia?

Our readings will not begin by arguing for this or that version of the true Australia. Instead we will begin by taking a step back and trying to see what is involved in the whole process of attempting to define a national identity. We will even take a few more steps back to ask just what a nation is — or at least how the concept of "nation" has been used over time. We can then approach attempts at defining the Australian nation with a more historically informed and critical mind.

In Reading 1, "Defining Australia", James Walter introduces the general problem of national identities through an initial analysis of the different "Australias" presented to us on such an occasion as Australia Day. He then discusses some of the approaches to defining Australia which have come from historians and other commentators. The writers he examines approach the question of Australian society or culture from a range of very different perspectives, some stressing traditions or values, some stressing ideas and institutions, others stressing political and economic relations.

One of the influences on Walter's discussion is the work of Richard White. In Reading 2, "Inventing Australia", White argues that we can never arrive at accurate or adequate definitions of national identity. We need instead to look at who is responsible for the production of such definitions, how they function in the society, and whose interests they serve. His argument overturns many of the received ways of thinking about national identity. As well as an Introduction in which White briefly sets out a general model for understanding how images of the nation are produced, we have selected extracts from two chapters in which he applies this method to particular periods, the 1890s and the 1950s. White's argument can be "tested out" against the four advertisements from the 1950s, from the *Australian Women's Weekly,* reproduced on pages 54-57.

Further reading

Alomes, S., and Jones, C., eds, *Australian Nationalism: A Documentary History.* Sydney: Angus & Robertson, 1991.

Fiske, J., Hodge, B., and Turner, G., *Myths of Oz.* Sydney, Allen & Unwin, 1987.

Hergenhan, L., ed., *The Penguin New Literary History of Australia.* Ringwood: Penguin, 1988.

McQueen, H., *Social Sketches of Australia.* Ringwood: Penguin, 1991 (2nd ed.).

Moran, A., and O'Regan, T., eds, *The Australian Screen.* Ringwood: Penguin, 1989.

Rowse, T., and Moran, A., " 'Peculiarly Australian' — The Political Construction of Cultural Identity". In *Australian Society,* eds Encel, S., and Bryson, L., Melbourne: Longman Cheshire, 1984.

Schaffer, K., *Women and the Bush: Forces of Desire in the Australian Cultural Tradition.* Cambridge: Cambridge University Press, 1988.

Turner, G., *National Fictions: Literature, Film and the Construction of Australian Narrative.* Sydney: Allen & Unwin, 1986.

Walter, J., ed. *Australian Studies: A Survey.* Melbourne: Oxford University Press, 1989.

White, R., *Inventing Australia: Images and Identity 1688-1980.* Sydney: Allen & Unwin, 1981.

Reading 1

Defining Australia

James Walter

One way of starting to think about defining Australia is to see what people say about Australia at a time when they are explicitly encouraged to think about what it means. Australia Day, which is supposed to serve such a function, provides a good starting point. Australia Day, 26 January, intended as a day of national celebration and a focus for collective Australian consciousness, always gives rise to a flurry of newspaper commentary. Press coverage of this day for any year shows uncertainty about both the nature of the ceremony and exactly what it is that is being celebrated. The debate was particularly intense at the start of the Bicentennial year, and some striking examples of journalistic approaches to the issue can be found in the major metropolitan newspapers of 23-26 January 1988.

One theme common to such passages is that the commentators are wrestling with how to arrive at a sense of ceremony and of "Australia" that will have a meaning for all Australians. The impulse of the debate is unity, the rhetoric is that of "the nation", and the goal is the establishment of boundary distinctions, a community distinct from others, a clear idea of what is Australian and what is not. But there are considerable difficulties:

> Let us consider whether the day marking the anniversary of British settlement of the penal colony of NSW has relevance as a national day, given that the Aboriginal people were here long before, that other States celebrate different founding days — and that a very large proportion of Australia's . . . population has no link with Britain's long-gone colonial activities. Looked at from those aspects, January 26 has more divisive than nationally unifying properties. [Editorial, *Australian*, 1 February 1982]

There is, as this passage notes, the problem of what this celebration means to the Aborigines:

> We have to remember that to the Aborigines, the first settlement was straight-out invasion. [Fred Daly, *Age*, 23 January 1981]

> I used to hate history . . . Aborigines were given only a few derogatory mentions in the books . . . When they [the white community] say

this is a grand nation they are liars. Certainly some don't know. It's been very well-hidden. I think the Bicentenary should be an occasion not to celebrate, but for Australia to face its history. Until they face it, we won't have harmony. [Eve Fesl, OA, *Age*, 27 January 1988]

If we who have arrived in the past two centuries are to identify with this land, we must also identify with those who, for perhaps as long as 60,000 years have been the repositories of its wisdom and secrets, its human presence. To deny them is to deny ourselves . . . ["Shadows behind the celebrations", *Age*, 27 January 1988]

Taking a historical viewpoint, it is evident that the Australia of the Aborigines (with their unique visions of country and society) was a different Australia from that understood by predominantly British settlers (with their European visions of country and society) between 1788 and 1988.

Even within the white community, understandings of Australia may have altered radically, for instance after about 1830 when free-born immigrants began to supersede convicts and their administrators, roughly after 1890 when the native-born outnumbered immigrants, and again after 1950 with the large influx of immigrants from diverse, non-English speaking cultures.

[The Australia Day Committee] . . . is emphasising the arrival of the First Fleet as *one* of Australia's three big waves of immigration. First came the Aborigines, then the British settlers, many of them in chains. Finally, there was the flood of migrants after World War II. Australia Day, the Committee says, must include them all. [*Age*, 23 January 1981]

From a contemporary perspective it seems that distinctive views of Australia may be held by different cultural groups. It may make sense to talk of the Aboriginal-Australian Australia, the Italo-Australian Australia, the Anglo-Celtic Australia, and so on. Even within the dominant cultural group, whites of British descent, there is a distinction between those who see 26 January 1788 as the primary event in our national life and those who would rather celebrate another event (the proclamation of the Commonwealth on 1 January 1901 and Anzac Day on 25 April are popular contenders: the first alleged to be the birth of the nation, the second said to represent our "coming of age"):

today is not an anniversary of nationhood, for it commemorates the foundation of a British convict colony, not the formulation of a free and independent nation. We have another 13 years to wait before we can celebrate . . . the centenary of federation and the creation of the Commonwealth of Australia . . . 1901 was the peaceful birth of a nation. [Editorial, *Age*, 26 January 1988]

Those who would stay with the British founding moment presumably see Australia in terms of links with an older culture, a dependent component in a broader British cultural grouping. Those who would prefer to celebrate nationhood or "coming of age" presumably wish to emphasise Australia as something unique, having distinctive qualities and an independent cultural life. Such attitudes, too, arguably imply different Australias.

The underlying issue here is that a national day must have a unified meaning, yet if Australia means different things to different people it is not surprising that there continues to be so much debate about Australia Day. What is important to our discussion here is to consider how to come to terms with the definition of Australia at all if it is subject to such variation. Australia Day alerts us to this larger issue, and indicates that defining Australia does present a real problem.

Does "Australia" mean "the nation"?

Discussion of Australia's national day — even if only as a means of introducing the problematic status of "Australia" — brings the issue of Australia as a nation to the fore, and goes back to one of the initial questions: Does "Australia" mean "the nation"? That suggests a preliminary question: Where does the idea of "the nation" come from?

One writer who has attempted to clarify the process of debate about culture and society by drawing attention to the history of the meanings of words is Raymond Williams. He elaborates the framework of ideas and the historical context of "nation":

Nation . . . has been in common use in English from the late 13th century, originally with a primary sense of a racial group rather than a politically organised grouping . . . It is not easy to date the emergence of the predominant modern sense of a political formation . . . Clear political uses were evident from the 16th century and were common from the late 17th century . . . There was from the early 17th century a use of the nation to mean the whole people of a country, often in contrast, as still in political argument, with some group within it. The adjective *national* (as now in *national interest*) was used in this persuasive unitary sense from the 17th century. The derived noun *national*, which is clearly political, is more recent . . . *Nationality*, which had been used in a broad sense from the late 17th century, acquired its modern political sense in the late 18th and early 19th centuries.

Nationalist appeared in the early 18th century and *nationalism* in the early 19th century. Each became common from the mid-19th century. The persistent overlap between racial grouping and political formation has been important, since claims to be a *nation* and to have *national rights*, often envisaged the formation of a *nation* in the political sense, even against the will of an existing political *nation* which included and claimed the loyalty of this grouping . . . In practice, given the extent of conquest and domination, *nationalist* movements have as often been based on an existing but subordinate political grouping as upon a group distinguished by a specific language or by a supposed *racial* community. *Nationalism* has been a political movement in subjected countries which include several races and languages (as India) as well as in subjected countries or provinces or regions where the distinction is a specific language or religion or supposed *racial* origin . . .[1]

Look first at the matter of dating. "Nation" and "national", like much of the terminology used to discuss culture and society, were first used in a political sense in the seventeenth and eighteenth centuries. Coincidentally, these developments parallel the first settlement. Keep this in mind and ponder how the emergence of the distinctively modern ways of thinking about society generally affected the development of particular ideas about modern Australia.

Second, note that the idea of nationalism became common in the mid-nineteenth century, that is to say at roughly the same time as the number of white, native-born Australians came to equal the number of immigrants (the native-born became numerically dominant in the 1890s). Around this time both the native-born, and those who felt their future to be bound up with the new country, began to seek a means of distinguishing colonial society in a positive way from the British mainstream. The tool that came to hand for this purpose was nationalism.

There is a paradox here, since those who identified with the colony were looking for a way of making a break from "the old country" in a distinctively Australian way, and yet the means of doing this came not from something particular to Australia, but through concepts that were current in Europe at that time. Something supposedly new, an indigenous culture, could only be understood through dependence on a shared western framework of ideas.

Most of the contemporary discussion of Australia as a nation has been in terms of a political formation (that is, a politically organised and unified grouping) which Williams notes is the predominant modern sense. But the sense of a racial group should not be ignored — persistent emphasis on "British stock", the arrival of the first fleet as the moment of our birth, the exclusion of the Aboriginal population from political participation in the society and in the denial of their rights, the White Australia policy from the 1890s until the early 1970s — all suggest the importance that has been given to the racial (indeed racist) connotations of nationalism.

Williams refers to the uses of the concepts of nation and nationalism as a means of politically mobilising subject groups within a country. These concepts have been used to persuade people in a country controlled by an outside political grouping (say, India by the English in the nineteenth century) that they have unified common interests and should resist such outside control. Such uses remind us of the impulse fostered by Australian nationalists to assert a distinctive identity in the face of British (or, after the Second World War, American) dominance. But perhaps more important has been the sense of the nation to mean *the whole* people of a country, given that Australia is a federation of formerly discrete colonies. Hence the growing debate over Australian nationalism in the nineteenth century included attempts to persuade the people of all the colonies that they had shared interests that transcended colonial boundaries. Indeed, contemporary emphasis on nationalism can be understood as reasserting this argument. It is reasserted because first, states' rights issues (for instance in Queensland, where Queensland rights versus Canberra's encroachments is a familiar topic) and, second, the many identities existing in national life, are seen as antagonistic to the "whole people, common interests" concept.

When people talk of "the nation" to imply the whole people of a country — without reference to the many identities or diverse interests within it — they are encouraging acceptance of what Williams calls "the persuasive unitary sense" of the nation: much discussion of Australia Day exemplifies this attempt to get people to forget their differences. The problem is to decide whether such persuasive unitary uses have positive or negative effects. This will depend very much on personal opinion. From one point of view, nationalism may be regarded positively when it is seen as a way of persuading a group within a country (or political formation) to oppose external control or oppression to protect its national rights . . . Similarly, nationalism may be a movement which opposes imperialist exploitation. Or, as in Australia, the sense of being the whole people of a country may be a step towards overcoming the economic inefficiencies of colonial fragmentation, and a step towards cultural distinctiveness as against simple derivativeness (second-hand Britishness); at least these uses of the term "nationalism" are familiar in discussions of Australian history.

Alternatively, "nation" and "nationalism" may be used in many ways intended to invoke exclusivist, even racist, attitudes. They may also be used to persuade people to subordinate the particular interests of their own group to the common interests of the whole country. Nationalism calls on people to give such allegiance to the broad political grouping that there is reluctance to question the status quo. Although some groups are always better served by the status quo than others, the disadvantaged groups are prevented from realising this fully by their sense of allegiance to the nation; to question the status quo would be divisive, implying that the nation is *not* the whole people. Hence most of the people in a country are easily persuaded that the claims of particular, identifiable groups within a country are merely sectional and selfish and against the national interest, as Williams points out.

Nationalism has been central to the modern political order. To understand why this has been so, we need not only Williams's etymology, but also a more extensive theoretical and historical understanding of the uses of nationalism in the world.

Benedict Anderson offers a helpful interpretation of the rise of nations and nationalism in his *Imagined Communities* (1983). A nation, suggests Anderson, can be thought of as an "imagined community", with limited boundaries, a sovereign state which is the nation's emblem, and a sense of fraternity. The turning point of Anderson's concept of the nation is the notion of a community which is tied not by religion (as in medieval Christendom) or by kin (as in tribal or some types of peasant society), but by its "imagined" status. Why imagined? "because the members of even the smallest nation will never know most of their fellow-members, meet them, or even hear of them, yet in the mind of each lives the image of their communion".[2]

* * *

Looking back at Williams's discussion on nationalism suggests some qualifications to Anderson's argument. Williams remarks:

> claims to be a *nation* . . . often envisaged the formation of a *nation* in the political sense, even against the will of an existing political *nation* which included and claimed the loyalty of this grouping . . . *national-ist* movements have . . . often been based on an existing but subordinate political grouping . . .[3]

The imagined community may therefore not be as cohesive as Anderson implies. As shown below, there have always been groups *contending* to represent Australia's nationhood. Equally, we should not forget that we belong to communities that operate a sub-national level (Australians are sometimes encouraged to see themselves as Queenslanders or Victorians rather than Australians, for example). Still, there is little doubt that Anderson is right in suggesting that as an *ideal* the nation (always represented as cohesive) is the most dominant form of imagined community in contemporary life.

How does such an approach accord with the questions already raised about Australia, and with the way the "nation" has been discussed in the Australian context?

The birth of a nation?

The radical-nationalist historians who concentrated on "the Australian legend" were very much involved in the construction of an "imagined community". It was because of their pro-Australian stance they came to be called the radical nationalists. Among their most prominent exponents were Brian Fitzpatrick, Vance Palmer, Ian Turner, Russel Ward and Geoffrey Serle (historians), and Nettie Palmer, A.A. Phillips, Stephen Murray-Smith and Tom Inglis Moore (literary critics). They decided that the history of Australia was the history of those influences that produced what they saw as an "essentially" Australian character, and that truly Australian literature was that which gave expression to this character. The issue, therefore, was to decide what were the typical features of the Australian character, and then put together the story of the origins of these traits. The most widely read version of this argument was Russel Ward's *The Australian Legend* (1958):

> *The Australian Legend* . . . advances in four stages. Firstly, Ward argues that there is something identifiably Australian, a proletarian "mystique" . . . Secondly, this mystique evolved out of bush life, especially out of the conditions of labour and leisure of the nineteenth century nomadic bushmen . . . Thirdly, this set of values was transferred to city people by osmosis, especially through the fiction of popular writers such as Lawson and Furphy. Finally, the advent of socialist ideas . . . after about 1880 was accepted by these men quite quickly, since mateship — an integral part of the mystique — was a "natural socialist ethos". . .[4]

The radical-nationalist project has been described as historicist and evolutionary because it postulates a set of historically evolving circumstances that, at a certain point, produced the essentially Australian attributes. (The "legend" was usually seen as fully flowering in the 1890s.) This approach has been called contextualist because it seeks to evaluate literature on the basis of how representative or expressive it is of the society it portrays.

There has been a strong stream of radical-nationalist writing in the disciplines of literature and history, and it has shown a capacity to create powerful myths and memorable narratives. But it has also generated controversy and opposition. It has been said that radical nationalism, with its emphasis on the bush tradition and the digger, leaves women, Aborigines and urban dwellers out of the picture. It has concentrated on the working class, where the tradition's values are allegedly embodied, to the exclusion of understanding how the powerful monied classes affect society and history. It has accentuated particular narrow characteristics at the expense of saying anything of value about experiences universal to humankind. It has valued social-realist depictions of life in literature at the expense of abstract and expressionist modes, and has concentrated so much on the context of literary works that it has overlooked entirely the intrinsic literary merits of texts:

> The chief weakness of this body of writing lies in its unexamined assumptions, its narrow range of reference, its tendency to draw on the same repeated examples of national character or national literature, its failure to recognise the wider historical context, its tendency to inter-

pret historic figures and texts unhistorically, confounding topical significance with universal value, its didactic and doctrinaire tone.[5]

The most fundamental flaw is that it tends to assume as a starting-
point what might be expected to be proved at the end of the enquiry, that is, the existence of an Australian character.

* * *

While criticisms of the radical nationalists have been noted, it is il-
luminating to look at the features of their argument in more detail
in the context of Anderson's analysis . . . First, why was the legend seen as important? R.M. Crawford (1955) argues that it provides a self-picture that enables Australians to act with
confidence.[6] It is perhaps an idealised picture, but as it encapsu-
lates positive values it gives Australians something to live up to. It
was inevitable that this picture would derive from the bush ethos.
When Australians turned from Britain in search of some element
unique to life in this country, and in particular when artists sought
inspiration from distinctively Australian sources, where could
they find them, argues Crawford, but in the bush? The bush ethos
was *distinctive*, not *representative*. Artists, particularly the writers
of the *Bulletin*, made the bush accessible and gave it expressive
meaning for all Australians. Thus, because it filled an imaginative
need, it entered the Australian consciousness and *became* the Australian legend. And the values that had their basis in the experience
of bush life — self-reliance, egalitarianism, mateship — were en-
capsulated in the national character.

Vance Palmer (1954) deals with another aspect of this argument, suggesting that the Australian people in the latter half of the
nineteenth century were united in their ideals and aspirations, and
that they were consciously isolationist, determinedly working at
an imagined community of their own devising and rejecting outside influences: "there is no doubt that . . . the Australian people
were acutely aware of their isolation, and were determined to turn
to account the freedom it gave them by building up something like
an earthly paradise for the common man".[7] Writing in the early
1950s, Palmer was reacting to the divisions and bitterness of the
post-war world; he sought to heal the rift by harking back to a pro-
totype of fellowship that had supposedly thrived in less sophisticated times, uncorrupted by cities and untainted by outside

influences. His message is that under those conditions, Australians were fused in a common dream of the future. Palmer seeks to formulate a common experience (albeit one in the past) to serve as a point of reference for the present. That is, he does not argue that we could or should resurrect the 1890s (he refers to that period as a "dreamtime"), but rather that reference to the legend can help us transcend contemporary divisions, to recognise that we are "a people" and can again share a common dream, build a common culture.

The radical nationalists provide an exemplary case of nationalist historiography as we might identify it from Anderson's argument. Their history builds a picture of a society (imagined community) characterised by unity, consensus, solidarity and fraternity: "the nation is always conceived as a deep horizontal comradeship".[8] Certainly the radical nationalists locate those characteristics in the past, in the 1890s, but their purpose in invoking the legend is, as Vance Palmer shows, to regenerate just such an imagined community in the present. That is, their history is not a *description* of nation-building, but a part of the *process* of nation-building. The question is, was our society, even in the 1890s, so unified?

One problem in the method of the radical nationalists was their failure to account for groups and values that were at odds with the bush ethos. They took no account of contending versions of the imagined community. Manning Clark was a pupil and then colleague of Crawford's, emerged from much the same background as the radical nationalists, and shared their concerns. Yet even while they were working on their histories he sounded a discordant note. His "A letter to Tom Collins" (1943) is a direct challenge both to the bush ethos, and to the picture of unity advanced by Palmer.[9] In his letter Clark addresses Tom Collins (the pseudonym of Joseph Furphy, whose novel *Such is Life* was taken by many to express the values of the 1890s) as the representative of "mateship". But Clark shows mateship to be a thin base for culture, indeed a source of vulgarity. Mateship did serve as a comforter in a foreign environment, but it also served as a blind to conceal the way in which European man in Australia turned to ravaging the land. It is as if, bereft of the "civilised" values of the European heritage, the pioneers went on a rampage of exploitative destruction — and then erected the gaudy monuments of Australian society to hide their guilt and despair. There is much to be unhappy about, but the unhappy want us to confess our failure, to embrace the "old faith" (in other words, renounce "Australia" and resurrect the "old faith" of the British heritage). The élite, scornful of the vulgarity of mateship, did embrace the old faith, and continued to emulate the European conventions, while the people aped the mate's ideal; there was a rift in national life.

Manning Clark returned to fill in the detail of this rift in a later essay, "The quest for an Australian identity" (1979).[10] He attempts to explain the factors which shaped the colonial quest for self-definition, and how these impinge on the contemporary nation. He argues that a fundamental experience for the white settlers was the vastness and strangeness of the land itself, which seemed so much at odds with the purposes of civilised humans (understood purely in terms of European conditions) that it quite dismayed the first observers. Clark suggests that the apparent uselessness of the land and the fact that its European inhabitants felt compelled to apologise for it instilled an initial sense of inferiority in them . . .

Such experience, Clark suggests, is the lot of all colonial people. What is important for the sort of culture produced is the way colonists react. In his view, Australian colonists reacted either by rejecting European ideas and standards to reassure themselves that they were a unique breed, or by claiming to be no different from the British mainstream. Those who adopted the first mode denied inferiority through absurd boasting, cruel mockery of the depraved and corrupt dandies of civilisation, and a refusal to accept responsibility for their circumstances. The others tried as much as possible to be the same as those at the centre of civilisation, and became the toadies and flunkies of the British, aping their life-styles and values. These reactions may be seen as the grounding for what would later be the assertive "ocker" style, versus the precious Britishness of some of the middle class and some intellectuals. Thus instead of unity, Clark emphasises a rift, and introduces the important qualification that there are sub-national groups in contention over the "imagined community".

What may seem especially striking to the contemporary reader of these debates about the origins of nationalism is their gender blindness. Both the radical nationalists and the historians who engaged with them at the time, like Clark, wrote histories of *man*'s experience in Australia as if that were the whole story. The radical nationalists concentrated on male mateship. Clark, for his part, marked his initial difference from them by revealing mateship to be a species of self-deception, but then elaborated what Lake and Allen would rightly describe as a "masculinist" quest for identity.[11] This is not to criticise the nationalist historians, but to establish the nature of the cultural assumptions that dominated the period in which they wrote. Such debates show the implicit claims of men to be the arbiters of cultural meaning, claims that are now increasingly contested. And to engage with the bush legend is to beg the questions of whether women's experiences were the same as men's, what women's roles were in the saga of nation-building, and what such notions as national identity can possibly have meant for women.

* * *

Another approach which avoids essentialist idealisation (such as that encouraged by the bush legend) is one that looks closely at the politics of nationalism at transitional points in our past. To focus on politics and economics is still to engage with the public rather than the domestic world, but it does avoid over-investment in "individual/typical" (and, as we have seen, usually male) experience.

* * *

Humphrey McQueen is a scholar who stresses political and economic dimensions of explanation. In the article discussed here much of his argument is captured in the title "The suckling society".[12] This is a metaphor of dependence and immaturity pointedly at odds with the radical nationalists' depiction of the nation evolving to maturity and impelled by a people working in isolation with their own resources. Indeed, McQueen argues that Australia is not a society in its own right and can never be understood by looking for a "genuine essence". His thesis is that Australians have enjoyed an economically privileged position, but only because of a relationship with larger powers, and that hence we have remained passive, dependent and imaginatively subservient to those larger powers.

The basis of our privileged position has been the reliance of the economy on primary products which brought high returns for low investment. We have depended on major capitalist imperial powers to buy these products (first England, then the United States, now Japan), but none the less have been able to maintain the lifestyle of a developed western country without suffering the dislocation, privations and social division that the older countries experienced to get there. Strong central administration (a hangover from colonial days) and "tame cat" unionism resulting from relatively good conditions have led to social passivity. The effect has been a strongly anti-theoretical streak in national life. The fact that rewards flowed on smoothly meant that theory never became an issue: "People become interested in theory when they encounter problems that cannot be resolved . . . in practice".[13] Australia's relative immunity from the ravages of war and economic privation has meant that Australians have avoided prolonged periods of self-questioning. The result: we are ill-equipped to think about social problems, tend to rely on rules rather than reason (and punish deviance from rules), and resort to piecemeal social tinkering rather than reform when problems are encountered.

In consequence, McQueen argues, Australia is derivative, dependent and closed:

> derivative — derived from another society and place in such a way as to seriously impede the evolution of an appropriate relationship with our geographic and political surroundings;
> dependent — flows on from the derivativeness, in the sense of seeking innovations from outside our environment rather than through creative adaptations to it;
> closed — indicates the absence of an internal critique and is based on the repressively homogeneous nature of Australian society.[14]

Australia in McQueen's view is more an imperialist outpost than a colony. Because we look back to the metropolis which dictates every economic development we are insufficiently attentive to the local context and environment. Dependence stops us from taking initiatives — we look for innovations from outside, from "the old country" (or from "great and powerful friends") to solve local problems. Because the society has been repressively homogeneous (dominantly Anglo-Celtic, free of the conflictive class relations produced by economic turmoil in the old countries, and intolerant of divisions) it is closed to the sort of currents that would give rise to an internal critique. Indeed, these problems have been accentuated because we speak English. Sharing the language of the major powers of the nineteenth and twentieth centuries (England, then the United States), we had no barrier to stave off direct penetration, nothing to prevent permeation by every influence from the metropolitan centres. Cut off from the ferment that produced major critiques in those countries, we were yet swamped by every vogue of the English and American mainstream and so precluded from producing anything unique and resilient of our own.

* * *

The writers discussed here have proffered different arguments about Australia. They have also used very different forms of evidence: the radical nationalists mine creative works — ballads, poetry, stories, paintings — as expressive of the Australian character; Clark relies on historical records of reactions to the environment; . . . McQueen looks at transnational economics . . . Still, there are common features: the concern with who gives expression to or articulates national identity; the dilemma of what weighting to give to external influence as opposed to local experience; the interest in the origin of ideas (metropolitan or colonial), and drives (native and developed in isolation, or the flow-on of European trends); the suggestion that the search is for something distinctive rather than representative. All of these writers parallel Anderson in seeing the nation as an intellectual construct, though there is a spectrum from those who see it having definable, material origins (the radical nationalists) to those who see it wholly as invention.

This reading suggests that debates over some important issues, such as ''Australia'', will never be resolved because there are no right or true answers to such questions as ''What is the 'real' Australia?'' But there *are* processes of cultural production through which versions of Australia are arrived at, and academic enquiry should alert us to these. All of the writers considered offer some insight into varieties of cultural production (the groups involved, their motives and needs, the material circumstances, the origins of ideas), but only Richard White suggests a coherent core: ''When we look at ideas about national identity, we need to ask, not whether they are true or false, but what their function is, whose creation they are, and whose interests they serve".[15]

This points to the importance of the *context* of debate. We have seen that historical period and cultural environment affect the debate. For instance that the debate over Australia in the late nineteenth century was about "the national type" depended on two features of the context: first, native-born Australians were becoming dominant and looking for a means of explaining their difference from the British colonizers; and second, the nineteenth-century preoccupation with categorisation gave rise to the concept of national type at the same time, so that it became available for Australians to construct just such an explanation as was needed. In the context of the 1950s, however, White shows that the concept of national type was less effective in serving such a purpose. It had been discredited by the master race theories of the Second World War, and so people looked elsewhere, to the notion of a "way of life", to explain what was important about Australia.

* * *

The issues of context and motive (or intention) should also be read into the academic debate . . . For instance, the Clark of 1943 ("A letter to Tom Collins") speaks differently from the Clark of 1979 ("The quest for an Australian identity"): doubt has been replaced by the certainty that we must emphasise "the Australian" in our cultural goulash. And it is no accident that White, writing at a time when economic problems and theories about them were at the forefront of attention, gives mainly economic reasons as the factors which determine different inventions of Australia. Feminist historians in their turn have alerted us to the gender blindness of much of the historical writing on which we have relied. Motives play their part in all of this, and indeed most of these historians make no secret of them. Crawford and Palmer, for instance, thought Australia had lost its way and that a new consciousness of national identity would help us regain our footing; that is why they tried to revive the debate. Historians of women have been intent on restoring women's part as integral to national history. McQueen and Clark sought to confront us with the origins of our limitations as a precondition for changing our society.

These contexts and motives cannot be avoided. Academic

writers are not omniscient beings, able to stand outside society and see it objectively. They write at a particular time in a particular society. They are part of (and not detached observers of) the imagined community, and part of the process of cultural production by which it is constantly being re-presented to its participants.

Inventing Australia

Richard White

This is the history of a national obsession. Most new nations go through the formality of inventing a national identity, but Australia has long supported a whole industry of image-makers to tell us what we are. Throughout its white history, there have been countless attempts to get Australia down on paper and to catch its essence. Their aim is not merely to describe the continent, but to give it an individuality, a personality. This they call Australian, but it is more likely to reflect the hopes, fears or needs of its inventor . . .

There are no prizes for getting it right. There was no moment when, for the first time, Australia was seen "as it really was". There is no "real" Australia waiting to be uncovered. A national identity is an invention. There is no point asking whether one version of this essential Australia is truer than another because they are all intellectual constructs, neat, tidy, comprehensible — and necessarily false. They have all been artificially imposed upon a diverse landscape and population, and a variety of untidy social relationships, attitudes and emotions. When we look at ideas about national identity, we need to ask, not whether they are true or false, but what their function is, whose creation they are, and whose interests they serve.

Historians seeking to explain the origins of the Australian identity have often contributed to its mystification. We must remember that historians can be image-makers too. Many have sought to hunt out the "real" Australia or the "typical" Australian and, with their eyes fixed firmly on what is distinctive about the land and its people, have ended their search among the convicts, the bushrangers, the shearers, the gum trees and the wide open spaces. But these are merely some of the materials with which the images have been constructed. To understand why they have been put together in the way they have, we need to look at other forces, not particularly distinctive, contributing to the making of Australian identity. Three are especially important.

Firstly, national identities are invented within a framework of modern Western ideas about science, nature, race, society, nationality. Not only is the very idea of national identity a product of European history at a particular time, but each addition to the Australian identity has reflected changing intellectual needs and fashions in the West. In other words, not only is the idea of "Australia" itself a European invention, but men like Charles Darwin and Rudyard Kipling have contributed as much to what it means to be Australian as Arthur Streeton or Henry Lawson. The national identity is not "Born of the lean loins of the country itself", as one ardent nationalist put it, but is part of the "cultural baggage" which Europeans have brought with them, and with which we continue to encumber ourselves.

The second influence moulding ideas about Australian identity is the intelligentsia, or that class of people — writers, artists, journalist, historians, critics — most responsible for its definition. As the composition and influence of that class changes, so does their image of Australia. The nineteenth-century man of letters, the *fin de siècle* professional artist, the mid-twentieth-century academic have all viewed Australia differently, and have all had an interest in claiming their image as the only valid one since it strengthens their position in society. To understand the images which they produce, it is necessary to keep in mind their perception of themselves as a group, and their economic relationship with the rest of society.

This brings us to the third influence on images of national identity: those groups in society who wield economic power. National identities emerge to serve a social function. While the intelligentsia create the images, they do not work in a vacuum. The most influential images are those which serve the interests of a broader ruling class, on whose patronage the intelligentsia rely. Every powerful economic interest likes to justify itself by claiming to represent the "national interest" and identifying itself with a "national identity". In this view of the world there is no room for class conflicts, and sexual and racial exploitations are also obscured. The "national interest" must appear to work for the good of all.

However the relationship between the "ruling class" and the "national identity" is much more complex than this suggests. For one thing, groups outside the ruling class can develop their own ideas of national identity, although they are unlikely to be dominant. For another, the ruling class is not united, but contains powerful economic interests often in competition with one another. The result is that the national identity is continually being fractured, questioned and redefined. The earliest debates about Australia's identity involved conflicting British interests. In Australia, from the late nineteenth century to the mid-twentieth, the competition was between the previously dominant pastoral interests and the increasingly powerful local manufacturing interests. Australia's flocks were being challenged by Australia's factories. It is no coincidence that this period saw the most effort being spent in the promotion of competing Australian identities.

So we will never arrive at the "real" Australia. From the attempts of others to get there, we can learn much about the travellers and the journey itself, but nothing about the destination. There is none.

* * *

Bohemians and the bush

From the 1880s . . . a conscious attempt was being made in Australia to create a distinctively national culture. At the same time, it should be remembered, literary, artistic and musical nationalists in Europe and North America were also ransacking history, nature and folklore to construct national cultures. It was an outcome of the rise of European nationalism and, as in Australia, it was often associated with the growth of local manufacturing industry and an urban bourgeoisie. In Australia this would result in a new image which was to prove more powerful than any other. It was essentially the city-dweller's image of the bush, a sunlit landscape of faded blue hills, cloudless skies and noble gum trees, peopled by idealised shearers and drovers. Australians were urged to respond to this image emotionally, as a test of their patriotism. For the first time, a basic distinction was made between the image of Australia created by Europeans, and that created by Australians themselves. New European images were condemned as necessarily alien, biased, blurred; only the new Australian image could be clear, pure, true. The irony was that this new image inevitably remained trapped, as we shall see, within a European intellectual milieu.

A cultural generation gap

The new image was painted in against a background of dramatic changes in Australian life. A series of liberal measures — payment of MPs, graduated income tax, old age pensions, wages boards — saw an expansion in the role of government, and made the colonies the world's social laboratory, a title they occasionally shared with Germany. The long boom, which had led to a steady improvement in the overall standard of living from the time of the gold rushes, came to a sudden end in 1891. In the depression which followed, amid the great strikes, the bank crashes, drought and unemployment, the old faith in constant progress collapsed. Labour parties were formed to carry the voice of the unions into the colonial parliaments, where they established themselves surprisingly quickly, and gave a new direction and tone to political life. At the same time, a middle-class federation movement held its first convention in 1891, and by the end of the decade, without much fuss or enthusiasm, the six Australian colonies had voted to become a nation.

These changes in political direction were accompanied by a new vitality in the development of art and literature from the mid-1880s. A new generation of writers and painters was giving creative expression to a fresh approach to Australia. It was claimed that the Heidelberg School of painters, which emerged after 1885, saw Australia for the first time with Australian eyes. The same was to be said of the coterie of writers and artists attached to the *Bulletin*: the Australia they described was supposed to be more "real", more in tune with the democratic Australian temper. Too often this vitality is explained by saying Australian culture had reached its adolescence, marked by youthful exuberance, cockiness, pimples and all. But the analogy is a dubious one because it implies that a national culture "grows" of its own accord, quite apart from the rest of society. The reason that cultural life changed direction at this time, and produced a new image of Australia, is much more complex than that.

In the first place, a new generation had arrived. Most of the writers and artists coming into prominence in the late 1880s and 1890s were born in the 1860s, as Australian society settled down after the upheavals of the gold rushes. In 1890, J.F. Archibald, the *Bulletin*'s editor, was 34, A.B. Paterson was 26, A.G. Stephens and Edward Dyson were both 25, and Henry Lawson, Bernard O'Dowd, Steele Rudd, Randolph Bedford and E.J. Brady were all in their early twenties; among the artists, Tom Roberts was 34, Fred McCubbin 35, Arthur Streeton 23 and Charles Conder 22. Of the previous generation of artists, writers, teachers and critics, whose cultural values were being challenged, Marcus Clarke, Henry Kendall, Adam Lindsay Gordon and Louis Buvelot were already dead. Rolf Boldrewood was 64, Brunton Stephens 55, Ada Cambridge 46, Tasma 42 and Rosa Praed 39. Among those who taught the members of the Heidelberg School, Eugene von Guérard was 79 and G.F. Folingsby 60. Among other artists of that generation, William Strutt and Nicholas Chevalier had returned to Europe and W.C. Piguenit was 54, while James Smith, the most influential critic of the day, was 70, and the young Charles Conder was looking forward to the day when "the irrepressible Mr. J.S. [would] be gathered to his fathers".[1] It was little wonder then that the younger generation saw themselves as rebelling against an outdated and stale set of cultural standards. They could believe they were presenting a vision that was new and fresh, and could make much of the virtue of youth.

The difference between the generations was accentuated by the fact that the older generation was centred in Melbourne while the younger generation generally looked towards Sydney. Indeed the sheer dominance of the cultural values of an older generation in Melbourne helped to drive many — Archibald, Julian Ashton, Roberts, Streeton, Victor Daley, and later Hugh McCrae and the Lindsays — to make the move to Sydney. There they found a more ready acceptance than in the Melbourne cultural establishment, centred on respectable journals or the National Gallery of Victoria. There was more work available for both writers and artists on the *Picturesque Atlas of Australia* — a large-scale project of the 1880s — and the *Bulletin*; and the New South Wales Art Gallery, with Ashton's encouragement, began to buy the work of the Heidelberg School. However, the differences between the generations and between Melbourne and Sydney, while emphasising the break made by the writers and artists of the 1890s, does not explain the direction they took.

What helps explain their direction towards what has been seen as a distinctively national culture, is the fact that the younger generation was more likely to be Australian-born. The Melbourne cultural establishment was largely made up of men who had arrived in Victoria around the time of the gold rushes, and who saw in culture a means of civilising and educating a materialistic democracy. The 1890s generation, predominantly native-born, felt more at home in the Australian environment and felt more need to promote an indigenous culture.

But this is a far from adequate explanation for the new direction, although some later writers have made do with it. Harpur, Kendall, Boldrewood, Praed, Tasma and Piguenit were all born in Australia or migrated as children, yet they still shared the cultural values of their immigrant contemporaries. On the other hand, important names among the new generation — although not the most important — were immigrants: Conder, Daley, Will Ogilvie, D.H. Souter and Price Warung all left Britain as adults. Both groups still looked to Europe for cultural attitudes and philosophies: Australia remained, undeniably, part of a broad Western culture. Both groups, in varying degrees, looked to Australia for imagery and inspiration, and although that perhaps came more naturally to the 1890s generation, it could still be artificial and painfully self-conscious, a matter of hunting around for "local colour". It is significant that the younger generation itself liked to attribute its image of Australia to the entrance of the Australian-born on to the cultural stage. However it is not enough to argue simply that a native culture had replaced an immigrant one.

The professionals' revolt

The real break between the two generations can be found in the changes taking place in the late nineteenth century — in Europe and Australia — in the role of the artist and his audience, in the way in which "culture" was produced, its *raison d'être*, the meaning of the word itself. The intelligentsia in Western society was being professionalised. Science, art and literature were increasingly the province of full-time professionals rather than educated amateurs or men of letters with a private income. Although the process was a gradual one, the sheer growth of the professional intelligentsia is striking. In Britain for example, the number of "authors, editors and journalists" listed in the census rose from 2148 to 14,000 in the 40 years after 1871.[2]

That increase owed much to the new readership created by virtue of the 1870 Education Act, and to technological changes which lowered the cost of paper and type-setting. The market for British writers, like the market for British manufacturers, was expanding internally. The new literature of Kipling, Conan Doyle, Rider Haggard and Robert Louis Stevenson catered for a new class of consumer, as did the new journalism with its illustrations, advertising, sensationalism and immediacy. The standard mid-Victorian novel — what Kipling called the "three-decker" because it normally filled three volumes[3] — was giving way to shorter novels, short stories and popular ballads in cheap illustrated editions. Their aim was not to moralise to the middle class, but to attract and entertain a mass market. At the other extreme, the aesthetic movement around Oscar Wilde and J.A.M. Whistler reacted to the same changes by promoting "Art for Art's Sake" and flaunting their intellectual exclusiveness and studied decadence. Even so, Wilde's *The Picture of Dorian Gray* could still appear in *Lippincott's Monthly Magazine* in the same year (1890) as novels by Doyle and Kipling.[4] A mass audience paid too well to be ignored.

The same changes were taking place in Australia and throughout the Western world. In Victoria between 1881 and 1891, the number of "authors and literary persons", including journalists and reporters, rose from 461 to 1292, while "artists" rose from 734 to 1502. After 1891 the census categories were altered, so they are no longer comparable with the earlier ones, but the figures given in the table below give a rough indication of what happened to the local "intelligentsia" after 1891.

Authors, editors,		1891	1901	1911
journalists:	NSW	530	595	955
	Vic.	534	606	702
Artists, painters,				
art students:	NSW	341	427	684
	Vic.	471	545	609

It is clear that the 1890s depression slowed down the growth of the intelligentsia in both colonies, but after that, the greater cultural vitality of New South Wales is marked. It is also noticeable that Australia was supporting a much larger "intelligentsia" for its size than was Britain: in 1911, authors, artists and journalists accounted for about one in 3200 of Britain's population, while in Australia the figure was about one in 2100.[5]

Most striking is the fact that a large new community of professional writers and artists had emerged in Australia in the 1880s.

* * *

Both writers and artists were forming part of a new intellectual community, a professional "Bohemia" in which they could see themselves as men committed to their art. In this way, through both their professionalism and their bohemianism, they distinguished themselves from those educated middle-class laymen who were committed to cultural improvement and had dominated the cultural establishment since the gold rushes.

Accompanying the developing sense of professional identity was a new attitude to the role of the artist and the purpose of art. The earlier dominance of the layman or lay critic as cultural arbiter had led to a utilitarian approach to art and literature. Art was seen as the servant of society: it served morality, it educated the people, it could even aid commerce.[6] Culture had become the great improver, the civiliser of nations, and so art galleries and libraries had been built in industrial Britain and materialistic Australia. John Ruskin, the epitome of the gentlemanly intellectual all-rounder, had dominated the British cultural establishment since the 1850s with his arguments about the moral function of art.

This view of art began to be challenged in the 1870s in Britain with the arrival of the "aesthetic movement", proclaiming that art existed, not for morality's sake but for art's sake . . .

As the artist became professional, he claimed art as his province alone, not that of laymen or critics whom he increasingly portrayed as philistine boors. In time the moral earnestness of Ruskin was to give way to the sensuality, cosmopolitanism and exclusiveness of the aesthetes, but only after a struggle.

* * *

The new writers associated with the *Bulletin* also openly rejected the old values of the British cultural establishment. Few could have been quite as irreverent at Ruskin's death in 1900 as A.G. Stephens of the *Bulletin*, who gaily debunked the "superfluous veteran" as one who "intellectually . . . does not count", and whose theories of art were "imaginative gibberish".[7] Irreverence provided the starting-point for the new image of Australia which the *Bulletin* writers helped create. The genial bohemianism, the scoffing at Victorian morality, the idealisation of the "Common Man", the commitment to naturalism, were all aspects of a common revolt against received literary values. They were not initially distinctively Australian. Even the *Bulletin*'s republicanism was based on an English radical tradition and Irish nationalism.[8] It had little to do with a sense of Australian identity or even the earlier Australian republican tradition derived from identification with America.

* * *

The new bohemianism centred on the *Bulletin* office, bohemian clubs such as the Dawn and Dusk Club in Sydney and the Cannibal Club in Melbourne, and the various artists' camps where the new generation of painters discussed their work, smoked, talked, shared picnics and enthusiasms with their friends, and taught their students, usually girls conforming to the style of the "New Woman". In a letter to Roberts, Streeton reminisced about one of the camps:

> How we made sketches of the girls on the lawn. The lovely pure muslin, and gold, sweet grass-seeds and the motherly she-oak with its swing, spreading a quiet blessing over them all . . . the silver dusk of night simplified the group of quiet happy boys and girls.[9]

Lionel Lindsay likened this happy life to "pagan Greece, before Christianity came to throw its ominous shadow of melancholia and 'purity' upon the blytheness of life."[10]

Their sense of community tended to be exclusive and elitist. They shared Clarke's scorn for Philistines, but extended it to nonprofessionals and "the public". As artists they claimed for themselves, as we have seen, a higher appreciation of art. As professional artists, they demanded more say on artistic matters in the established art societies, which were dominated by amateurs and laymen intent on cultural improvement. The result was that in 1886 the younger professionals left the Victorian Academy of Art to form the Australian Artists' Association, and in 1895 a similar group split off from the Art Society of New South Wales to form

the New South Wales Society of Artists. The names of the new societies were significant, for they implied the recognition of professional interests which needed protection . . .

The Dawn and Dusk Club was also exclusive. Its membership
included writers (Daley, Lawson, Brady, Bedford) and artists
(Roberts, Mahony), but excluded "the detestable Philistine", as
one member put it, in order "that soul may commune with soul
alone" . . . They were also exclusive in that they tended to be
young single men, firmly rejecting middle age and respectability;
when they did get married it was often to the sisters of their fellow
bohemians.[11] In contrast, the older generation of writers was
often linked by marriage to the colonial gentry.[12]

France, Bohemia and the Bush

These then were the dimensions of the new generation's revolt:
professionalism, youthful hedonism, fellowship and a rejection of
the Victorian era's values. By the 1890s, "Victorian" was already
a derogatory term.[13] Out of that revolt — almost as a by-product
since the same revolt was taking place in London — the new image
of Australia emerged. It was not seen then as being particularly
nationalistic. The rejection of the values of the British cultural establishment did not necessarily involve the celebration of peculiarly Australian ones. Indeed the revolt could take other
directions altogether.

There was, for instance, an attraction towards France. As in
Britain, French realism in both literature and art was an important
influence on the younger generation. Paris was the new centre of
the art world, and French literature was considered by people such
as A.G. Stephens and Francis Adams as setting new standards for
local writers. It went deeper still. The *idea* of France appealed. As
O'Dowd put it:

> A wind hath spirited from ageing France
> To our fresh hills the carpet of romance.[14]

Archibald, the greatest Francophile of all, changed his name from
John Feltham to Jules Francois, allegedly because of his "inborn
objections to everything that sounded English".[15]

* * *

A bohemian outlook could also lead towards a generalised political radicalism: republicanism, free thought and socialism of a sort found recruits among *Bulletin* writers. A series of "progressive" causes were linked by the *Bulletin* and, later in the 1890s, by the emerging labour parties, and these were contrasted with prevailing conservative British values. But that radicalism, and the contrast, were themselves imported from Britain as part of the international urban culture. It is significant that labour parliamentarians were more likely to be recent immigrants and less likely to be native-born, than their non-labour colleagues, a point that is often lost in discussion of radical nationalism.[16] It is also worth noting that both bohemianism and radical republicanism were essentially urban, part of a world of artists' studios, cafes, bookshops, boarding houses and political meetings which could only exist in large cities such as Sydney or Melbourne.[17] Victor Daley acknowledged the allure of this world:

The town's confined, the country free —
Yet, spite of all, the town for me.[18]

In rejecting the values of the cultural establishment, the new generation could turn to the idea of France, or the idea of bohemia. Most importantly, they could also be attracted to a cluster of symbols and principles which they associated with Australia: sunlight, wattle, the bush, the future, freedom, mateship and egalitarianism. This, like other images of Australia, was essentially artificial. It did not spring, in full bloom, from the Australian soil, but rather grew out of a set of attitudes to which the new generation had attached themselves and which provided a reference point for their revolt. They generally found this new Australia, which they thought of as the "real" Australia, in the outback.

While this image of Australia was usually developed in the city, there were occasional forays into the bush to gather material. For his most consciously "Australian" works — *Shearing the Rams, The Breakaway* and *The Golden Fleece* — Roberts visited sheep stations to make sketches, then finished the paintings in his city studio. His response was typically romanticised: "If I had been a poet . . . I should have described the scattered flocks on sunlit plains and gum-covered ranges, the coming of spring, the gradual massing of the sheep towards the one centre, the woolshed".[19] Henry Lawson too found what he had wanted on his trips, except that he had gone with a different set of expectations and in a season of drought:

> Further out may be the pleasant scenes of which our poets boast
> But I think the country's rather more inviting round the coast.
> Anyway, I'll stay at present at a boarding house in town
> Drinking beer and lemon squashes, taking baths and cooling
>   down.[20]

The most ludicrous expedition was surely that undertaken by four self-styled bohemians associated with the Dawn and Dusk Club. One of them, George Taylor, a *Bulletin* artist, described it in his nostalgic *Those Were the Days*:

> It was decided that a real back-country adventure should be experienced. What was the good of posing as Australian artists or writers unless one had been "there". Harry Lawson got his "local" color[sic] through personal experience, so it was up to the other Bohemian boys to do something in that line.

They took a train to Byrock, the first time any of them had been so far from Sydney. They waved wildly to any swagman they saw "as if to a 'brother of the track' " but ended up hiring a horse and buggy to carry their portmanteaus and other gear. On the road, they were soon depressed by the "soul-destroying sameness", relieved only by "dreams of city pleasures and delights", so they turned off the track to the Bogan River. On reaching it,

> It was only the work of a minute for Jessie to be unharnessed, and with four naked, joy-wild excitedly shouting Australians, to be trotting down to the welcome water to drink, to bathe and splash around with the very joy of living.
> Ah, it was worth while living in the back country to have such sport. "City life holds no joys like these", said Artie. He was going to string some impromptu rhymes together, but thought better of it.
> Oh, those were the days!
> Time can never efface the joy times spent by the bank of that Bogan River. Gone were all thoughts of Gongolgan and Bourke . . . It was unanimously agreed to stay by that lovely river till it was time to go home.

Then they returned.

> Back to Sydney! Back to Bohemian haunts; and four happy chaps brought back the "local" color [sic] to tinge their story, verse and picture for ever more.[21]

Taylor's account of getting "local" colour is a good illustration of just how self-conscious and artificial the process could be. The bush simply provided a frame on which to hang a set of preconceptions. At the same time it shows how the sense of freedom, comradeship and youthful spirits associated with the bush overlapped with the values which they infused into their bohemia. Thus, while it is possible to isolate the different directions rebellion could take, the various strands — outback Australia, bohemia, even France — were in fact closely interwoven. There were differences of emphasis, but men such as Francis Adams and A.G. Stephens could quite comfortably combine passionate attachments to France, the bush, radical politics, the artist and Australia, all to some degree based on a rejection of dominant British cultural values.

* * *

Even the masculine exclusiveness of the bush ethos was repeated in the bohemianism of the 1890s. Women were as out of place in the Dawn and Dusk Club as they were in the shearing shed. George Taylor's emphasis on being "Bohemian boys" together, for example, excluded all women except an artist's model, "our sexless pal". For Arthur Jose, the romance of Sydney's bohemia was on the whole:

> devoid of feminine interest . . . It was not that kind of romance. There were a few girls among the Boy Authors, but they were tolerated there mainly because they made tea and organised refreshments.

The only women writers who managed to penetrate that particular charmed circle were Louise Mack, who "was on the whole taken as a joke by her fellow Boy Authors", and Amy Absell, who married the artist George Lambert and then "absorbed her ambitions in her husband's".[22]

One reason for this smothering sexism was that "feminine" values were associated with the "respectability" which the young bohemians condemned: they talked of Melbourne's literary circles as being "obsessed with respectability, the respectability which they believed fervently to be of the ruling English type, for which Ada Cambridge wrote her polite and soothing novels".[23] Another reason women were excluded was that their interest was assumed to be "amateur" when the men were striving to protect their professional interests. Finally the 1890s generation joined in the idealisation of the "masculinity" of "The Coming Man", and helped forge his image: Streeton, for example, when he watched railway builders in the Blue Mountains, admired the "big brown men . . . toiling all the hot day", "the big, stalwart men . . . big and bronzed".[24] There were women of this generation, notably Mary Gilmore and Barbara Baynton, who competed effectively as writers, but necessarily on the men's own ground. Women artists, although they actually outnumbered males at the National Gallery School, were not awarded the major prizes or scholarships, and generally failed to break into the professional bohemia of the period.[25] It is significant that at a time when women were making advances in politics and education, they were largely excluded from the newly professional artistic community of the 1890s. They had received more recognition in the earlier generation, and were to become prominent again after World War One.

The real Australia

Thus this new intelligentsia carried into their image of the bush their own urban bohemian values — their radicalism, their male comradeship, their belief in their own freedom from conventional restraints — and presented it as the "real" Australia. They also projected on to their image of the bush their alienation from their urban environment: they sought an escape from what the city represented. A few escaped in other directions, Brady to sea, Becke to the islands, and found there a similar freedom. Most chose the bush as an imaginative refuge. The contrast between the cramping, foetid city and the wide open spaces became a cliché for that generation: Paterson's "Clancy of the Overflow" was its most famous expression. In part it represented a personal response to the poverty endured by many of the artists and writers, the sort of life which, as Lawson put it, "gives a man a God-Almighty longing to break away and take to the Bush".[26]

But it was more than this. The city could be identified with the values of the older generation, their respectability, their philistinism, their faith in progress which had turned sour in the depression. Even in 1885, Francis Adam's objection to Sydney had been that it was "the home-elect of the six-fingered and six-toed giant of British Philistinism".[27] Later he would turn with relief to the bushman, his version of "The Coming Man", as Australia's savi-

our from the soft, debilitating city. Paterson also contrasted
Clancy, the drover, with the city:

> . . . the hurrying people daunt me, and their pallid faces haunt me
> As they shoulder one another in their rush and nervous haste,
> With their eager eyes and greedy, and their stunted forms and
>   weedy,
> For townsfolk have no time to grow, they have no time to waste.[28]

It is important to note that this city-bush contrast was expressed
in very similar terms to those used by Kipling in depicting the relationship between the metropolis and the fringes of empire. Lawson resented any comparison with Kipling. However they were
writing for similar audiences, and as a result had the same relationship to the dominant literary culture and adopted similar literary forms. The cheap, popular editions of the work of Lawson
and others of his generation, published and tirelessly promoted by
the *Bulletin*, Angus and Robertson and, later, the New South
Wales Bookstall Company, were modelled on the early Macmillan
editions of Kipling.[29] The two writers also espoused many of the
same values, particularly in the identification of their heroes of the
wide frontier — Kipling's bearer of the "white man's burden",
Lawson's "real" Australian — with the cluster of ideas embodied
in "The Coming Man" . . . The attachment of Lawson and others of his generation to the bushworker, as opposed to the older
generation's preference for the squatter, was also parallelled in
Kipling's idealisation of the "Common Man" over the educated
English gentleman.

Russel Ward has pointed out that the "noble frontiersman"
provided Western culture with a symbol of escape from urban, industrial civilisation, a romanticising of imperial expansion, and a
focus for patriotic nationalist sentiment, especially in "new" societies.[30] Ward himself was concerned with the third element, and
argued that the nationalist image of the Australian bushman had a
distinctively Australian inheritance in the nomadic bush-workers
of the outback. However all three elements are so closely interwoven that the isolation of any one is distorting. We have already
seen the contribution of urban bohemianism to the imagery of
bush life. It must also be remembered that the bush-worker was an
integral part of empire and, when he was ennobled as "the
Bushman" and his capacity for drunkenness and blasphemy for-

gotten, contributed much to imperial ideology. Even the London *Times* could "value him as a part of the Empire . . . to leaven with his fine youthfulness our middle-aged civilisation".[31]

The imperial significance of the bush-worker rested on two points. Firstly the bush-worker, rather than the urban or agricultural worker, gave Australia its identity in the empire. The economic basis of empire was that the colonies provided a variety of raw materials for English industry. Australia's main contribution was wool. With that in mind, the suggestion could be made in 1849 that in the decoration for the new Houses of Parliament at Westminster, Australia should be represented by mines and sheep stations.[32] Australian shearers and squatters featured prominently in the literature of empire. Like the furhunter of Canada and the backwoodsman of the United States, they had been in the vanguard of white settlement of new frontiers: they had entered an alien landscape and made it profitable.

In the late nineteenth century the Australian economy was diversifying. From the imperial point of view the wool industry remained of special significance, and its drovers and shearers continued to contribute to the romance of empire. However, in the colonies, local manufacturing interests, particularly in Victoria, were increasingly influential in directing economic policy in their own interests. The idealisation of the bush-worker by Tom Roberts, A.B. Paterson and others was a reaffirmation that the wool industry was the "real" basis of the Australian economy and of Australian prosperity, despite its imperial connections.

The second contribution that the bush-worker made to empire was in his role as "The Coming Man" on whom the new imperialists pinned their hopes. The qualities which he was believed to display were the newly-respectable qualities of "The Coming Man" on the fringe of empire: comradeship, self-confidence, generosity, restlessness, resourcefulness. It was to such men, "the men who could shoot and ride" as Kipling put it, that the empire looked for its superior cannon fodder. So Australia chose contingents of "Bushmen" to send off to the Boer War, and was thrilled when Chamberlain was impressed enough to ask for more.[33] In this light, bush-workers were respectable enough for a contingent of mounted shearers to be selected to lead the procession at the Federation ceremonies in 1901. They had the full approval of the conservative *Sydney Morning Herald* which praised the shearers as:

> men that could be sent anywhere to do anything, from shearing to soldiering — men who would give a good account of themselves in any company in the world . . . fine-looking backblocks men with a certain freedom of bearing and suggestion of capability that was very effective.[34]

So when the professional writers and artists of the 1890s contributed to the idealisation of the bush-worker, they did so within a more general context of changing Western ideas, tastes and attitudes, which included new imperialism, Social Darwinism and the exalting of the common man, as well as the desire to create a nationalist symbol.

Much the same can be said about the image of the Australian landscape popularised by the *Bulletin* writers and the Heidelberg School artists. In terms of expressing what was distinctively Australian, the new generation dealt with little that was entirely new. The lost child, for example, almost a Jungian archetype in the Australian landscape, was used by McCubbin and Furphy, as it had been used earlier by Marcus Clarke and Henry Kingsley. Bushfire, flood and drought, pioneering, campfires, bush and station life, even the artistic problems of the gum tree, can all be found in the literature and art of both generations. Both were aware of the problems of "local colour" and of the temptation to reduce Australian literature to conventional wattle and bushrangers, a temptation which a few writers in both generations managed to resist. Both generations realised that it was possible to be "too" Australian, by unnaturally adding swagmen and gum trees at every opportunity.[35] Just as the younger generation owed institutional debts to their elders, they also owed much to their sketching-in of the possibilities for the writer and artist in Australia.

The differences between the generations in their depiction of landscape were essentially differences in taste. In terms of subject, for example, fashions had changed. Ruskin had turned the Swiss Alps into "monuments of moral grandeur"[36] and Chevalier, Piguenit and von Guérard had done the same to the mountains of Tasmania and northern Victoria. By the time of the Heidelberg School, fashion demanded a more intimate approach to landscape, with gentler scenery and more attention to colour values, space and sunlight than to careful drawing, dramatic romanticism or heroic gloom. Similarly in poetry, Kendall's romanticism had attracted him to the eastern seaboard and fern-filled gullies; by the 1890s, fashion led Paterson towards sunlit plains and wide open spaces.

Changes in taste also demanded a different treatment of the landscape. By the 1890s, many critics were condemning one of the classic descriptions of the Australian landscape:

> What is the dominant note of Australian scenery? That which is the dominant note of Edgar Allan Poe's poetry — Weird Melancholy . . . The Australian mountain forests are funereal, secret, stern. Their solitude is desolation. They seem to stifle, in their black gorges, a story of sullen despair . . . The lonely horseman riding between the moonlight and the day sees vast shadows creeping across the shelterless and silent plains, hears strange noises in the primeval forest, where flourishes a vegetation long dead in other lands, and feels, despite his fortune, that the trim utilitarian civilisation which bred him shrinks into insignificance beside the contemptuous grandeur of forest and ranges coeval with an age in which European scientists have cradled his own race . . .[37]

Marcus Clarke had written this in his preface to the poems of Adam Lindsay Gordon in 1876 but it had been adapted from descriptions of paintings by Buvelot and Chevalier which he had written earlier. From the 1890s on, this preface was continually held up as typical of a negative, alienated "English" view of the Australian landscape, and compared unfavourably with the cheerful, sunlit vision of the 1890s generation. They professed to be seeing the landscape positively for the first time, because they saw it with "clear Australian eyes", ignoring the fact that the settlers of the early nineteenth century also had a favourable image of the Australian landscape.[38] . . .

Making a legend

From where, then, comes the legend that it was only in the 1890s that writers and artists first gave expression to the "real" Australia, seeing it for the first time with "Australian eyes" rather than with the eyes of an alienated exile? It was a common view after the Second World War, when many intellectuals sought to give the national identity a radical heritage. It was a common idea too in the 1920s, when national insularity sought a pure and uncorrupted Australian golden age. But the legend can be traced even further back, to the "Bohemian Boys" themselves. They simply created their own.

After all, their commitment to naturalism required them to portray the "real" Australia with the implication that all other versions of the landscape were artificially contrived. It was also a matter of self-interest. The *Bulletin* created its own legend as a sensible commercial enterprise: self-advertisement was part of the new journalism. For the writers and artists, it was in their professional interest to adopt and popularise a nationalist interpretation of Australian cultural development, to perpetuate the idea that the particular image of Australia which they had created was somehow purer, and more real, than any other.

* * *

In effect, Australian intellectuals were doing what Australian manufacturing interests were doing when they sought to protect local industry by tariffs, and advertised local products as superior to foreign imports. Once they were aware of themselves as a professional group, writers and artists began to make a claim for a sort of intellectual protectionism, seeking support for the local cultural industry. When faced with the argument that "creative intellectual work" could easily be imported from Britain,[38] they retorted that the local product was superior, at least in Australian conditions. Joseph Furphy sub-titled his *Rigby's Romance* as *A "Made in Australia" Novel.* In 1889, Victorian artists asked the Minister for Customs to impose a £10 duty on imported paintings. In 1910, one group formed an Australian Writers' and Artists' Union to protect their interests, but they were superseded by the Australian Journalists' Association. In 1912 writers and artists demanded tariff protection from imported magazines and novelettes to save "the pioneers of culture" in Australia from "semi-starvation".[39] The irony was that the pastoral industry, which played such an important role in the national image developed by this generation, was always staunchly opposed to protectionism.

The link between economic self-interest, as a professional group, and their nationalist credentials as interpreters of Australia, is most explicit in E.J. Brady's account of Australian cultural development, written during the Great War:

Once it was unfashionable to recognise Australian science, applaud

Australian literary effort, or praise work of Australian artists.

A persistent preference for the foreign article so discouraged local genius that it grew timid and deprecatory, or else fell a prey to a melancholy which reacted upon all its aesthetic output . . .

Australian writers of my own generation have . . . loved our young country and realised her. In spite of social and monetary disadvantages, under which we all laboured, we have endeavoured, to the best of our abilities, to express our free and glorious motherland.

A few years ago a little group of writers and associate artists, who mostly found expression through the Sydney "Bulletin", struck the first definite national note in Australian literary and artistic thought. Their influence has grown beyond expectation . . .

Literary and artistic genius of the next generation will not suffer the neglect and opposition which made life's highway more flinty to our feet . . . It is possible that a majority of them will be enabled to reap an adequate harvest from their life's efforts.[40]

As a spokesperson for his generation, Brady had impeccable credentials: a participant in the maritime strike, a balladist with the *Bulletin*, bushman and bohemian, he also had links with the next generation of nationalist writers who came into prominence after the Great War. His generation passed on to the next a national self-image, forged, they said, out of their Australianness, although in fact as we have seen there was little that was distinctive in it. It had already begun to sour.

* * *

Everyman and his Holden

The Australian Way of Life as seen by Her Majesty the Queen can be yours . . . as the Modern Emigrant.
                Slogan in Australia House, London, 1954[41]

During the 1940s, the basis of the Australian identity changed. The idea of a racial or national type, a fundamental part of what it meant to be Australian since the early nineteenth century, was replaced by a new concept, "the Australian way of life". Although only invented, it seems, in the 1940s,[42] the term proved so popular that by 1950 a columnist could complain that she was "sick and tired of hearing people bleating about The Australian Way of Life".[43] Not that she deterred anyone: in 1953 alone, three significant general surveys of Australia appeared, one called *The Australian Way of Life*, and the other two containing essays on the subject where similar books before the war might have included chapters titled "The Australian Type".[44] Throughout the 1950s, the new concept was central to any discussion of Australian society.

Selling a way of life

The idea of a "Way of Life" fulfilled both general Western needs and more specific Australian ones. George Caiger's *The Australian Way of Life*, published under the auspices of the Australian Institute of International Affairs, was the first volume to appear in a UNESCO "Way of Life Series" which later included such titles as *The South African Way of Life, The Pakistani Way of Life* and *The Norwegian Way of Life*. They represented a broad shift in Western thought which was closely related to a new Cold War outlook. In that Cold War context, Australia was becoming an important bulwark of "freedom". Australia's racial identity became less important than its alliance with the United States in the Cold War.

As a concept, a "way of life" was more effective in defending the status quo than "the national character" or "the national type", which radicals had actually been associating with social change. The Cold War defensiveness inherent in the concept was spelled out in the introduction to another of the 1953 analyses of Australian society, W.V. Aughterson's *Taking Stock*, which suggested that "our way of life in Australia is a miracle for this kind of world, and . . . the danger lies in thinking of it as 'natural' and likely to endure without a passionate determination on our part to preserve and defend it."[45] Similarly, in 1951, when the Commemorative book celebrating the fiftieth anniversary of the Commonwealth dealt with "The Australian Way of Life", it stressed stability and congratulated Australians on their lack of a revolutionary heritage.[46]

The defensiveness was partly a continuation of the obsessions of the 1920s, but then the stress had been on the purity of Australia, the foreignness of Bolshevism, and the fact that it undermined a British civilisation. Now, with the greater strength of the Communist Party within Australia and the dissidence of many intellectuals, the Cold War outlook encouraged the pursuit of internal ideological warfare. As in other Western countries, fear of the external threat posed by "Russian expansionism" gave it added impact. Thus in 1949, the Institute of Public Affairs, which helped formulate Liberal Party policy, inserted full-page newspaper advertisements stating: "It is the communist influence within the Labour Party that is lowering production. This dangerous influence must be eradicated if the Australian way of life is to survive".[47] "The Australian Way of Life" was what was "at stake" in the Cold War, and was used by conservatives against internal as well as external opposition.

The concept of "the Australian Way of Life" was central to another issue that dominated the 1950s — immigration. The large-scale post-war assisted immigration begun by the Chifley government and continued under Menzies was the product of earlier "populate or perish" fears, the Japanese threat during the war and the decision to industrialise Australia. What distinguished this from earlier immigration schemes was not only its size and effectiveness — between 1947 and 1964 more migrants were added to the population than in the 80 years after 1860[48] — but also the fact that a large proportion of migrants were not British. In this context, "the Australian Way of Life" again played a crucial role.

In the 1920s, non-British immigration, like communism, was essentially an external threat; "undesirable" migrants were kept out by the "White Australia" policy, while British immigrants were exhorted to "live up to your British tradition and aspire to emulate the Australian spirit of Anzac".[49] Now, however, the non-British immigrant was a problem to be dealt with within Australia, and "the Australian Way of Life" provided the basis for government policy. Assimilation, required of both migrants and Aborigines throughout the 1950s, assumed a common, homogeneous Australian way of life which would be threatened unless outsiders conformed to it. Successive ministers for immigration made the same point. In 1945, Labor's Arthur Calwell thought it "economically unsound to bring migrants to the country until there is . . . proper housing and other social amenities to help them fit themselves quickly into the Australian way of life".[50] In 1950, the Liberals' Harold Holt stressed that "We can only achieve our goal through migration if our newcomers quickly become Australian in outlook and way of life".[51] In 1957, in John

O'Grady's very successful novel, *They're a Weird Mob,* migrants were told

> There are far too many New Australians in this country who are still mentally living in their homelands, who mix with people of their own nationality, and try to retain their own language and customs . . . Cut it out. There is no better way of life in the world than that of the Australian.[52]

In this way the concept was used to discriminate against migrants in Australia. Since it was never really defined, and often was simply a formula for expressing a general prejudice against outsiders and a distaste for non-conformity, all migrants could be criticised for failing to adopt "the Australian Way of Life". It not only denied the possibility that the cultural traditions of migrants might enrich Australian life, but also denied the existence of different "ways of life" among Australians themselves. Cultural differences were an affront to a society which demanded social uniformity, if not equality. "The Australian Way of Life" proved a useful tool of intolerance because it was so vague a notion, but it was rare for an Australian to point out how meaningless it was. One who did was Elizabeth Webb, a Brisbane journalist and commentator, who wrote:

> When it comes to The Australian Way of Life every foreigner I have met is completely at sea. To quote one — "What is this Way of Life? No one yet tells me what this is! Yet always they tell me I must adopt it . . . perhaps I began to behave like you behave in pubs. I drink beer until I am stupid. Or learn to 'put in the boot' and bash the other fellow with a bottle . . . Is this the way of life I must learn? Thank you. No. I stay a bloody Reffo!"[53]

The idea that "the Australian Way of Life" might in fact only boil down to beer and gambling disturbed some writers. They wanted to define its true essence, but they simply repeated the vague rhetoric of Cold War politics. George Johnston, for example, argued that "the beer-swilling spectacle in any Sydney pub ten minutes before closing time" was not "a true or even partly true picture of the Australian way of life", but he could only define its essence as "something which for all its uneasiness and confusion seems to talk of true democracy of the spirit".[54] Another article on the subject explained that "the Australian way of life" was "something much deeper than words can depict", that it embodied some "inner principle" which, although difficult to define, was related to "the freedom, the security, the justice and the individualism of life in this sunburned, muscular continent".[55]

Although the stated definitions were vague and contrived — like earlier definitions of the Australian "type" — it did not matter because what was important was not the meaning of the term but the way in which it was used. It provided a mental bulwark against communism, against change, against cultural diversity; it could call forth a common emotional response to the Cold War and to immigration, in defence of stability and homogeneity. In this, it was more effective than the concept of an Australian "type", as a 1955 Australian News and Information Bureau pamphlet implied, when it reinforced the idea that Australia was united and classless:

> What is a "typical Australian"? Even few Australians agree on this point, for the development of the land has brought with it a great diversity of occupation and outlook. Many Australians have a distinctive accent; many have not. Many conform to the popular overseas picture of the tall, lean, sun-tanned stockman; but more spend their lives in the crowded cities. Yet throughout this wide-ranging land, where outback station and city night-club are equally part of the social fabric, and where opal gouger, crocodile hunter, city clerk and atomic scientist are all members of its community, one language prevails; and its people are united in customs, character and tradition. Few are so rich that they need not work; none so poor that he cannot enjoy recreation.[56]

It is significant that egalitarianism, seen by left-wing writers as a radical impulse in the national "type", is here presented as merely another factor which makes for cultural unity.

Again, although it lacked definition, the image of "the Australian Way of Life" was closely related to the image of Australia as a sophisticated, urban, industrialised, consumer society. This suited the needs of an Australian manufacturing sector which was increasingly aligning itself with the United States, and which had been strengthened in the industrial expansion promoted by the war. Whereas the Australian "type" had been seen as an extension of the British "type", and Britain had set the standard against which the developing Australian character was measured, it was the United States which provided the standard against which Australia, and other Western nations, measured their "way of life". After all, "the American Way of Life" was the original, the most glamorous, the best publicised. Hollywood and, after 1956, television had seen to that.

The break with Britain among conservatives was quite sudden. In 1953, one of the older generation, F.W. Eggleston, could still write of Australia as "a British community . . . following the English way of life . . . England is 'Home' ".[57] At the same time another observer of Australian life was remarking that the habit of calling Britain "Home" was dying fast.[58] Brian Fitzpatrick thought the habit had died during the Second World War.[59] Its death, however, did not signify the leap towards a confident national independence for which many radicals yearned. For many conservatives, economic, cultural and military dependence on Britain was replaced by similar dependence on America, and the concept of "the Australian Way of Life" simply disguised the switch. Australian conservatism was impressively unsentimental about its change of allegiance, despite the Anglophile rhetoric of Menzies. In 1958, at a time when both radicals and old conservatives were critical of American influences, a Gallup Poll found that only 29 per cent of voters thought that "the United States is influencing our Australian way of life too much", and these were more likely to be Labor than Liberal voters.[60] Typical of this new conservatism was Donald Horne, who saw anti-Americanism as the bad feeling of a deluded Left and a "mindless", sentimental Right. For him, "Australia was the first country in the contemporary world to be saved by the Americans" and he looked forward to a "quite massive relationship with America".[61] While his republicanism would have been too iconoclastic for many in the 1950s, his shift of outlook towards America was common. There were even suggestions that Australia should become the fifty-first state.

A second feature of the "Australian Way of Life" which tied it to the manufacturing sector was its urban character. The national "type" eulogised in the past had been a rural "type" but the "Way of Life" was undeniably urban, or rather suburban. The city had lost the pejorative connotations it had had in the past, when it was viewed as a festering sore corrupting and debilitating the national type. Now suburbia was an ideal. In 1951, the Commonwealth celebrated its jubilee with an article on "the Australian Way of Life" written by a refugee:

> What the Australian cherishes most is a home of his own, a garden where he can potter, and a motor car . . . as soon as he can buy a house and a garden he . . . moves to the suburbs. This accounts for the enormous size of Australian cities — and also for the overwhelmingly middle-class outlook and way of life.
>
>   A person who owns a house, a garden, a car and has a fair job is rarely an extremist or a revolutionary.[62]

Not only was "the Australian Way of Life" specifically urban; it was also increasingly identified with Sydney. Before the phrase was commonly used, Sydney had been seen as exceptional rather than representative. Bohemians had left Sydney to find their "real" Australia. Lawson described Sydney as

> She, of Australian cities
> The least Australian of all!
> Greedy, luxurious, corrupting
> Her sisters one by one.[63]

In the 1930s, Thomas Wood had expected to find Sydney "the centre of Australian thought", but instead found it "worlds apart from . . . the men who plough and shear and mine — and keep Australia going . . . Sydney lives its own life: a city life with city interests and city pleasures, and Australia may go hang".[64] By the 1950s however, Sydney was seen as "the most 'Australian' of Australian cities", although (or because) it was also considered the most American.[65] Constantly writers on "the Australian Way of Life" would refer to Sydney to describe what was typically Australian. Increasingly, in books about Australia, photographs of Sydney — Bondi, Manly, busy Pitt Street, cosmopolitan King's Cross, the Bridge, the Harbour — were challenging the familiar iconography of outback Australia — the homestead, the sheep, the lonely gum and the proud Aborigine. In 1953, for example, Caiger's *The Australian Way of Life* had as its frontispiece "A Sydney Street Scene", and contained seven photographs of rural scenes, six of Sydney, two each of Newcastle and Canberra, one each of Adelaide and Perth, and none at all of Melbourne. Melbourne was the centre of attention when the Olympic Games were held there in 1956, but its glory was momentary. By the 1970s the

Sydney Opera House had become easily the most popular symbol of Australia, both here and overseas.

For the manufacturing sector, the most important feature of "the Australian Way of Life" was its identification with consumerism. It was no coincidence that the Official Commemorative Book for the Commonwealth Jubilee in 1951 should illustrate its article on "the Australian Way of Life" with photographs of the major city department stores. The familiar picture of suburban family life, with its focus on home and garden, and on a catalogue of family possessions such as refrigerators, washing machines, radiogrammes, television sets and, of course, the family car, was the basis of post-war affluence and the vast new consumer economy which the manufacturers and governments encouraged. Home ownership in Sydney rose from 40 per cent in 1947 to 60 per cent in 1954 (when homes were easier to buy than ever before or since), and to 71 per cent in 1961.[66] An Australian white goods industry expanded rapidly after the war so that the household appliances which had been luxuries before the war were now available to almost everyone. In 1949-50, Australia produced 31,638 washing machines, 150,878 refrigerators and 1070 petrol lawn mowers; ten years later the figures were 201,873; 237,328 and 246,721 respectively.[67] And then there was "Australia's own car", Australia's own in the sense that all the capital investment involved was Australian and only the profits went to America. The first Holden was produced in 1948. The Labor Prime Minister, Ben Chifley, was photographed next to it but, appropriately, Essington Lewis was invited to buy it.[68] Lewis more than anyone was identified with Australia's industrialisation. By 1962 one million more Holdens had been sold, and in 10 years car ownership had increased from one for every nine people to one per three and a half.[69] It was all accompanied by advertising campaigns structured around the imagery of "the Australian Way of Life".

Both major political parties encouraged this manufacturing boom and the consumerism which went with it, although the Liberals more successfully identified with it. In 1949, the last year of the Labor government, a Liberal Party think-tank, chaired by the large retailer, G.J. Coles, demanded for Australia "the American attitude of mind . . . leaders who can bring the nation to a new way of life".[70] Fifteen years of Menzies' government later, they looked back with some satisfaction at "improvements" in "the Australian way of life":

> democratisation of the motor car with its side effects of road conges- tion, numerous, immaculate petrol stations and modern-architectured motels . . . multiplication of modern, attractively designed factories . . . houses comprehensively equipped with the labour-saving and en- tertainment-giving "gadgets".[71]

As late as 1977, one of Malcolm Fraser's academic advisers, David Kemp, explained the ALP's failure to win office as due to its association "with what are still perceived as significant threats to the Australian way of life".[72]

The role of women in this vision of Australia was two-edged. On the one hand they were central to the new identity, in a way they had not been to the old Australian type. They, more than men, were conceived by the advertisers as the great consumers, dominating family, home and garden, and the consumer economy was structured around them. In 1947, for example, the *Argus* Women's Magazine had told its readers that "the American Way of Life is Easy for the Housewife", and described how

> Big New York stores trade exclusively in household gadgets. Seven and eight floors are devoted solely to them.

The reporter hoped "to interest manufacturers here and get into production small labour-saving devices for the Australian housewife".[73] For the next two decades women were inveigled into buying small labour-saving devices and persuading their hus- bands to buy larger ones.

However this role was a very restrictive one. Men had many outlets in "the Australian Way of Life", as workers, fathers, sportsmen, beer-drinkers, home handymen. Women were part of it only as full-time housewives and mothers. The variety of experi- ence which women could have outside family life was denied, yet in 1961 a quarter of factory workers were women, and a third of females over 15 were not married.[74] Women had at last been given a role in the dominant image of Australia, but it was one that worked to keep them in their place.

The image needed to be fairly static, but it also embraced two great symbols of development which caught the imagination of Australians in the 1950s and 1960s. One was the Snowy Mountains

Scheme, a major government enterprise set up in the late 1940s. It reflected the changing balance of the economy: its main purpose was to generate electricity for Canberra and for industry in the cities, while a secondary feature was irrigation farther west. The idea of migrants from many countries contributing to this great national enterprise seems to have had particular appeal to many Australians. In fact their work in the snow and mud was providing power for suburban washing machines. The scheme added to the exuberant self-confidence of the development ethos. George Johnston later described its impact on a thinly disguised version of himself:

> The yellow tractors against the glaring drifts of snow, the beards and mackinaws, the polyglot babble of smoke-hazed mess huts, the tingling atmosphere of a collective excitement; these as much as the sheer audacity of the concept had a profound effect upon Meredith . . . "It's like coming to an oasis in a desert, when you've been thirsting for something of promise, something to believe in. It's magnificent, darling! It's exciting! It's the only *visionary* thing I've seen since I've been back in this bloody country . . . I'm going down *there* to work . . . then write it as a novel. It could be the greatest bloody novel ever. It *could*, Cress. It's the most fabulous theme. It's got everything. *Everything*!"[75]

The other acknowledged symbol of development was Canberra. As one government adviser put it in 1965, Australians should be encouraged to look on the city "as a place where growth and development are being initiated, not only in local projects but in national policies".[76] Itself a monument, Canberra was also a city of monuments, and as each one rose up, as rural peace gave way to the suburb beautiful, the changing image of Australia was put on record. The Australian War Memorial, designed in the 1920s under C.E.W. Bean's inspiration, but postponed in the depression, was opened in 1941. It continued to be extended until 1970, paying tribute to the lingering significance of the digger legend. The Australian National University was established in 1946, reflecting that period's heightened respect for the intelligentsia. In 1954, it was time to recognise Australia's place in Cold War politics: when the Australian-American monument was built it was situated between the Department of Defence office blocks. In the same year a Senate Committee recommended the establishment of a National Capital Development Commission which, when it was established in 1958, turned Canberra into the fastest growing city in Australia. Here was the suburban ideal made manifest. Ironically it was based on leasehold rather than freehold principles: even the most suburban of dreams could not be consummated through private ownership, and even Menzies recognised it. Planning was centred on the car, the family, the garden and a uniformly middle-class life-style — "the Australian Way of Life" in all its glory. Filling the lake in the early 1960s was like providing one gigantic backyard swimming pool. But that ideal began to pall. The 1960s and the 1970s saw efforts to develop a more sophisticated cultural identity, and cultural monuments, such as the National Library, the Civic theatre complex, the School of Music and the National Gallery began to appear.

New images

. . . Gradually through the 1960s the racial exclusiveness and intolerance associated with "the Australian Way of Life" showed signs of weakening. In Aboriginal policy, in theory at least, "integration" replaced "assimilation", and although official attitudes to "Our Aborigines" remained paternalistic, they at least allowed for the maintenance of the sort of cultural identity which Aborigines themselves were developing. The same change of outlook, from "assimilation" to "integration", could be seen in official attitudes towards migrants in Australia. "Pluralism" was a convenient way of coping with the refusal of minority groups to accept "the Australian Way of Life" as their own.

In addition, strict adherence to the "White Australia" policy was quietly replaced by a policy which admitted a small number of non-Europeans in the late 1960s. But it was only in the 1970s, particularly under the Whitlam governments of 1972-75, that Australians recognised the fact that they lived in a "multi-cultural" society, to such an extent that "multi-culturalism" itself could become something of a fad. The "White Australia" policy was formally abandoned and "self-determination" became the new stated policy on migrants and Aborigines. Ethnic radio and, by 1980, ethnic television recognised the existence of more than one culture within Australia, although the attitudes of some conservative politicians suggest that they see such initiatives as a means of exerting more effective social control over minority groups.

By the early 1970s, Australia was being promoted as a pluralistic, tolerant, multi-cultural society, although it did not reflect any real improvement in the position of Aborigines and migrants, most of whom remained on the lower rungs of the socio-economic ladder. This image coincided — somewhat paradoxically — with what Whitlam referred to as the "new nationalism" . . .

The "new nationalism" was never clearly spelled out, but it related to a general pride in Australian achievement, particularly cultural achievement, and an increasing disquiet at the extent of foreign investment in Australia. From the mid-1960s, the founding of a Fellowship of First Fleeters, the expansion of the National Trust's role and the appearance of native shrubs in suburban gardens had all heralded a new confidence in being Australian. In 1979, even the New South Wales Higher School Certificate succumbed, and Australian History became an acceptable subject for 17-year-olds. (It had been taught in other states at that level for some time.) Intellectuals no longer felt themselves to be quite so alienated . . . For Geoffrey Serle, in his cultural history of Australia published in the same year, we had finally arrived at "mature nationhood".[77]

The irony was that, although many of the plays, novels and films produced in the 1970s were intensely critical of aspects of Australian life, they were absorbed by the "new nationalism" and applauded for their Australianness. Thus the film, *The Chant of Jimmy Blacksmith*, was an indictment of Australian racism and a critical success at Cannes; its overall impact was to induce pride in the local film industry rather than shame at the treatment of Aborigines. Similarly, the figure of the "Ocker" originated as a satire on Australian boorishness, but became an affectionate tribute to the national identity and ended up as the most effective way of selling cigarettes to children.

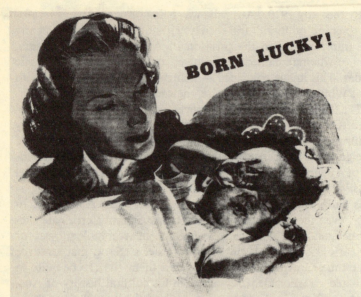

BORN LUCKY!

Yes, baby, you were born lucky—simply in the fact that you were born an Australian.

Unlike babies being born in many parts of the world, you will grow up in a free and sunny land. The bounty of the earth and the fruits of invention will be yours; the opportunities to win and enjoy the good things of life will be assured to you—if we secure your future as our forefathers secured ours.

★   ★   ★

That the future of Australia, and of all democratic countries, is gravely threatened can no longer be doubted. It is abundantly clear that the forces of communist aggression are ever poised, waiting to strike wherever and whenever a weakness appears along the democratic front.

Only in military strength is there any guarantee of a secure future. The Navy, the Army and the Air Force need the services of every available man—not only men for the permanent forces, but also men who will, by volunteering for part-time training, help to build up the large reserve strengths necessary. And backing these forces must be a united population determined to produce the materials and supplies required.

To help make Australia strong—that is the supreme duty and responsibility of every Australian at this time.

What we do over the next few years will determine the fate and future of Australia

Issued by the Government of the Commonwealth of Australia.

Advertisement from the *Australian Women's Weekly*, 16 December 1950, p.55.
Commonwealth of Australia copyright reproduced by permission

Advertisement from the *Australian Women's Weekly*, 23 September 1950, p.2.
Reproduced by permission of Unilever Australia Ltd

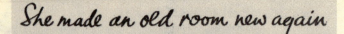

She made an old room new again

WHY A VANTONA IS BEST FOR YOU.
You need a bedcover that gives your
room an air of luxury and elegance.
Vantona will. You must have a bedcover that will drape smoothly day
after day, without a single crease.
Vantona does. One that will keep its
loveliness throughout the years. Vantona gives you this and more. A
Vantona bedcover is English crafts-
manship at its very highest.

VANTONA
Bedcovers

Three styles — one to suit every purse . . .
VANTONA COURT . . . VANTONA RUSTIC
VANTONA HOMESTEAD

MADE IN MANCHESTER . . . THE HOME OF FINE FABRICS

Advertisement from the Australian Women's Weekly, 1 July 1950, p.51

Advertisement from the *Australian Women's Weekly*, 8 July 1950, p.6. Reproduced by permission of CSR Ltd (CSR Wood Panels).

Part Two
White Australia Has a Black History

Readings 1 and 2 suggest some of the ways in which Australian identity has been put forward in images that are predominantly male, white and "Anglo-Celtic". Despite being the original occupants of the land, Aboriginal Australians were given no part to play in the most widespread and influential versions of what it meant to be an Australian.

Aborigines have begun to assert their own sense of identity or Aboriginality against the definitions which white society has imposed upon them. This development is strongly linked to community and political consciousness, especially around such issues as land rights. Non-Aboriginal Australians, in response, have questioned some of the legal, political and cultural foundations upon which their own national identities have been based. A slogan during the Bicentenary year insisted that "White Australia has a Black History".

Reading 3, by John Rickard, is from the first chapter of a general history of Australian culture. By beginning his book with an account of Aboriginal society and culture, and by insisting on its diverse and continuing presence, Rickard challenges many of the earlier accounts of Australian history — although he insists that a history written from an Aboriginal perspective would be very different again.

In Reading 4 Colin Tatz examines definitions of Aboriginality in certain examples of legal, administrative and academic language which tend to be based on racist notions of colour or blood. He argues instead for a notion of Aboriginality based on self-identification and community acceptance.

The final reading for this section, "Raised to Think White", comes from an ABC Radio series in which a group of Aborigines talk about what being Aboriginal means to them. This is of particular interest as these Aborigines were separated from their families and brought up in a white environment.

Further reading

Bowden, R., and Bunbury, B., comp., *Being Aboriginal: Comments, Observations and Stories from Aboriginal Australians*. Sydney, Australian Broadcasting Corporation, 1990.

Davis, J., Muecke, S., Narogin, M. and Shoemaker, A., eds, *Paperbark: A Collection of Black Australian Writings*. St Lucia: University of Queensland Press, 1990.

Morgan, S., *My Place*. Fremantle: Fremantle Arts Centre Press, 1987.

Reynolds, H., comp. *Dispossession: Black Australians and White Invaders*. Sydney: Allen & Unwin, 1989.

Reynolds, H., *Frontier: Aborigines, Settlers and Land*. Sydney: Allen & Unwin, 1987.

Aborigines

John Rickard

For the Aborigines the earth had always been there. It required no explanation. Myth interpreted the shape and appearance of the world the Aborigines knew and inhabited. Rocks, trees, waterholes, animals, birds: such objects, intimately experienced, were integrated through myth and ritual into a spiritual universe of extraordinary richness.

There were — are — spirit beings which expressed themselves in creating or actually becoming the physical detail of the Aboriginal world. In doing so they gave meaning to the land and to life. These spirit beings had an independence and unpredictability which were also beyond explanation. So they might appear male or female or draw on the sexuality of both; and human might, at will, become animal; nor was their force diminished if they transformed themselves into the features of the landscape.

So the rainbow-serpent, which is found in most Aboriginal mythologies, is commonly depicted in its terrifying, animal form, with a kangaroo-like head and crocodile teeth, ears or crown of feathers, long, spiked body and fish tail. Usually inhabiting waterholes, the serpent is also the arching rainbow in the sky. Thus the rainbow-serpent is a symbol of water and life; sometimes it is also an ancestral being. For the Gunwinggu it became Ngalyod, a woman, who, with her husband, Wuragog, travelled the country carrying her digging stick and net bag. When Wuragog sought to lie with her, Ngalyod was apt to return to her serpent form, but their union produced children who were the first Gunwinggu. For the Murinbata the rainbow-serpent became a man, Kunmanggur, who made the musical instrument, the didjeridu, from a bamboo stalk. He blew on it hard, and with the reverberation of its strange music several flying foxes flew out of its end. Kunmanggur decided to make people, and when he blew again a boy and girl emerged.

In some myths the spirit beings who created the familiar world of the Aborigines came across the sea from another place. So in the Djanggawul epic song cycle two sisters and a brother came from somewhere far away, but the journey celebrated is from Bralgu, the island of spirits. Reaching the mainland they continue their journey, making wells and trees, and through such acts investing the land with meaning. Then, following proper ritual preparations, children are removed from the wombs of the sisters. The world of the Yirrkala people had begun to take shape.

It is myths such as these which are the source of what Aborigines call the Dreaming. The myths are not fables of "long ago", for the Aborigines have, in the European sense, no concept of history. The past does not so much precede the present, as lie contained within it. The Dreaming paths mapped out by the spirit beings continue to determine the pattern of Aboriginal life, for the Dreaming is a relationship between people and land which forms the basis of traditional society. The myths serve to unite the creativity of the source with the continuing reality of life. So a man can say of a particular site, with certainty rather than wonder: "This is a place where the dreaming comes up, right up from inside the ground."[1]

The frequent association in myth of origins with canoe journeys over sea is historically suggestive. The Aborigines have been in Australia at least 40,000 years. Human evolution could not have taken place separately in Australia, for there is no evidence of the existence here of the ape-like predecessors of *homo sapiens*; therefore the first Aborigines must have come from elsewhere, most likely South-East Asia. Sea-levels were then much lower, and although the Australian continent was never joined to Asia, New Guinea was part of a mainland which was relatively close to the chains of islands pointing from Java and Borneo. Most islands were within sight of each other, and even over the last and longest gap it is likely that smoke from natural bushfires on the Australian continent would have been visible. Whatever the background to this migration, and whatever the precise route followed, the journey required a combination of technical skills and high motivation. Setting foot on the unknown land the first inhabitants had to learn to understand a new, though not totally unfamiliar, environment. Northern Australia shared some of the plant life of Indonesia, but its animals were strange and different. The newcomers had to, like their spirit beings, "make" the country in their own image.

How long it took for the Aborigines to spread out over the vast island continent is not known, though it might have been as long as 10,000 years. Preferring at first the kind of coastal terrain familiar to them, they were unlikely to have sought out less hospitable regions until forced to by circumstances. Twenty-three thousand years ago another drop in sea-level united Tasmania to the mainland, and almost immediately, it seems, Aborigines ventured into what was then a harsh, cold environment, with glaciers paving its mountains and icebergs floating along its coast. Ten thousand years later the sea rose again, and the Tasmanians were marooned, but in what was now a more congenial environment. As for the desert regions of central Australia, so often associated with the archetypal Aborigine, these were probably the last to be occupied: there is no evidence of habitation far inland older than 26,000 years. By 1788 it is thought that there might have been a total Aboriginal population of about 750,000.

Over many thousands of years, therefore, the pattern of Aboriginal settlement emerged. Eventually there came to be possibly between 500 and 600 dialects and languages. These might be spoken by as few as 100 people, or as many as 1,500: each such group was a society unto itself. The world was largely defined through a particular people's relationship with its land. Myth did not need to explain the life and culture of other people, since they impinged only incidentally on this world. To travel beyond your country was to go outside your world — it was hazardous spiritually, as much as materially. Aboriginal culture is, then, many separate cultures. Even physically, Aborigines vary considerably: the Tasmanians, for example, were distinguished by woolly hair and reddish-brown skin colour. Although the similarities remain important, the diversity of Aboriginal experience is one born of 40,000 years in a continent of great physical variety, from lush tropical rain forest and fertile, grassy plains to desert wastelands and wild mountains.

"Tribe" is an inappropriate word to describe an Aboriginal community. There was no chieftain, and the community came together infrequently, and usually only for ceremonial purposes. Yet within each society relationships were governed by a complex web of structures. At the base was the family — a man, his wife or wives (for marriage was not necessarily monogamous) and their children. For purposes of daily hunting and foraging the family was part of a band, usually comprising no more than fifty people. But beyond the family a range of groupings was organised according to descent, relationship to the land and particular sites within it, and totemic association. The total community was usually divided into moieties which had important social and ritual functions. So all were aware of their position in society, and accordingly the nature of their relationship to other members. In some ways this was restrictive — marriage, for example, was governed by an elaborate hierarchy of rules — but it also made for ease and security. This did not mean that Aborigines were mere captives of custom: there was still much scope for negotiation, bargaining and making decisions. But the entire society was like a family in which the individual member had a clear knowledge of the obligations and responsibilities of social intercourse. So it was possible to live your whole life without meeting anyone who was, literally, a stranger.

A casual observer watching an Aboriginal band absorbed in its daily concerns could hardly guess at the complex social structure which conditioned it. Even the movements of the band from camp to camp reflected a pattern born of a long spiritual and material association with the land. To describe the Aborigines as nomads is misleading if it suggests aimlessness, and indeed in the more fertile regions Aboriginal communities were much more settled. In the south-east there were even villages of stone dwellings, close to lakes and rivers where there was good fishing with elaborate systems of weirs, channels and nets. But even where, as in the arid zones, greater distances were crossed, the essence of these cyclical movements was to "look after" the country, both in terms of husbanding its resources and caring for its religious sites. The gathering of food was a material and not unpleasant necessity, but it also kept the Aborigines close to the spiritual source of their culture.

In the daily routine the men hunted, with much ingenuity, their game being kangaroos, wallabies, emus and a range of smaller marsupials; fishing, too, was often important. Women and children were primarily responsible for gathering vegetables, fruit, eggs, shellfish and honey; sometimes they hunted smaller game. Their tasks too, demanded considerable skill in recognition and selection. Various foods required cooking or preparation: meat was lightly cooked, often in earth ovens, while some tubers and the fruit of the cycad palm, for example, required quite complicated processing. The diet was one of surprising variety, though this was naturally affected by the seasons. The seasonal availability of a particular food might provide the occasion of a gathering; so in the summer when clouds of small brown Bogong moths took shelter in the southern alps many Aborigines, some travelling great distances, pursued them there for a time of sociable feasting. Food generally was shared: the band was a cooperative unit.

* * *

So life went on, and somehow this society functioned with little evidence of overt government. Partly this was due to the interlocking network of social structures which set the rules for conduct. But partly it was due to the consensual mode of making day-to-day decisions, a mode encouraged by the realities of nomadic life. Respect was accorded older people, because their knowledge was greater, particularly in matters of ritual. Ritual, of course, was concerned with conditioning behaviour, so in this sense the old presided over the young. But their authority was not formalised, outside the context of ritual itself. When someone offended against recognised standards of conduct — say, in breaching a sacred tabu — the penalty was usually a customary one, though it might be carried out in a casual manner without ceremony. So a man who had offended might, when hunting in a group, suddenly be speared in the back by a companion: the nature of this act as punishment would be understood by all concerned.

In one sense men had more power and privilege than women. They could take more than one wife, while a woman was not similarly able to acquire husbands. Moreoever a husband exercised certain rights over the disposal of his wife's sexuality. Men were more likely to exercise authority and to preside over ritual, and they assumed that hunting had more status and glamour than gathering. Yet women had their own ritual life, their own sacred knowledge; and their work as food gatherers was fundamental to the economy.

The relationship of woman to man was not, in practice, one of subservience. In one myth Minala, whose totem is the tortoise, is married to Wimu who is extremely possessive, and does not want to share him, somewhat to Minala's chagrin. He goes to seek the magic which will turn her into a tortoise, and thus rid him of her, but the determined Wimu follows and observes him, and later profanes his magic, with the result that it is Minala who becomes a tortoise. Wimu is now overtaken by remorse and wants Minala turned back into a man, but she is told that there is no magic strong enough; the only solution is for her to become a tortoise. Such a tale might be interpreted as a warning to wilful wives, yet ultimately it is Minala who is the loser.

It is notable, however, that while many of the creative spirits of the Dreaming are female, the myths seemed to feel a need — or, one should say, the tellers of the myths did — to explain a disparity between the status of woman as the source of life and her tribal situation. So in the Djanggawul cycle the brother steals the sisters' sacred basket and emblems, and thus appropriates a particular ritual. The sisters appear neither resentful nor humiliated, for they still retain important roles, but the myth can be interpreted as validating male control of a female-derived ritual.

* * *

It was part of the balance of Aboriginal life that there was plenty of time for social activity. Except in times of drought, hunting and gathering did not take up many hours of the day, so that conversation, storytelling and ritual were easily accommodated. Ritual, however, had more than a social function, for it was vital to the maintenance of the community. Much care and time were taken in the preparation for and performance of rites. Some rites were dramatic re-enactments in song and dance of the deeds of the spirit-beings or heroes; some were concerned with replenishing the natural environment, and therefore were seen as fundamental to immediate survival; others were essentially rites of initiation or death. All were characterised by great energy and commitment; there was a real sense in which the community was revitalised by their performance.

* * *

Music, dance, painting and culture were all essential to ritual. Indeed, "art" was not something to be juxtaposed against "society", in the sense that "leisure" is often contrasted with "work". Art was fully integrated with the social process: it always had a utilitarian purpose, whether in terms of immediate function (as with a spear or a dilly bag) or ritual significance (as with body painting and sacred objects). There were no professional artists, and little distinction between "art" and "craft". Certain skills were required of most people — in making implements, for example, and body painting — and if some gained particular reputations as artists, songmen or dancers, it was because of the opportunities their position in the community afforded them, rather than any special response to an artistic calling. To play the didjeridu called for the development of considerable technique to maintain a continuity of sound and produce, simultaneously, two pitches, but such a player, however important to his community, was in no sense a professional performer.

The importance of art was assumed: it needed no justification. Indeed, art was so important that there was a constant process of production rather than any sense of amassing artistic treasures. For communities on the move there was no point in *objets d'art*, except, of course, for the few essential sacred objects. Bark paintings might simply be left to decay or, if used in rites, deliberately destroyed, though sometimes a sacred object would be hidden at a site for later use. Sand sculptures, made for mortuary and healing rites, were as ephemeral as the sound of the didjeridu itself.

There were, however, the great galleries of Aboriginal art in caves and on rock faces, which were often part of the Dreaming and had, in that sense, always been there. So the Aborigines were certain that they themselves had not painted the extraordinary Wandjina figures, with their white faces and red haloes, found in the Kimberleys. For in the Dreaming the Wandjina came from the north, making waterholes and shaping the landscape; each Wandjina then painted his own image on the walls of a cave before making his home in a nearby waterhole.

* * *

The meanings of Aboriginal paintings or sculptures were usually intricate. The geometrical motifs might represent landscape features such as waterholes and rivers; they might also have other deeper symbolic meanings. To fully understand a particular work one would need to be a member of the particular group within the people from which it came. Although the graphic code language upon which artists drew might have some universal characteristics, precise meanings were localised in context. So a sacred object, the significance of which was located in ritual, might only be capable of full interpretation by a very few. It was not so much that knowledge was "secret", in an elitist sense, but that an Aborigine's expectations of "understanding" a work of art were conditioned by circumstance.

Traditional Aboriginal society was imbued with a religious view of life, and ritual and art were harnessed to its expression. Particular people acquired ritual responsibilities, but just as there was no chieftain, so did religion lack secular organisation. So personalised by culture and experience was the Dreaming that there was no *need* for such organisation to maintain it. Nor were the spirit-beings worshipped in a formal sense.

* * *

Aboriginal religion was life-oriented. It contained no sense of sin or personal salvation, and death, while it did not destroy the spirit, offered no promise of a heavenly after-life. Death was, therefore, something of a puzzle. At one level there was a tendency, particularly if a person died short of old age, to blame the exercise of malevolent power — the sorcery of another people, for example. At another level myth sought to explain how death had come to the world. According to the Murinbata, Crow and Crab argue about the right way to die. Crab, a very old woman, shows how she would do it, crawling into a hole where she remains for some time changing her shell. When Crab emerges from the ground everyone is happy except Crow. "That way takes too long", Crow protests. "There is an easier way to die. This is what we should do."[2] Whereupon he rolls his eyes, falls over backwards and dies instantly.

Similarly for the Maung, there is the myth about Possum and the Moon, when they were both men. They fight with yam sticks and Moon mortally wounds Possum. As he dies, Possum says that all who come after him will, like him, die for ever. Moon protests that Possum should have let him speak first, for although he, too, would die for a few days, he would return in the form of a new moon. Both Crow and Possum were responsible for Aborigines having to follow the example they had set. The option of renewal, offered by Crab and Moon, had been pre-empted. There was no particular moral to be drawn from this, but the myths suggest that while for Aborigines life was natural death was not — people had to be taught how to die.

Aboriginal beliefs did not altogether discount the prospect of renewal, but there was little sense of the human personality surviving death intact. The spirit was, in effect, dispersed. Part of it lingered in the land, always having the potential to haunt the living; but the main energy of the spirit travelled to the land of the dead, losing its individual identity, and awaiting some later re-birth. Death, in the personal sense, remained an austere reality. In most places the name of someone who had recently died could not be uttered: the tabu might apply for years.

The mythology of death points to a fundamental feature of Aboriginal culture — its lack of concern with motivation and "morality". It was not pertinent to ask *why* Crow or Possum behaved the way he did: the myths did not operate at this level. There was no attempt to explain the need for death. Rather, the mythology simply defined the alternatives as they existed, and nominated the fate which Aborigines had to accept. It is not surprising, therefore, that Aboriginal culture was not noted for proverbs or saws, for they would have had little point. Behaviour was not governed by moral precepts, argued out a theoretical level. Ideas about "right" and "wrong", or appropriate and inappropriate behaviour, derived from a complex interaction of social structures anchored in the land itself.

So the spirit-beings of the Dreaming were sources of energy and life, and performed great deeds, but moral majesty was not part of their aura. They were feared and marvelled at, and their ways had to be respected, but they were not adored. Often, indeed, there was a moral ambiguity to their behaviour. The *mimi*, for example, were sometimes credited with having taught the Aborigines their skills, yet they were also seen as being capriciously hostile to human beings, and likely, if given the chance, to take them captive.

There was no room, in such a culture, for a sense of tragedy. Suffering, like death, had to be accepted. But just as there is an almost abrasive matter-of-factness in the compelling myth of Crow and Crab, so, too, suffering was not an occasion for moral grandeur. The point of suffering was its material reality. It was made bearable by a religious understanding of the world which was underpinned by myth and sustained by ritual.

In its acceptance of the realities of survival, Aboriginal culture could to the outsider sometimes appear harsh. Infanticide was practised, though its exact extent remains uncertain. Babies with deformities were killed, and in the case of twins the weaker seems to have been discarded. If this was population control, it was only so in the immedite sense of the family and band meeting the difficulties of raising children in a semi-nomadic situation. Such decisions, ratified by the culture, did not pose moral dilemmas; in any case the spirit of the dead baby simply returned to its source. In some areas cannibalism occurred, usually associated with rites of internment. Token parts of the flesh of the dead body might be eaten by certain kin, who would draw strength from this communion. A dried piece of flesh might also serve as a kind of talisman, helping, for example, a man in his hunting. To describe such customs as uncivilised only obscures their cultural significance; they were not so much aberrations from an otherwise "civilised" society, as logically compatible aspects of Aboriginal civilisation as a whole.

Aborigines had no concept of material wealth. Objects and implements had to be made all the time, to satisfy not only the requirements of daily life and ritual, but also to meet kinship obligations. There was no point in seeking to amass a surplus, for it would have been more a physical impediment than an instrument for power over others. Hence competition for wealth though not necessarily power was notably absent from Aboriginal culture. It was partly for this reason that society did not have the sorts of institutions of government usually needed to regulate such competition.

Disputes and fights were more likely to be concerned with matters such as sexual relationships. The organisation of Aboriginal life did not preclude opportunities for aggression. Sometimes rites and ceremonies would allow for physical contest. Just as the Aborigine was proud of his hunting prowess, so too he respected bravery and loyalty. Although territorial disputes would appear to have been infrequent — bound to its own land, a people had little motive for expansion — there were other occasions for dispute, particularly deriving from the tendency to blame the sorcery of another people for the ills of one's own. But just as the Aborigine's religion lacked the structures of church and priesthood, so their society did not encourage a warrior tradition. Violence and killing were not absent from their society, but for the 40,000 years of their uninterrupted occupation of the continent, the Aborigines had not found the need to develop the structures and strategies of formalised war.

Above all, Aboriginal culture was characterised by a fusion of the material and spiritual. The tasks of daily life were themselves imbued with religious meaning, while the function of the great rites was to reaffirm and sustain the community's relationship with the land. The technological simplicity of Aboriginal society was matched by a cultural complexity, as much evident in the subtlety and opaqueness of its mythology as in the intricate pattern of its kinship systems. As a non-literate people the Aborigines found their history in the power and beauty of art, myth and ritual. The land itself was a kind of text, a scripture, which each Aborigine learnt to read. And in their painting and sculpture the Aborigines not only expressed their aesthetic sense but also wrote, and wrote again, their cultural messages. In all of this there was the continuing reality of the Dreaming. When they celebrated the spirit beings the Aborigines were celebrating life in its diversity — Ngalyod, the rainbow serpent woman, the Djanggawul paddling their canoe from Bralgu, Crow and Crab, Possum and Moon, the yam people, the *mimi*, all represented the spiritual energy of the universe. The Dreaming ultimately unified everything, and from that unity the Aboriginal people drew their strength.

* * *

Such a sketch as this of a "traditional" society is bound to convey a static quality — a sense of the endless repetition of daily routines, of myths being retold and rites re-enacted over the centuries. In fact Aboriginal society did change, even if the pace of that change was necessarily slow, and even if much of it can only be inferred or guessed at.

The coming of the Aborigines had a significant impact on the environment. The Aborigines have been called "fire-stick farmers''[3]: they set fire to bush not only to keep tracks clear and flush out animals for hunting, but also, it seems, as part of a larger strategy for regenerating the land. The persistence of this practice established a new ecological balance. On the west coast of Tasmania, for example, ancient rain forest gave way to heath and sedgeland. The centuries of fire contributed to the dominance of the eucalypt which adapted best to the Aborigines' land use.

Changes in climate compelled adaptation, just as the casting adrift of Tasmania committed the Aborigines there to a separate history. About 4000 years ago a tabu emerged, for reasons unknown, on the eating of scale fish, and the Tasmanians ceased making bone tools; they had, however, satisfactorily established their own accommodation with their island environment.

At the same time the mainland was witnessing some significant innovations. New small tools — points, backed blades and adzes — were introduced to the technology, and though it seems likely that these were imported, the possibility of local development cannot be entirely discounted. The dingo, or native dog, was definitely an immigrant, possibly 4000 years ago and thought most likely to have been brought from south Asia; the Aborigines readily incorporated this animal into their culture. The dingo was semi-domesticated, often taken from the bush as a pup, to become for a time a pet of the camp, later returning to the wild. On cold winter nights the warmth of the dingo's company was much prized.

It must also be remembered that the evolution of the settlement pattern of the continent, with its variety of languages and dialects, must have been a long historical process. Contact between different societies remained important. Although the spiritual universe of each people tended to be self-contained, taking little account of what lay beyond its own country, there were often overlaps, as in the case of a site which might have religious significance for more than one people. Just as two communities might be able to understand each other's dialect, so too they might share sections of a myth. At a practical level there were patterns of trade by which all benefited, pearl shell from the Kimberleys, for example, finding its way right across the continent.

Myth and ritual were not unresponsive to the changing needs of their guardians, nor could they be. Sometimes elements might be discarded, so that eventually cave paintings of past generations could lose their original significance, or be endowed with a new one. With each myth there were always varying versions and emphases, and often these suggest the continuing vitality of oral tradition. Myth and ritual existed always in the present, constantly reinterpreting the Aborigines' relationship to the land of their Dreaming. A tradition, after all, only reveals its strength by its capacity to adapt and modify.

So as the Aborigines occupied the continent, and came to terms with the changes of environment and climate, their culture evolved and adapted, in all its variety. Nor can it be assumed, as the coming of the new small tools and the dingo warn us, that once they set foot on Australia the Aborigines were isolated from the rest of the world. The cultural overlap between the Aborigines of Cape York Peninsula and the Papuans (the Torres Strait islanders representing an amalgam of both) provides evidence of extensive contact between Australia and New Guinea, though for how long a time before 1788 remains uncertain. The contact was strong enough, however, for Papuan technology and customs to penetrate some 300 kilometres down the Cape. We know of the regular visits of the Macassans from Indonesia to northern Australia possibly from the sixteenth century or even earlier. They took advantage of the north-west monsoon to guide their praus (dugout sailing canoes) to the Australian coast where they fished for the valued trepang or béche-de-mer. The processing required, which included boiling and smoking, meant that they needed to establish themselves for a time on the shore, building, it seems, villages of leaf-thatched houses for their stay. Although there were instances of hostility from the Aborigines, there is also evidence that they were most interested in the visitors, their technology and customs. They may even have helped the Macassans in their work. The iron implements which the Macassans brought with them were sought after, and their dug-out canoes were adopted in Arnhem Land. Perhaps even more significantly, Macassan words entered Aboriginal languages, and the visitors had a noticeable influence on Aboriginal music and art. Thus Aboriginal culture responded creatively to both the Papuan and Macassan influences.

It would seem that the voyages of the Portuguese in the sixteenth century (when they may have sighted Australia) and of the Dutch in the seventeenth century impinged little on Aboriginal consciousness. In 1629, however, a mutiny by survivors of the wrecked *Batavia* resulted in two of the rebels being marooned on the mainland. Nothing is known of the fate of these, the first known European inhabitants of Australia. Some Tasmanian Aborigines mostly likely saw Abel Tasman's party when it "discovered" Tasmania in 1642, but if so they discreetly secluded themselves. Aborigines certainly witnessed the Englishman William Dampier's forays in 1688 when he visited the north-west coast, but they kept at a distance and deliberately avoided contact. Irritated, Dampier concluded that they were "the miserablest People in the world". And when Captain Cook explored the east coast in 1770 the Aborigines' reaction was more one of suspicion than hostility. But perhaps influenced by the lusher environment of eastern Australia, Cook disagreed with Dampier's assessment:

> From what I have said of the Natives of New-Holland they may appear to some to be the most wretched people upon the earth: but in reality they are far more happier than we Europeans; being wholly unacquainted not only with the superfluous but the necessary Conveniences so much sought after in Europe, they are happy in not knowing the use of them. They live in a Tranquillity which is not disturbed by the inequality of Condition: The Earth and sea of their own accord furnishes them with all things necessary for life; they covet not Magnificent Houses, Household-stuff &c. they live in a warm and fine Climate and enjoy a very wholesome Air: so that they have very little need of Clothing and this they seem to be fully sensible of for many to whom we gave Cloth &c to, left it carelessly upon the Sea beach and in the woods as a thing they had no manner of use for. In short they seem'd to set no value upon anything we gave them nor would they ever part with any thing of their own for any one article we could offer them this in my opinion argues that they think themselves provided with all the necessarys of Life and that they have no superfluities . . .[4]

If Cook's portrayal of the Aborigines suggests a romantic image of the noble savage, he nevertheless grasped something of the atmosphere of Aboriginial society before European contact.

How the Aborigines viewed these occasional curious visitors is difficult to surmise, though their ships, great white birds on the horizon, sometimes provoked alarm. Their visits were infrequent and fleetingly brief. They came and went away, leaving almost no imprint compared with the Macassans. Life went on.

And then, in January 1788, these visitors from another world, another dimension even, came again — and stayed.

Reading 4

Aboriginality as Civilisation

Colin Tatz

Changing labels or attitudes

Heinrich Heine[1] once said that Judaism was not a religion but a misfortune. What would the poet have said of Aboriginality? A people not yet generally articulate in English, Aborigines are submerged by the sovereignty and sway of our written and spoken words about them. Their image in white eyes — often in their looking-glass self eyes[2] — is that of the Different Ones, the Differently Coloured Ones: pre-historic, pre-literate, tribal, clannish, once noble, still savage, now a remnant people, leaderless, odorous, of late doubly squeezed between (for the most part) lip-service social justice and (for the most part) rabid racism, between their once-upon-a-time culture and Progress.

My object here is not to devise a new language, consisting of new names or labels for familiar things. I am aware of the trap of assuming that by changing labels one thinks one is changing essences. My aim is to find a framework and the right words with which to get across a *perception of people* — a consciousness and an attitude — different from that which has kept Aborigines inferior, aberrant, inept, oppressed, depressed, suppressed both in image and in reality. Working with governments, missions, mining companies, talking with teachers, lawyers, police officers, students, academics, indeed Aborigines themselves, I see an urgent need of a new frame of reference for and about Aborigines. If the change is simply one of label — replacing "culture" or "race" with "civilisation" — in order to describe the essence of what demarcates Aboriginality, then the skeptic could well ask whether the substitution will change others' perceptions of Aboriginality. But enough men and women who read earlier versions of my treatment have said this exploration has changed either their romantic or their caricature image of Aboriginality. Such value as this analysis may have lies in the topics and contentions it poses for thought rather than for what it resolves, or even prescribes at points. It may bring about changes in perception, in viewing, in attitude. It is an *essay* in the true sense: an attempt, an endeavour to present both reality and ideas.

* * *

Perceptions of Aborigines

Aborigines as a Race. Aborigines have indeed been an object of the taxonomy-of-physical-types industry. The 18th and 19th centuries saw the first serious attempts to correlate social with physical characteristics, to relate whiteness to western civility and blackness to alien barbarism.[3] (Modern Australian thinking on these correlations is discussed later.) Much has been written about Aborigines as *Australoids*, about their unique physical anatomy. One major legacy has derived and survived from all this: race came to mean "full-bloodedness", "purity" of blood. Based on some dubious genetics and even more spurious haematology, "blood" was divided into and equated with social characteristics on the premise that somehow blood could be titrated in a laboratory and filtered into full drops, half drops, white drops (or strains). We defined degrees of mixture and alleged "impurity" *on the sole criterion of what our eyes told us was full or half or quarter or eighth*. South Africa's criteria for race classification include appearance or skin colour, descent or origin (the so-called test of blood), general acceptance and repute and mode of living (including associates, habits, dress, place and conditions of residence and customary language).[4] The following modern examples show how heavy has been Australian reliance on the skin colour test, or the *appearance of descent* criterion:

- In Queensland until 1972 Aborigines were full-bloods, persons with a preponderance of full-blood, part-Aboriginal spouses of Aborigines already defined, and residents of reserves! Part-Aborigines were those with one full-blood parent and one with no strain of the blood of the indigenous inhabitants, and those whose parents both have a strain of the blood and who themselves had no more than 25 per cent of such blood but not a preponderance of it.[5] *Strain of the blood*, while conveying notions of origin or descent, was nevertheless determined by the eye of the beholder.
- Paul Everingham, then Chief Minister of the Northern Territory, told a House of Representatives Standing Committee in

1979: "The description of a person arrested as Aboriginal depends on the observation of the arresting officer and includes people who are part-Aboriginal."[6]

- From 1957 to 1964 the *Welfare Ordinance* was in force in the Northern Territory. Throughout its 83 clauses it managed to avoid the word "race" or "colour" or "Aborigines". It created the concept of "ward", that is, the provision of assistance for individuals who because of their manner of living, their inability to manage adequately their own affairs, their standard of social habit, behaviour and personal associations, needed such assistance.[7] All this had a South African flavour and intent. But by the expedient of declaring that voters, people who would become voters at (then) 21 or who would become voters when naturalised, *could not be declared wards*, this meant that only (then) voteless Aborigines could be so declared. Following a round-up based solely on the appearance of descent, 17,500 full-bloods (and a number of part-Aborigines seen to be close enough) were declared wards *en masse*.

- In June 1972 a Perth magistrate had before him a self-identified Aborigine on a charge of failing to register for National Service, then in force and from which Aborigines were exempt. He said:

  There's no evidence of his living in a native camp, and he apparently lives at a normal address in Perth. *I must also take notice of his appearance.* I'm going to convict him. [my italics]

Colour — rather than race — was and still is the major criterion of Aboriginality. The "scientific" equation was, till recently, the fuller the blood, the darker the skin, the closer to barbarism, savagery, heathenness, "myalness", "bushness": the consequence of which is that the less full the blood, the lighter the skin, the nearer one stands on the scale of civility, civilisztion and enlightenment — and therefore the greater the rights to grog, to voting, to sex, marriage, freedom of movement etc.

The notion of descent from Aboriginal ancestry rather than colour begins legally in Victoria in 1966 and in the federal sphere in 1969, i.e. the idea that an Aborigine is anyone descended from Aborigines who claims to be and is accepted as such by other Aborigines. Possibly Australia is about to come of age in these matters. The 30 June 1981 census form asked this first ever sensible question: "Is the person of Aboriginal or Islander origin?" The wording of the subsidiary question, while well-intentioned, still carried "blood" overtones: "If the person is of mixed origin, indicate the one to which they consider themselves to belong."

Aborigines as a class (and as a class of colours). Aborigines have been, and in Queensland many still are, a separate legal class of persons, separate not by virtue of their desire to be so but because of barriers set down by government in law. They were (and are) separate in that they became minors in law, wards in law, with all the attendant disabilities of that class. They could not drink, possess or supply alcohol or methylated spirit, nor come within two chains of licensed premises, marry a non-Aborigine without permission or have sex across the colour line. In Queensland they could not enter into contracts, establish businesses, draw from savings accounts or make wills without official permission. In many cases they were subject to penalties, including imprisonment, for offences which only their class could commit: leaving a reserve, entering one when barred, refusing to work, being cheeky, telling tales, writing salacious letters, committing adultery, and playing cards.

In the Northern Territory recently I came across the following archival gems: they add to that great low-water mark of the Welfare era, the case of Gladys and Mick,[8] in which white Mr Daly was initially refused permission by the Director of Welfare to marry black Miss Namagu. The Senior Constable at Lake Nash Station, writing on 21 September 1959:

> There is now one half-caste here living with a lubra. He is not married to her, but has been living with her for about six years. I was under the impression, until last week, that they were married. I don't know what Welfare policy is in matters of this nature but as they have four children it seems to be a little too late to do much about it. There are two or three other half-castes employed on the station who are believed to cohabit with the lubras when at the station. This is very hard to stop, even to detect, as it is condoned by the management . . . I intend to carry out a full investigation into these matters . . .

Again:

> X is a Queenslander . . . he has been made aware of the provision of the Welfare Ordinance and realises that he will be prosecuted if any offence is detected. It was explained to him that if he wished to marry

any female ward and his wishes were reciprocated, the Director would consider an application from him; however, illegal unions are frowned upon and he could be prosecuted if he entered into any such union.

This gives an equation something like this: Aboriginality equals colour and gradations of colour equals class of minors with disabilities in proportion to their gradations of colour (except, as we saw from the Queensland definition, those who could be called reserve bloods!).

Aborigines as a Culture. Edward Tylor's *Primitive Culture* was first published in 1871. The work has been criticised, particularly by the eminent Australian scholar V. Gordon Childe. Tylor, he says,[9] didn't see human societies as functioning wholes "but as isolated activities, or aspects, of societies". Nevertheless Tylor's definition[10] is one that is apt in this context: "Culture or Civilization, taken in its wide ethnographic sense, is that complex whole which includes knowledge, belief, art, morals, law, custom, and any other capabilities and habits acquired by man as a member of society." Two points must be made: firstly, unlike Childe I believe that here Tylor sees culture as a total phenomenon, holistic in concept and in reality; secondly, I accept his broad definition as explaining culture only. Civilisation is something more than Tylor says it is and to appreciate Aboriginality we need to see just how much more than culture — as defined here — it is.

Aboriginality as culture has been portrayed in grossly simplistic terms by government officials, missionaries and pastoral property employers. The following can be said to be their "old" (but held until very recently) view:

"Myalls"	The white cultural perception is one of cere-
"Bushies"	monial forms (mortuary rites, circumcision
"Tribals"	and sub-incision rituals) and family practices
"Heathens"	that are essentially barbaric, uncivilised, un-Christian, un-Australian and anathema — in spite of having full equivalents in our culture such as circumcision, funeral ceremonies and incest prohibitions. Such customs are seen to permeate, and be embedded in their cultural configuration.

"Half-castes"	The white cultural perception is one of light-
"Quadroons"	ness, or their having "lost" the above config-
"Octoroons"	uration on the infusion of white drops, of
	their being "enlightenmentable", assimilable,
	Christianisable, civilise-able, nearer-to-God-
	go-thee kind of people.

All these qualities were perceived as being fixed, immutable and therefore transmittable from one generation to the next. Government policy was predicated on these notions, or *sights* rather than notions. Culture is seen as related to and contingent upon gradations of colour. Rights were, of course, dispensed in accordance with these perceptions.

We now have a picture of their "new" view, one admitted at the start of the last decade, resulting from Aboriginal assertiveness about identity, decision-making, land rights and the recognition of Aboriginal culture. But the new forms whites are prepared to accept are still only those that are aesthetically pleasing or comfortable: One Pound Jimmy on our postage stamps, Albert Namatjira and his legacy of water colours, bark paintings on our dollar notes, goannas and turtles on an endless array of table linen, traditional corroboree performances for concert export.

A different but equally simplistic set of dogmas to bedevil the issue has derived on occasion from the work of social anthropologists. In 1979 I wrote this perhaps unduly harsh criticism:[11]

> For Aborigines the ultimate indignity is the sovereignty of those who control the gathering and dissemination of the written and spoken word concerning their situation. White reconstruction anthropology (and some ethnocentric history) has provided a mental straitjacket for whites and blacks: a physical prototype, head-banded, bearded, loin-clothed, sometimes ochred, one foot up, a clutch of spears, ready to hunt or exhibiting eternal, mystical vigilance. Libraries of material — often of great value and scholarship — have helped create, or re-create, a pristine, pure, before-the-white-man-came-and-buggered-everything, idealised type. THAT, says the academic orthodoxy, is Aboriginality: any deviation therefrom gives white society licence to deny people that which they are and believe themselves to be.

Some academics showed a vested interest in keeping things as they were thought to be. The tradition of what I call "reconstruction anthropology" permeated the Australian Institute of Aboriginal Studies from its inception in 1961 until the mid-1970s. With the enactment of its statute, (then) Senator John Gorton said: "the permanent Institute will not be concerned with current problems as they affect Aborigines". Perhaps the men rather than the discipline were at fault but there was a pervasive attitude that said: avoid part-Aboriginal communities and their problems, eschew all research involving matters of policy, politics, legislation, administration, welfare. For that very reason Monash University, with the Institute's blessing, established the Aboriginal Research Centre in 1964: to do the very things the Institute did not consider "safe". In the 1960s a handful of theses ventured into the realm of social change studies. Even then most of the few tended to be more concerned with the degree to which the subjects studied were holding on to *themness*, resisting white values and intrusions. With Aboriginal assertiveness has come a change in research direction. Marcia Langton's review of this literature should be heeded. Her critique[12] centres on the academic treatment and "location" of urban Aborigines: "We are exploring our own Aboriginality and are finding that the white social scientists cannot accept our view of ourselves." The major point, however, is that the legacy of the "reconstruction era" — which in another sense has made a most important contribution, as discussed later — will endure as *the* image of Aboriginality for a long time to come.

Such is the authority of these academic images, such was and is the hegemony of white knowledge and white dissemination of all things Aboriginal, that some of these perceptions have been enshrined in what is otherwise the most positive piece of legislation in Aboriginal history, the *Aboriginal Land Rights (Northern Territory) Act* 1976. It embodies several anthropological orthodoxies. Section 50 requires the Aboriginal Land Commissioner to ascertain whether Aboriginal claimants are the traditional owners of any unalienated Crown land claimed. The Commissioner is obliged to "have regard to the strength or otherwise of the traditional attachment by the claimants . . ." Traditional owners are then defined as "a local descent group of Aboriginals who . . . have common spiritual affiliations to a site on the land, being affiliations that place the group under a primary spiritual responsibility for that site and for that land; and . . . are entitled by Aboriginal tradition to forage as of right over that land."

Mr Justice Toohey has said "there are some objective criteria by which to measure but in the end the assessment [of strength of spiritual attachment] must reflect a large element of the subjective, an attempt to understand the feelings and attitudes of the people, an attempt to see things as they see them".[13] An examination of the transcripts of some of the claims to date, and of the reports of the Land Commissioner, show just how much importance is placed on anthropological evidence as to spirituality and strength of attachment. Intended or not, the *wording of the Act* in my view has resulted in practice whereby the techniques and taxonomies of the anthropologists loom larger than the articulation and overt behaviour and social history of the Aborigines themselves (as most who observed the lengthy Uluru [Ayers Rock] land claim would agree). In an arbitration proceeding (which is what a land claim is meant to be), or even in an adversary situation, the level of "proof" adduced by anthropologists seems weightier and more determining than that required of expert witnesses in other fields. Objective proof of cancer by an oncologist is one thing; objective or even subjective proof of spirituality is quite another. I do not attack the notion of applied anthropology or the use of academics in politically and morally virtuous pragmatic action. But where else in the world, where else in the collective experience of minorities seeking and obtaining land rights, has an external discipline been inserted to such effect over and above the (internal) living claimants in order to establish such personal and elemental phenomena as descent, spirituality and strength of such attachment? Where else in a land rights context have such criteria as prior occupation, settlement, conquest, adverse possession or prescription, plain possession, gift, deed, grant, cession or reservation (as in Southern Africa, Canada, the United States) been totally excluded from consideration?

This is now the equation: Aboriginality equals full-bloodedness equals darkness equals but-at-least-it's-the-true-culture; part-Aboriginality equals lightness equals closeness to enlightenment equals but re-identification (let alone identification) is not possible because they're not full-blood equals it's a "mixed" culture equals the best we/they can do is take the best from both worlds. These perceptions of colour turn blacks and whites away from seeing and comprehending an enduring truth: that being a full, participating member of a group, an identity, a culture, *can involve the capacity to be proud of those values even in the very process of abandoning them, or having abandoned them.* Colour, or gradation thereof, is irrelevant. Unless this is understood most of those who presume to know and who declare their concern will persist in making invidious distinctions between "real" Aborigines and others, between "traditional" ("culture-ful") Aborigines and others.

Among themselves, Aborigines show differences in the quality or quantity of their religious or traditional practice, of their place of domicile, in their sense of where and to what they belong. Two examples illustrate the point[14]: (i) An Aboriginal man, tearing off his shirt ready for a fight: "Come on! I'm not mission blackfella, I'm not myall, I'm not drunken town blackfella, I'm station man!"; (ii) "You go away! You rubbish! You nothing! You only boy!" — this, from men of the 20 to 30 year age group to a man of 50 who hadn't been initiated. But despite the differences they perceive, that we perceive, they are collectively *other*, other as an entity in white eyes, white culture, in white society. As it relates to white mainstream society, it is this very otherness of Aboriginality that is in jeopardy when non-Aborigines (or even some Aborigines) make distinctions based on colour, blood, geographic location and social history. The great fight Aborigines have on their hands is to save the varying forms of Aboriginal life, the otherness that ranges from "station man" to Ms. Langton's "living actuality", her "inside story of Aboriginality". The differences between Aboriginal groups is something they have to take care of. (At times it may be appropriate for whites to become involved in some of those internal differences.)

Other perceptions of Aborigines. As a religious group? There are Aboriginal communities where religion is an integral part of their social and familial organisation. Recognition of the sacredness of aspects of their religion has come about recently with efforts to protect sacred sites and objects from vandalism and despoiling. Religion, in the sense of spiritual attachment, has figured largely in Northern Territory land claims. In the Alyawarra and Kaititja claim, Mr Justice Toohey, while finding white witnesses helpful, turned to "the claimants primarily": "The obvious enthusiasm of those people for their country and the disclosure of important places and sacred objects was compelling".[15] The Warlpiri presented a "clear picture of a very strong traditional attachment",[16] one which "showed itself in the ceremonial life of the people, the concern expressed for country, the wish to return to it to live or for a time or to be buried there, and attempts and proposals to set up outstations".[17] But important as religion is here, it is no more central to the essence or the totality of Aboriginality than is Jewish religion to the phenomenon of Judaism and Jewishness, where the latter two can be said to be the composite of the collected thoughts, sentiments and efforts of Jewish people (however different).

As a minority in a multicultural society? We now have a rampant fashion in Australia: the placing of "ethnicity" and all things "ethnic" on a pedestal — all of it, without undue cynicism, devoted to an avowed wooing of the migrant vote. Establishment of Aboriginality has been a tremendous battle; as a result, Aborigines don't wish to surrender this recognition by being consumed or subsumed by a generalised multiculturalism. There was a period when a few anthropologists and several civil servants postulated the poor-whitemanship of Aborigines, arguing that they exhibited all the problems and symptoms of existence and existing as shown, for example, by Welsh coalminers. Mercifully for all, these perceptions died before they really were born. There is, lamentably, another so-called "poverty": the "culture of poverty" with which so many academics seek to endow part-Aborigines, especially those in urban centres.

As members of a nation state? In the Coe case it was argued that an Aboriginal nation (state) existed prior to white arrival and held sovereignty over all Australia, some of which sovereignty, it was claimed, still exists. In this particular context, international law requires three things for a nation state to exist: population, territory and the absence of any outside control in the determination of the population's affairs. Clearly today Aborigines do not form a nation in that sense. Do they have *nationhood* in the sense of a separate identity, as Palestinians and Kurds claim to do? Yes, in the sense that I use the term civilisation; no, in the very real sense that white Australians concede "partial" identity by virtue only of strains and fractions of blood — no Kurdish nation so to speak, but half-Kurds, quarter-Kurds, mixed Kurds.

Aboriginality as "Race-Civilisation." My initial interest in

Aboriginality as civilisation was stirred rather than stimulated by a front page headline in a Darwin newspaper.[18] Captain Tom Milner, president of the Automobile Association of the NT, said in relation to the very high road death rate that we don't need random breathalyser tests. We all know, he said, that the Aborigines are the killers:

> All men are not equal in the sight of the bottle. Western man has been using alcohol since the introduction of settled agriculture 7000 years ago while Eastern man has been using mind-blowing drugs for the same period. Aboriginal man, never having developed any form of agriculture, can handle neither, as he has proved quite convincingly since contact with western man a mere two centuries back.

What Aborigines are up against — amongst the many other things they are up against — is this kind of "race-civilisation" analysis, the kind which General Hertzog established as the fulcrum of modern apartheid in South Africa in 1926, the one which postulated the Africans as being in their "nonage": "as against the European the Native stands as an eight-year old child next to a man of greying experience — a child in religion, a child in moral conviction; without art and without science; with the most primitive requirements and a most rudimentary knowledge of how to supply these needs . . ."[19]

"Race-civilisation" theory has serious and often disastrous consequences for those defined as different. Following the mere assertion of the differences between "adult" and "child", Hertzog was able to legislate for differentials in every facet of life and its conduct. We have already seen something of the similar consequences for Aborigines who were legislated for in similar vein.

"Race-civilisation" comes not only to the common but also to the sophisticated intellectual mind. In his *Social Evolution*, V. Gordon Childe[20] adopts the framework devised by Lewis Henry Morgan in 1871[21], namely, that in the evolution of society as a whole there is a sequence by which the position of any observable society can be recognised. The three "ethnical periods" in the sequence are "Savagery, Barbarism and Civilisation". However, this framework is used to assess only *technological* change.

Aboriginal history is replete with garbled ideas about evolution, sequences, ages and stages. In Arnhem Land Dr Carmel [Schrire] White[22] documents 25,000 years of human occupation, with evidence of a stone technology using edge-ground axes — a technological advance of thousands of years upon the development of European man. Yet both before and after her work, the best and the worst of commentators have engaged in this kind of "race-civilisation" thinking, in equating Aboriginal behaviour and characteristics with savagery and barbarism.

In 1913 Professor W. Baldwin Spencer wrote[23]:

> The aboriginal is, indeed, a very curious mixture; mentally, about the level of a child who has little control over his feelings and is liable to give way to violent fits of temper, during which he may very likely behave with great cruelty. He has no sense of responsibility and, except in rare cases, no initiative.

They never realised that the kangaroos they caught and ate could provide them with skin clothing against the cold; "the native has no idea whatever of the cultivation of crops nor of the domestication of animals". In this respect "he is far lower than the Papuan, the New Zealander or the usual African native". Their customs were sometimes "revolting to us", such as their highly complex system of incest prohibition within marriage: but we shouldn't interfere with it "until we can give them something better and something that they can understand".

Thus the views of the eminent professor of biology at Melbourne University 68 years ago. In 1979 we have the views of Father Eugene Perez, a Benedictine, whose writings on Kalumburu Mission earned him the highest of accolades from the Premier of West Australia.[24] Sir Charles Court writes of Perez and his colleagues as lives "spent in unselfish dedication" in the "most sustained attempt by West Australians to incorporate Aboriginal people into the community at large".

The people Fr Perez works with are, in his words, the "East Kimberley Primitives" who correspond to the Paleolithic Age: "Australian primitives [who] remained dwarfed to the bare essentials of human existence".[25] The missionaries who came as "messengers of the Good News of Christian civilisation and Western culture" maintain their original aim to this day: "to humanise the remnants of the unfortunate and forgotten tribes of a stone-age."

Aborigines, *inter alia*, have "inborn cunning", "lack interest and ambition", show "undeniable immaturity"; they are not "a productive, but rather a consumer society", with "no definite purpose in life'', a ''decomposed society''.[26] Our way of life demands ''concepts and responsibilities beyond their powers of comprehension'' and they can't be ''trusted with the serious responsibility of planning, or of looking after, their own affairs and destiny''. Their ''unsound ambitions'' lead them to expect — under new policy ideas like self-management — the unattainable EL DORADO, coming to them on a silver tray''. Even the reintroduction of tribal laws among ''the more pure Aborigines'' seems to him ''to be rather suspect''. Finally:

> Completely destitute of any constructional ability — beyond the paper-bark-shelter of their walkabout pilgrimages; ignorant of any kind of agricultural activity — not knowing any other ecology than the one of their reduced hunting grounds . . . housing and care had to be supplied for them, is being supplied, and they would expect that it will continue to be supplied, and this at increasing cost to the tax payers. Most improvident, as the Australian Aborigine always was . . . he takes all this and everything else for granted, not appreciating its value. With no thought of the morrow . . . he would go now, with the greatest of ease, through any amount of provisions . . . With no sense of balance or proportion . . . he will continue to want ''today'' what cannot be given till tomorrow, regardless of the nature or value of handouts in money, implements or property — like the toy given to a child, which will soon be reduced to bits, and thrown into the rubbish dump.

[In September 1981 the Roman Catholic Bishop for the North-West removed Fr Seraphim Sanz as superintendent of Kalumburu Mission. Notwithstanding his claim that ''the Aborigines want me at the mission forever'', his dismissal was triggered when large numbers of Aborigines left the mission, crying ''enough'' at 42 years of Fr. Sanz' practice and Fr. Perez' ideology of ''race-civilisation''. A month later the West Australian mining magnate, Lang Hancock, said ''half-caste Aborigines should be sterilised by drugging their water supply . . . and so breed themselves out''.[27] These are the people Fr Perez describes as ''the so-called 'Aboriginal minority' generously favoured by recent liberal interpretations of blood count''.]

Aboriginality as civilisation

In 1952 Kroeber and Kluckhohn[28] assembled 164 definitions of culture. Now there would be only slightly fewer treatments of the similarities and differences between civilisation and culture.

Aboriginality is culture but it certainly comprises and embraces more than that. It is important to show it is more because far too often white society equates Aboriginal culture only with facets of their ornamental culture, such as bark paintings.

I have chosen two approaches to civilisation. One allows the ready slotting in of Aboriginality; the other is complex and fraught with problems of both wording and understanding. Both are based on an analogy — but not an identification — with the Jewish experience, because that phenomenon is relevant enough and well-known enough to help convey what constitutes Aboriginality. As with some Jews some Aborigines live in a "homeland", or at least in a pervasively Aboriginal domain; others are in the Diaspora, scattered, dispersed, seeking constantly to establish and maintain an Aboriginal milieu and atmosphere, their sustaining social contacts and interaction.

Briefly, here are the ideas of Ernest J. Hull SJ, editor of the *Examiner,* published in 1916:[29]

> Civilisation . . . I define as a state of social organisation which bonds together a race or people into a unity under a definite social code . . .: a code of government, a code of police, and a code of manners . . . (T)he government code regulates the action of the whole nation towards other nations, and the action of the citizens in relation to the state. (It regulates conduct towards government in such things as allegiance and paying tax, and conduct towards each other as in commerce.) The police code is nothing but a practical enforcement of the government code where the laws are infringed or neglected. The code of manners is something not created officially but by custom and convention, and determines how the citizens ought to behave towards each other outside the margin of obligations and of law . . . In short, civilisation is essentially the reign of social law.

Hull describes the manner in which indigenous peoples were civilised in these senses: "they had tribal laws of great precision and observed them with unflinching rigour; and these laws covered a considerable area of government, police and manners". Every tribe member could "thus count on the conduct of his fellow tribesman under various circumstances": in short, there was a reign of social law. Just as civilisation is a collective idea, so its opposite, savagery, is an individualistic one. Civilisation is a stable social condition of things; savagery an unstable one. The former is the reign of law, the latter the absence of law. "Savagery is that state of things in which the individual is a law to himself, and the only law."

All else, he asserts, lies outside civilisation and is perhaps irrelevant: "Civilisation means neither clothes, nor houses, nor industries, nor science, nor culture, nor taste, nor literature, nor art." Much of these are present but they stand outside the essential idea of civilisation: they belong to it "materially", not "formally" (intrinsically). "A primitive people needing no clothes and no houses, eating the things which nature provides for them, without literature or art or industries, would possess a perfect civilisation, provided they agreed to live at peace with each other and in due consideration for each other's rights and liberties."

Culture he defines as the application of human faculties to some object: there is mental culture (sustained use of the intellect or the senses in issues of knowledge or science); technical culture (the exercise of some industry or art); ethical culture (which means the exercise of the will on the lines of moral principle); aesthetic culture (the appreciation of the beautiful in nature, manners or in art); and physical culture (the cultivation of the body and its movements). Culture is partly the cause and partly the effect of civilisation. Civilisation does not have to mean progress, he says. And where there is progress, it may be cultural or technological — not civilisational.

There is no need for me to labour the point that Aboriginality fits well these descriptions and prescriptions. There was Aboriginal civility and civilisation for perhaps 50,000 years before 1788. Even after white settlement, expansion and "pacification of the natives", civilisation remained. There was good reason for a scholar like William Lloyd Warner to call his study of the Murngin people of Arnhem Land *A Black Civilisation*.[30] Despite my earlier stricture on "reconstruction anthropologists", those researchers performed one signal service: they reconstructed and presented aspects of Aboriginal civilisation in Hull's sense. Kevin Gilbert's recent comment[31] would not really have been possible without their work: "But when we compare the stability and level of true civilisation, the ennobled state of Aborigines, the length of our civilisation, to the British, Chinese, Germans etc. we find that we rank not only amongst the most civilised and most socialised, but also as the longest unchanged, continuing civilisation in the world.''

The difficult approach centres on "Diaspora" Aborigines finding a satisfactory ideology of Aboriginality, one that enables them to sustain themselves against the opposition of all around them. As it relates to Aborigines, I look at civilisation in this schematic way:

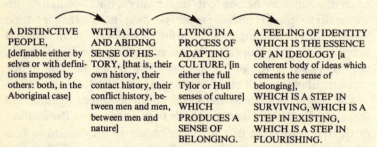

| A DISTINCTIVE PEOPLE, [definable either by selves or with definitions imposed by others: both, in the Aboriginal case] | WITH A LONG AND ABIDING SENSE OF HISTORY, [that is, their own history, their contact history, their conflict history, between men and men, between men and nature] | LIVING IN A PROCESS OF ADAPTING CULTURE, [in either the full Tylor or Hull senses of culture] WHICH PRODUCES A SENSE OF BELONGING. | A FEELING OF IDENTITY WHICH IS THE ESSENCE OF AN IDEOLOGY [a coherent body of ideas which cements the sense of belonging], WHICH IS A STEP IN SURVIVING, WHICH IS A STEP IN EXISTING, WHICH IS A STEP IN FLOURISHING. |

Aborigines have a definable population. It wasn't always counted in the census; and even when official counts began in 1971 they have been bedevilled by concerns as to fractions of colour. Aborigines have their own history, which includes the history of black-white relations. Their history is often a painful one but it is assuredly part of the social cement that holds together a society and a civilisation. One must reject the nonsense of those civil servants and academics who talk of the need to forget the past. Minorities oppressed and decimated in the ways Aborigines (and Jews) have been cannot and do not forget.

Across Australia Aboriginal groups live in a cultural environment of Aboriginality — however different, orthodox, revisionist, however strong or diluted — *irrespective* of white interpretations of their colour correctness. From Oenpelli in Arnhem Land to Framlingham in western Victoria, from Strelley in remote West Australia to Tingha in northern NSW, Aboriginality — albeit of different kinds and different manners — is being lived daily. Kitaoji's thesis[32] on Kempsey, NSW describes the high degree of maintenance of the traditional family among Aborigines whom even whites want to accept as having "passed". The Tingha girls still go down to Sydney with aunty escorts to see they don't contract a marriage to a male of the wrong skin group. The Strelley people proclaim their vision and practice of a spartan, stern, almost Hasidic orthodoxy and denigrate (as whites so often do) all part-Aboriginality, not so much on account of colour difference but because of what they see as religious ignorance. Yet the recipients of this abuse are doing precisely what the Strelley people are doing: establishing community schools for the express purpose of preserving their distinctiveness. The collectivity and continuity of Aboriginality — divorced from fictions based on colour — need to be appreciated. It is this essence of Aboriginality that is denied by myths based on fractions of caste or blood.

Some people have told me they cannot conceive of any two kinds of people more apart, remote and different than dual Masters degree holder Margaret Valladian and tribal elder Jacob Oberdoo from Strelley. However, they are bound together by their religion, their religious present or religious past; they are bound because of their immediate, secular history, their different but nevertheless painful and discriminatory history; by their common heroes, their common (often identifiable) enemies, their common contemporary predicament, their common myths and needs, their common concern for the future and well-being of the people they see as Aborigines, by the common positive as well as negative aspects of their otherness, the otherness that is often foisted upon them whether they like it or not, even the kind they seek themselves.

There is, of course, one *internal* difference between Jacob Oberdoo and Margaret Valladian. He lives in a society with its own laws, social sanctions, *mores*, schools, one which maintains a separation of values, where the domain in which he lives is *his*. Margaret Valladian lives in the geography of a white world: she has to *create* the domain of Aboriginality. Her battle, and that of so many like her, is *to raise the level of consciousness of what they already have*, both for themselves and for those who perceive them as the fractional, "lost-culture" people.

How do Aborigines think about themselves? What in their view sets them apart and what are their changing perceptions of self-hood? No one has asked them in any systematic way. If anyone does, it will have to be a tortuous, circuitous approach given the very different communities. Some Aborigines have a clear-cut ideology of blackness or Aboriginality within their groupings. It may be expressed within the communities or it may be so much part and parcel of their lives that it does not need special articulation.

Sometimes it is expressed poorly, or even suppressed because they lack the words and the skills with which to address it to the other world. What Aborigines have not done yet — and one may argue that they shouldn't have to do it — is to enunciate an *ideology of Aboriginality* that is addressed to the white world, that expresses a coherent body of thoughts and ideas that embraces their interaction and involvement with our world. In short, there is as yet no intellectual and/or religious dynamism that conceptualises black consciousness and voluntary separatism to the white world, perhaps even to themselves. *And such is necessary if they are going to be perceived differently.*

The land rights "movement" is an important example of the need for a coherent ideology addressed to and capable of comprehension by the white mainstream. Aborigines, and many concerned white supporters, have used land rights as the rallying point to focus attention on the Aboriginal condition. A banner has to have substance; a solid basis for a cohering and cementing into something tangible, viable, developing, growing. Those involved have virtually stopped at land rights: at the need to attain such generally, at the political-mechanical problems of attaining land in West Australia and Queensland, of holding on to what has been attained in the Northern Territory. But once land, *what are the goals, the aims*?

There are many forms of political nationalism and some are concerned with land as a base and as a basis. Simon Dubnow[33] distinguishes three types of nationalism: tribal, politico-territorial and, probably the highest form of all, cultural-historical or spiritual (in the Zionist sense). The May 1980 Land Rights Symposium arranged by the Australian Institute of Aboriginal Studies was indeed a low-water mark in this sense. The content of the resulting publication[34] attests to the lack of cohesion, framework, philosophy in this area, to the ignorance of elementary political processes by many of the protagonists (several of whom wear the label of social scientists). In July 1981 an advertisement appeared in support of land rights in NSW.[35] The criteria of and for support are to "confer on Aboriginal people not only justice and compensation" but also to "provide an economic base on which to build a future". Are these the real criteria as Aborigines feel them? Or are they a white-influenced attempt to express the kind of economic considerations that will evoke a sympathetic response from the major society? My view is that land rights *as a movement*, not land rights as rights, is no longer sure where it came from, is not certain where it is and is undecided about where it is going.

Some of the black domains are intact. There ceremonial life can and does maintain an ideology in this civilisational sense. Their struggle is to perpetuate what they have in the face of such intrusions as mining and tourism. There are no more than twenty Aboriginal writers, mainly poets, published to date (in English that is). It is a start but it doesn't as yet provide an intellectual-religious dynamism for cohering. Some of the best Aboriginal minds have been pressed into civil service. Therein they become part of what Michel Crozier calls the "bureaucratic rhythm", one in which conformism and retreatism are more common than innovation.[36] Such innovators as there are, he says, tend to be legislators rather than discoverers. Civil service employment is an activity hugely different from the stimulation, dynamism and the relative freedom needed to be involved in pressure group politics.

Cohesion, in my sense, means survival. It is of much greater importance than the usual white, ethnocentric, economic concern about how Aborigines can survive as a minority amidst the invasion of white technology and greed. The Aboriginal literature to date is a plea to us to hear their demeaning and hurt. Perhaps the next generation will assert a more aggressive, chauvinistic, nationalistic and arrogant view. It has just begun. And as it continues it may eventually convince white Australia that Aboriginality is many-sided, multi-faceted, rich, complex, enduring, suffering, surviving. It is patently not what its historical treatment has been: the arithmetic of colour, the division of people into halves, quarters, eighths, sixteenths and almost full people whose fractions of the blood determine their degree of civility, the degree to which they are aberrant, inept, unable, pathological, the degree therefore to which they are entitled or are allowed to participate in the benefits, rights and values of white civilisation.

Being Aboriginal: Raised to Think White

Compiled by Ros Bowden, with the voices of Coral Edwards and Lola, Joy, Robyn, Cherie and Kevin

"My mother was Aboriginal. The policy was to separate children, especially fair-skinned children, from the mothers as soon as possible. On my Certificate of Removal it said 'Take the child from the association of Aborigines as she's a fair-skinned child.' I think the rationale behind that was to raise me as white."

"I was adopted when I was, I think, about twenty weeks old to a white family in Sydney and that's where I grew up. They were a middle-class family and I grew up with one younger brother. We grew up on the Northern beaches of Sydney so it was a very middle-class suburb and there were no other Aboriginal people around that I knew of."

"I know for a fact that I was adopted when I was only a couple of months old. When I was younger I didn't want to have anything to do with Aborigines. I sort of thought of myself as being a white person. In fact, if ever I heard the word Aborigine I'd back away, so to speak, but that was when I was much younger, and then as I grew older and wiser I came to terms with it."

* * *

"When I found out that I was Aboriginal, one of the biggest things that I had to start doing was looking really closely at all the things that I'd learned and the stereotypes. [I had to look] at things like being taught by white people — I don't just mean by that my family, I mean the school that I went to and the newspapers and just everything around me — the white culture that I grew up in. I had to start questioning all the things that I'd learned through growing up like that. I felt really frightened that I'd take all those judgments home with me and put them on my family, because they're wrong and an absolutely bad place to start from in trying to get to know your family. It's hard enough getting to know strangers anyway, let alone putting all these judgments and rubbish on them.''

''I was 36 when I started to think that I was black, in my mind, because I had been working and living in white society for so many years. I've been discovering my Aboriginality since 1983 and there's no way that I will again think white.''

''It took a long time to get over that thing of black not being a colour of your skin. I'd been taught to believe that to be black you have to have really dark skin. That's partly also why, growing up, it was harder for me to identify as Aboriginal, see myself as Aboriginal, because I thought that I didn't look Aboriginal enough to be Aboriginal. And all those things like, 'You're so fair you can't be Aboriginal', and 'What about the part of you that isn't Aboriginal?', and 'What percentage of you is Aboriginal?' — all those qustions were what I'd grown up with around me, so it is actually quite a long process, feeling that I could comfortably identify as black.''

''How many times have I heard said, 'How can you really consider yourself an Aboriginal person when you had a white father, or if you've got white blood in you?' You cop it all the time from white Australians and I just say to them, 'Look, you are what you are and I am what I am. I'm an Aboriginal person. What are you?' 'I'm an Australian', they say. But what are they, really? What are white Australians? They're always questioning our identity and we always have to prove our Aboriginality, but when have white Australians ever proved their identity?''

Carol Edwards says it's hard to explain the need to find out about being Aboriginal.
''It just drives you. It takes over your whole life. You want to belong so much and you've got no base to start on, because if you start mixing with Aboriginal people the first thing they're going to say is, 'What's your name and where do you come from?' And if you can't answer those two questions then you're gone. People can't connect you into the Aboriginal network because they don't

know the name, or you don't know the name, so they sort of shut the door straight away. That's why it's really important for us to get to know what the natural name is, because as soon as we've got that name we can pick the area. For instance, my family name is Edwards and there are only three places in New South Wales where there are Edwards families. We talk about our country, our spot . . . Aboriginal families didn't move far from those areas. People say, 'Edwards — where are you from? Are you from Bourke or from Balranald or Tingha?' and I say, 'I'm a Tingha Edwards', and people just click you [in] because they know. One of the most common Aboriginal names probably would be Williams. Now, there are Williams not connected with each other, different Williams families from the North Coast, South Coast, out West, and Smith is another one and Johnson's another — we know Johnsons only come from certain areas. And so that's why it's really important for people to have that name so we can just click them in.

"If someone came to us and said their name was Williams, for instance, we would contact those areas and not just ring up. We don't ring up, we actually drive to that town and go and see the people, because it's the right thing to do, and find an older person who'll remember. And the thing with children being taken, people remember that. It's not something that's just forgotten, like yesterday's birthday party. They say, 'Oh, yes, so-and-so had a child taken, you know, thirty years ago, or something like that, and she's married to, say, someone else now, but was a Williams'. People remember. You just don't forget something like a child being taken.

"People contact us through word of mouth. They ring through or write letters. A lot of welfare agencies — Aboriginal Child Care agencies, Youth & Community, any government offices, in fact, any enquiries at all now, they just put them on to us."

* * *

"With relationships there are certain things in the Aboriginal society that you just don't do, and I'm learning those — what to do and what not to do. You can refuse a biscuit or a piece of bread or a piece of cake or something, but you never refuse a cup of tea. There are people that you go and see first, not a pecking order, but

there are people you go and see first and people you spend a certain amount of time with. There are some that you can talk to about certain things and others who can talk about other things.''
''Aboriginal families are so extended — that's the biggest thing I think, getting used to having heaps of people in the house, cousins, aunties, uncles. There might be ten living under the same roof. There might be a lot of them living on benefits. Some of them don't. A lot of them work some time. Always, if you've got money and your brother hasn't and he needs money to go down to the shop and get something, well, you'll just give him money and you'll give everyone money. If they need something they're very unmaterialistic. Money isn't an issue. It's surviving, you know, and we've all got to survive, so you give it away so everyone can survive.''

''I was put through the hoops a couple of times. I made one horrendous mistake when I went back by myself the second time and Janie's fridge was empty. So, big magnanimous me, I decided to go out and do a whole lot of shopping and spent about $80 to $90 on groceries and filled up the fridge. That was in the morning. In the late afternoon nearly all the food was gone and I said, 'Jane, look, all those bloody kids are running around eating this food that I bought for you. There's only one loaf of bread left.' Then I opened the fridge and I went through everything that was left, I knew the fridge had been full and she said to me, 'Listen here, little woman, you didn't buy all that food just for me, you bought it for all of us. Once one of us has got the food, we all have the food. Those children out there are just as hungry as my children are in this house, so,' she said, 'don't come up here with your high-falutin' ideas of thinking you're doing me a favour, otherwise you can just piss off now.' That was the most marvellous thing she ever said to me because if she could talk to me like that it showed me she really cared and that she wanted me to learn how things were done, not how to *be* but how to *show* I'm Koori.''

''In the white culture not to look someone in the eye all the time that they're talking to you is rude; it's like you're not paying attention. But to look Aboriginal people in the eye the whole time you're talking to them is rude, because you're staring at them.

That was really hard to get used to. It takes a long time to accept that something you learned as good manners in one culture is wrong in another, a long time to be able to do that and feel comfortable, about doing it. It's like being in a no-man's-land in a way, because you don't know Aboriginal ways enough to feel comfortable and to know that you don't sort of stick out as someone who doesn't know quite what they're doing half the time. You're trying to watch other people and trying not to make mistakes and laugh at the wrong things . . . your whole body language is different. I'm sure I stick out like a sore thumb to people and they wonder, they think, this woman's a bit strange. Also I found that I lost a lot of contact with the white people I'd spent a lot of time with. That was a long process, partly because they didn't understand why it was so important to me to find out where I was from and also because it became an absolute obsession that I just had to know everything that was to do with who I was. And because most of the white people I knew didn't really understand that, I lost a lot of contact with them. You're a bit in limbo for a long time, I think.''

''There's a natural bond that I feel toward Aboriginal people that when I was thinking white was never there. I've re-discovered that. You'll just nod, even if you don't know them, if you see them somewhere, in a restaurant or in a pub, or walking down the street. It's 'Cous' or 'Sis' or 'Brother'. You just do it.''

''Aboriginal people are getting a lot stronger. They're feeling like their own people. They're uniting more. And they're doing a lot to rejuvenate the culture, just bring it to people's eyes. Once people know about where they come from — their country, their tribes — and they've met their families, then they've got it inside, and they know a little bit about traditional society and how traditional people lived: that's all they need.''

''I want to say that I feel I'm regaining my Aboriginality. To me at the moment it means that I know where I'm from, I know who my people are, I'm starting to know who all my relations are and to meet them and get to know them as my aunts and uncles and cousins and my grandfather. I'm learning very slowly the history of the area that I'm from and it *is* a sense of belonging, and unless you've felt that you *don't* belong, it's really hard to explain how important it is and how precious it is knowing where I'm from.''

"When we got to Arambi Mission I was told to stand and look all around, which I did, and they said 'Now, all of that's yours'. It's all bounded by natural boundaries. None of it, before the *gubs* (white people) got here anyway, none of it was subdivided for individual use.

"This is part of the land rights question. We never *had* subdivided for individual ownership: that territory was bounded by natural boundaries.''

"I had to know the history, to know where I came from and to be really knowledgeable. There are a lot of Aboriginal people that wouldn't know what I know, although they know it in a different way than I do. A lot that I know is from books, but they know it because they've lived it or their father or grandfather lived it and it's been passed down that way.

"I have to know things because when you get with Aboriginal people they talk about the old times a lot and you like to be able to participate, too. It's good to sit there and listen and learn; it's also good if you know a little bit, even if it is from a book.''

"As an Aboriginal person it will give me something to identify myself by to know that I do have a family. When I'm with other fellow Aboriginals I feel a certain bond, a certain magic. I feel like I'm part of their family. It's a wonderful feeling, actually: a feeling of joy, a feeling of pride.''

"Aboriginality means to me that you come from the land. It's your land, Australia, the trees, the grass, the seas, the deserts, the rainforests, are all linked with yourself. It's something nobody can take away from you.''

Part Three
A Multicultural Nation?

The ethnic make-up of Australian society has been significantly altered as a result of large-scale immigration since World War II. Australia is now a multi-ethnic society, a "multicultural nation". One of the results of large numbers of migrants and their children becoming Australians is the questioning or revision of traditional images of what it means to be an Australian. An Australian might still be a Man from Snowy River, but he or she might also be a man or woman from Italy or Turkey, Ireland, Lebanon or Cambodia.

Government policy and popular national images have changed in response to immigration and multiculturalism, both of which have been controversial areas for public debate. Some have welcomed large-scale immigration for its economic effects or celebrated multiculturalism; others have argued that "the Australian way of life" is under threat. Whatever the position, images of national identity are closely involved in the debates.

Jock Collins, in Reading 6, provides a brief overview of Australian immigration followed by a survey of the development of multiculturalism and opposition to it from different sides of politics.

Castles, Kalantzis, Cope and Morrissey, in Reading 7, provide a more contentious argument. They see the idea of a multicultural nation as an improvement on earlier, racist ways of conceiving Australia; but they are also critical of certain aspects of multiculturalism, especially in so far as it is still tied to "older" ways of thinking about national identity.

Further reading

Bottomley, G., and de Lepervanche, M., eds, *Ethnicity, Class and Gender in Australia*. Sydney: Allen & Unwin, 1984.

Castles, S., Kalantzis, M., Cope, B. and Morissey, M. *Mistaken Identity: Multiculturalism and the Demise of Nationalism in Australia*. Sydney: Pluto Press, 1988.

Collins, J. *Migrant Hands in a Distant Land: Australia's Post-War Immigration*. Sydney: Pluto Press, 1991 (2nd ed.).

Jupp, J., ed., *The Australian People: An Encyclopedia of the Nation, Its People and Their Origins*. Sydney: Angus & Robertson, 1988.

The federal Department of Immigration and the Office of Multicultural Affairs also publish excellent booklets, available through Commonwealth Government Bookshops.

Migrant Hands in a Distant Land

Jock Collins

Australian immigration

The impact of international capital and migration on the Australian economy has been more significant than on almost any other advanced capitalist country, with the exception of Israel. These factors have fundamentally shaped post-war Australian society.

The basic tenet of Australian immigration policy for over 100 years was "White Australia". Before Federation, the Colonies introduced anti-Chinese immigration restriction acts as a response to the influx of Chinese during the Gold Rush. Federation was accompanied by the 1901 Immigration Restriction Act, better known as the White Australia policy. Black labour from the Pacific Islands, the "Kanakas", were expelled from Queensland sugar plantations and the Chinese were to be kept out. Australia needed immigrants, but only whites were welcome. This policy was reiterated by Arthur Calwell who, as the first Minister for Immigration, launched the post-war immigration program. It was only in 1972 that the White Australia policy was formally buried. The Australian immigration story is inextricably linked with racist laws and practices.

By 1947, with a population of just under seven million, Australia had nearly three quarters of a million overseas born residents, the majority of whom were British. Immigration policy had achieved a "White Australia"! Only a small percentage of non-British migrants had managed to enter before and during the days of the White Australia policy, with Chinese, Italians, Greeks and Germans being the most prominent. Australia had selected its migrants to ensure that a racially homogeneous society would confront the challenges of the post-war era.

The post-war immigration program was to be the largest planned immigration intake in Australia's history. By 1981 the net intake from immigration was just under three million. At that time 21 per cent of the Australian population was born overseas, with another 20 per cent the Australian-born children of at least one migrant parent. More than four out of ten Australians today — some six million people — are therefore direct products of the post-war immigration program.[1] Immigration has thus had a greater impact in Australia than in any of the other major countries experiencing post-war immigration. Only Israel, with its unique history as a state created for the resettlement of Jews from all over the world, can exceed Australia in this regard.

The Australian immigration experience is notable not only for its relative size, but also for the ethnic diversity of its post-war migrant intake although this was not the intention of the architects of the post-war immigration program. Arthur Calwell emphatically planned to continue White Australia and preserve the homogeneity of Australian society. He gave assurances that "for every foreign migrant there would be ten from the United Kingdom".[2] But even in the first years of the program, insufficient British migrants were available and Calwell turned to Eastern Europe and the "Displaced Persons" (refugees from the Second World War) to fill immigration targets.

This pattern of the desired ethnic composition of the immigration intake undermined by availability was repeated throughout the following decades as immigration targets were undersubscribed by the preferred British. The immigration net was, reluctantly, cast wider and wider: first to the "more cultured" migrants from Northern Europe; then Southern Europe; the Middle East; and so on until the early 1980s, when the Indo-Chinese were the largest ethnic group in the immigration intake.

A policy which had initially been planned to continue a homogeneous and racially pure society had, by default, produced one of the most ethnically diverse of all immigration programs, with migrants from over 100 nationalities and ethnic groups making the long journey to Australia . . .

Although they were the largest birthplace group in the immigration intake, British migrants fell well short of Calwell's "nine-out-of-ten" ideal. Indeed a major feature of post-war immigration is the relative decline of British migration. Assessing Australia's net settler intake (arrivals minus departures) for the period 1947 to 1980, demographer Charles Price estimated that just over one third were from the United Kingdom and Eire. Just under one fifth came from Southern Europe, with the Italians and Greeks the largest birthplace groups after the British. Another 13 per cent came from Eastern Europe, with the Yugoslavs the next largest birthplace group. The other third of post-war migrants came from a great diversity of countries, as the Australian immigration net had been cast to most corners of the globe.

"Populate or perish" was Calwell's catchcry to sell his immigration program. The Australian population has more than doubled, from the 7 million in 1945 to over 16 million today. Of this population increase, more than three million were born overseas. Between 1947 and 1973 immigration contributed nearly 60 per cent of Australia's population increase, if the Australian-born children of immigrant parents are included in the calculation.[3] This enabled Australia to have the highest population growth rate of all the OECD countries in this period.

As was the case in Western Europe, immigration in Australia is closely tied to labour market needs. Migrant men and women were the major source of workforce growth in the post-war period, particularly in the 1950s and 1960s. By January 1987, 25.2 per cent of the labour force was born overseas, with overseas-born men 26.2 per cent of the total male labour force and overseas-born women 23.8 per cent of the female labour force.[4]

Comparing the Australian-born workforce with the overseas-born workforce taken as a whole there seems to be little difference in terms of occupational and industrial distribution in the labour market. However there is a distinctly different labour market profile between migrants of different ethnic origin. A useful distinction is that between migrants from the main English speaking countries (ES migrants) and those from non-English speaking countries (NES migrants).[5] ES migrants closely approximate to the labour market profile of the Australian-born, while NES migrants are disproportionately concentrated in the "dirty jobs" of unskilled or semi-skilled manual work associated with migrants in many other countries. The major exception to this generalisation are the Northern Europeans who, while not English speaking, appear to have a labour market profile more similar to ES migrants and the Australian-born. Any discussion of Australian migrants as if they were a homogenous grouping, that is all "dirty workers", misses the most salient aspects of Australian immigration: differences within migrants in Australia are as important as differences between migrants and the Australian-born.

The major problems faced by NES migrants relate to the economic domain. They are concentrated in the worst paid, hardest, most monotonous, dangerous and dirtiest jobs of the male and female segments of the labour market, particularly in the manufacturing sector. Consequently NES migrants have the lowest income, highest incidence of poverty, and highest rate of unemployment in non-Aboriginal Australia. It seems clear from the available evidence that NES migrants bore the brunt of the economic recession that has gripped Australia intermittently over the last decade. Even the most recent period of economic recovery seems to have bypassed the NES migrants, with the evidence that the improved labour market conditions of 1984 benefitted the Australian-born and ES migrants to the exclusion of NES migrants. But even here generalisations are difficult: the newly-arrived NES migrant groups — particularly the Indo-Chinese, Turkish and Lebanese — are much worse off than the Italians and the Greeks who arrived decades earlier.

This difference between ES and NES migrants is not limited to the labour market. Studies of the major socio-economic indicators such as income inequality, poverty, housing, health, education and access to legal services are unanimous in suggesting that NES migrants are severely disadvantaged when compared to ES migrants. This is mirrored in all dimensions of Australian society, whether it be the political, economic, social or ideological. This disadvantage seems to persist over time, although their children, the second generation migrants, appear to move into white collar jobs and achieve greater educational success.

NES migrants have had greater problems adjusting to Australian society. Language and cultural differences — small obstacles for ES migrants — become major hurdles for NES migrants. These problems relate not only to the workplace, but also to the home and community. Intergenerational conflict between migrant parents born overseas and their Australian-born children, worries about religious and social customs in an alien Australian environment and a sometimes hostile or indifferent reception by others — be they Australian-born or other migrants — all provide day-to-day problems for NES migrants. So, too, do gender relationships.

The subordination of women in cultures from the Mediterranean and Middle East, for example, and the dual role of migrant women as mothers and workers in a new society are often sources of conflict and difficulty, particularly as most did not work in the "old country".

Nevertheless, Australia's NES migrants seem better off than their counterparts overseas in terms of status in their new countries. Welfare services are available on arrival in Australia. Citizenship is a mere formality with the residential qualifying period being reduced from three years to two years in 1983 for non-British migrants, while political rights are available to all migrants once they are naturalised. Not all migrants avail themselves of this privilege; only 1.5 million of the overseas-born were citizens at the 1981 Census.[6] Nevertheless, the right to citizenship in Australia is in sharp contrast to recent Western European government actions to restrict further migrant rights, that are already limited, when compared to the indigenous population.

Australia's post-war migrants also seem to have escaped the sharp edge of racist attacks and anti-immigrant mobilisations that characterised community relations in many other countries over the last decade. Post-war migrants did of course enter a country with an entrenched history of racism, embodied in immigration laws and practices by the state, and in deep-rooted attitudes of prejudice and intolerance in the Australian people. Community opposition to newly arrived migrants achieved public attention during what has been called "the Blainey debate". Blainey argued that the majority of Australians opposed the increase of migrants from Asia.

In many ways it seems surprising that the large change in the ethnic composition of Australian society in the post-war period — and in particular the Indo-Chinese intake which dated from 1975 — did not give birth to such debates earlier. It took just under a decade of economic recession before public concern and debate raised immigration policy from a curiosity to national controversy. While far-right political groups such as the National Front agitated around "Keep Asians Out!" slogans, the failure of the Blainey view to achieve widespread support suggests that Australia's experience of anti-immigrant feeling is of a different order to that experienced in some overseas countries recently.

The rise of fascist groups, and the extent of popular support for and the intensity of racial violence in Western Europe and the UK, had no parallel in Australia. Indeed, one of the most remarkable features of Australia's rapid growth into one of the most multi-cultural countries in the world is that it has been achieved without serious social turmoil. This has not been because of an enlightened government, public, or trade union movement, nor because Australia is a "lucky country". Like the diverse ethnic composition of the immigration intake, Australia has managed to avoid serious racial conflict directed towards migrants more by default than by design.

*   *   *

Multiculturalism: uniting or dividing Australia?

. . . What has been the theory and practice of government in relation to the new migrant settlers? Perhaps here is the answer to the success of post-war Australian immigration. Is it the case that the Australian state has had an enlightened attitude to migrant settlement, responding to the increasingly multicultural society with sensitivity and generosity? Has the state been quick to recognise, and respond to, migrant disadvantage? And has government promoted models of migrant settlement designed to advance equality, acknowledge and respect cultural differences and thereby tackle prejudice?

The term multiculturalism has come to mean much more than an empirical description. It refers to the officially-sanctioned philosophy of the place of migrants in their new country.

Multiculturalism is the current ideology of migrant settlement, reflecting government attitudes and policies to post-war migrants once they arrive in Australia. In the mid-1970s, multiculturalism replaced the ideologies of assimilation and integration and while it is still supported by both major political parties in Australia, it has been severely criticised by the Right and the Left of Australian politics. Critics from the Right and the Left have argued that multiculturalism is a conspiracy designed to serve the interests of their political enemies.

The view from the Right is that multiculturalism is a radical conspiracy, promoting the interests of "ethnics" above those of the Australian-born. According to the most vocal right-wing critic, Professor Geoffrey Blainey, multiculturalism is a "confidence trick" imposed on the mass of unsuspecting Australians who are opposed to multiculturalism. Blainey claims the result is that the public is very suspicious of immigration policy and increasingly uneasy about migrants themselves. In *All For Australia* he stated, "An immigration system set up originally to serve the nation had been undermined. Now it is the nation that exists to serve the immigrant."[7]

At the other end of the political spectrum, those on the Left often take the view that multiculturalism is a means of maintaining conservative political control. They argue that multiculturalism's function is to keep migrants in their place by funding conservative parts of the ethnic communities at the expense of radical groupings, and by stressing peripheral "cultural" aspects to the neglect of workplace inequalities. One of the most trenchant left-wing critics, sociologist Andrew Jakubowicz, refers to multiculturalism as "one of the most innovative dimensions of conservative political strategy."[8]

* * *

The multiculturalism debate is not just academic; it affects the provision of migrant services and programs and the lives of previous, current and future migrants. More generally, the multiculturalism debate is a platform for reassessing the role of migrants in Australian society and the relationship between migrants and the Australian-born. At stake, according to the protagonists, is a united or divided Australia . . .

Assimilation and monoculturalism

In the first decades of post-war immigration, assimilation was the dominant philosophy of migrant settlement. This was a "non-policy"; the "new Australians" were expected to conform to Australian cultural norms, including language, and quickly discard their "cultural baggage". Billy Snedden, who was an immigration selection officer in Italy and England from 1952 to 1954 and subsequently Minister for Immigration in the conservative Coalition government, commented as late as 1969:

> We must have a single culture. If immigration implied multi-cultural activities within Australian society, then it was not the type Australia

wanted. I am quite determined we should have a monoculture with everyone living in the same way, understanding each other, and sharing the same aspirations. We don't want pluralism.[9]

Initially assimilation was a reassurance for Australians that non-British immigration would not undermine their way of life. When 180,000 Displaced Persons arrived in the late 1940s, promises to retain a British/White Australia could no longer be guaranteed, but as Harold Holt, Immigration Minister in 1952, stated in an address to the Third Citizenship Convention:

Australia, in accepting a balanced intake of other European people as well as British, can still build a truly British nation on this side of the world. I feel that if the central tradition of a nation is strong this tradition will impose itself on [the various] groups of immigrants.[10]

One way of maintaining the Australian tradition was to expect all "new Australians" to adopt the Australian culture completely. This entailed a break with the "old country", its language, traditions of dress, dance, cultural ceremonies and social relationships. As Jean Martin argued, this would ensure that non-British migrants "could be as readily assimilated as the British: that is, they were capable of being absorbed without strain."[11]

The ideology of assimilation not only helped reduce public antagonism to an immigration program that, in terms of ethnic composition, had failed as soon as it had begun, but it also absolved the state of the responsibility to introduce services to help "new Australians" settle. Assimilation asserted that migrants had no problems with Australian settlement, that assimilation was rapid and trouble-free. To provide "new Australians" with special services was an anathema to the ideology of "sameness". Treating migrants no differently from other Australians was at the heart of assimilation.

One of the clearest manifestations of this was in the area of education and language. Most of the Displaced Persons were not fluent in English, but pamphlets directed to these "new Australians" were written in English. In response to claims that the material would be better understood if the migrants could understand it, T.H.E. Heyes, the first secretary of the Department of Immigration and a powerful bureaucrat who did much to shape Australian immigration policy, replied:

A knowledge of the English language is the first prerequisite for a European migrant to help his assimilation into the community. Any obstruction to his learning the language should be strongly resisted. We think that catering for him in his own tongue would constitute such an obstruction.[12]

This view permeated education policy for migrant children. Despite their language problems, the assimilation ideology asserted that it was not necessary to introduce bilingual teaching aids, or to provide extra educational resources for teaching non-English speaking migrant children. To treat these migrant children differently would run counter to the policy of Anglo-conformity. As one primary school headmaster in a migrant holding center stated in 1951:

> The child must learn to think in English from the start . . . English is to be the basis of all instruction. It is the avenue to mutual understanding. It is the key to the success of the whole immigration project . . . English must be spoken to the pupils and by them, all day and every day, in every activity, in school and out of it.[13]

Migrants were trapped in a Catch 22. They had to learn English to successfully assimilate, yet they were not given any special support in this process.

The ideology of assimilation permeated all government services and programs. In areas such as health, welfare and the law there were no provisions for translation, no bilingual material produced, no special resources allocated to overcoming migrant difficulties in settlement and no recognition of the problems that migrants' cultural pasts incurred. However, contradictions between the official, confident pronouncements of successful assimilation and the experiences of those who worked with migrants began to emerge. Rather than successful settlement, it was a case of disadvantage and difficulty, particularly among those migrants from NES countries. By the mid-1970s special migrant assistance in areas such as education, health and welfare was being demanded.

This was exacerbated by the spreading of the immigration net from the Eastern European refugees to Northern and Southern Europeans. Not only were non-English speaking migrants coming in larger numbers, but they arrived from numerous countries, with different languages, cultural backgrounds and traditions. The gap between the rhetoric and the reality of the assimilation ideology became increasingly apparent, not least to the migrants themselves.

The area in which this credibility gap was first exposed was in the schools. By the end of the 1950s, only South Australia had recognised the difficulties that NES migrant children were experiencing at school. Other states were less perceptive. Harold Wyndham, the Director General of Education in NSW, stated in 1958, in response to requests for special reading material for migrant children, that the "great majority" of NES children had made "such rapid progress with the language that they have little need for special reading material".[14] Subsequent evidence dispelled such confident pronouncements and confirmed the lower academic achievement and persistent language difficulties of NES children, particularly in schools with a high migrant density.

Independent evidence of migrant disadvantage in the schools corresponded to individual experiences, causing the ethnic communities to become increasingly vocal. They began to demand the right to maintain their own cultural traditions rather than having them discarded and insisted on resources to overcome educational disadvantage. The self-proclaimed success of assimilation was increasingly being challenged, much to the distress of the "anglo-conformists". An ostrich-like response from the government was increasingly difficult under mounting evidence and mobilisation against migrant disadvantage.

Growing government concern over the difficulties of migrant settlement was not based solely on humanitarian considerations. The Immigration Department was experiencing difficulty in attracting and keeping migrants. While the Immigration Department underestimated the departure rate of migrants, Charles Price estimated that for years 1959-65 settler loss was over 16 per cent. By 1966, more than one-fifth of all post-war German migrants, 18 per cent of Dutch and 13 per cent of Italian migrants had abandoned Australia.[15] Improving conditions in Western Europe made it difficult to attract new migrants from Northern and Southern Europe, particularly given the increasing competition from Western European countries seeking "guest-workers" from Southern Europe. Many British migrants also became disillusioned about settlement in Australia — the origins of the "whingeing pom" stereotype — and returned home in significant numbers.

Clearly Australia had to improve its treatment of newly arrived migrants. The ostrich-like, assimilation approach to migrant problems may have been useful in dispelling Australian fears of the "new Australians", but it did not endear the migrants themselves to this land of "endless opportunity". The stage was set for a more enlightened response by the Australian government, an approach which recognised the problems of migrant settlement, particularly for those from non-English speaking countries.

Integration: the second phase

In the period from the mid-1960s to the early 1970s, assimilation broke down and a multicultural policy gradually emerged. This was a period of transition, and is often referred to as the period of "integration", the second phase of official government attitudes to migrant settlement. This shift in policy was symbolised by a change in name for the appropriate section within the Department of Immigration. The Assimilation Section became the Integration Section in 1964, although the actual policy changes were less clear.

Integration seemed to imply that migrants no longer needed to totally and immediately discard their cultural past and become part of an homogenised Australian culture. As Jean Martin pointed out, in the mid-1960s integration was not much more than a "two-stage" assimilation process, a recognition that it would take time for migrants to fully assimilate.[16] Cultural differences were seen as valid in the short term, but the expectation was that they would eventually be merged with the mainstream. This phase of integration was associated with a belated recognition of migrant disadvantage and of the need for government policy to redress the most blatant examples.

The government lifted its head out of the sand to acknowledge the concerns of increasingly vocal migrant communities. The Department of Immigration began to fund migrant welfare via Grant-in-Aid programs channelled through ethnic community organisations such as the Italian agency Co-As-It in the late 1960s. In 1970, Phil Lynch, the Immigration Minister, announced that the government would fund a child migrant education program in state and independent schools, with the government assuming the responsibility for teacher training and providing appropriate materials. However, these developments were an ad hoc response rather than a systematic, philosophical, policy orientation. This was to occur in the early 1970s.

Multiculturalism: the third phase

By the mid-1970s a new political consensus emerged. Both major political parties supported a policy shift as multiculturalism became the official guiding principle for migrant settlement. Distinctive migrant cultural trappings such as dance, dress, food, religion, language and social relations, were to be celebrated and encouraged as multicultural enlightenment and diversity replaced assimilationist homogeneity. Cultural pluralism had replaced monoculturalism. Or to use the terms popularised in the United States, the "melting pot" was replaced by the "salad bowl". No longer were migrant cultures expected to disappear and melt into some sort of homogenised ockerism. All the different cultures could be maintained, each adding a distinct "flavour" to the salad.

Michael Liffman, in a paper to the 1983 Committee of Review of the Australian Institute of Multicultural Affairs, suggested that there were six key factors in the emergence of multiculturalism in Australia.[13] First, the "undeniable reality" that Australia was a multi-cultural society in its ethnic composition. Second, "the phobia of many Australians was waning". In other words, prejudice was slowly being translated into tolerance as the reality of living with migrants began to outdistance the stereotypical fears. Third, the migrant communities themselves were becoming more confident and articulate, with young second and third generation professionals emerging as strong and effective advocates of multiculturalism. Fourth, this led to the expansion of migrant and ethnic community groups and a broadening of their concerns from "cultural" to welfare and political issues. Fifth, the Labor Party's Immigration Minister from 1972 to 1975, Al Grassby, acted as an important catalyst and, finally, the early 1970s followed decades of full employment and economic boom, allowing social reform to rise in the political agenda.

There are two sets of landmarks on this road from assimilation to multiculturalism. One relates to the individuals and publications which promoted the concept of a multicultural society and cultural pluralism; that is multiculturalism as theory or ideology. The other relates to the institutional response, or multiculturalism in practice.

Multiculturalism as theory

Al Grassby, the flamboyant, British-born Minister for Immigration in the Whitlam Government was, as Liffman suggests, an important catalyst in the promotion and acceptance of the notion of a multicultural society. In 1973 he issued a statement entitled *A Multicultural Society for the Future*, which set out the concepts of ethnic heterogeneity and cultural pluralism.[18] Grassby suggested that without such a multicultural society, NES migrants would become "non-people". He advocated the concept of "the family of the nation" as a means to stress the contribution of migrants to Australia and of the need to recognise, rather than dismiss, their distinctiveness.

Academics further developed the concept of cultural pluralism and multiculturalism. Most prominent was sociologist Jersy Zubrzycki. In 1977 Zubrzycki argued that the lack of equality of opportunity for migrants in Australia was one of the key reasons for the high departure rate of migrants. He promoted the need for equal opportunity for all Australians, migrant and non-migrant alike. This required the acceptance in theory and practice of "cultural pluralism", since "justice for all Australians" was only possible "within the framework of cultural pluralism but not structural pluralism and that ethnicity, ethnic ties, and primordial ties play a major and constructive role in this nexus."[19]

The Australian Ethnic Affairs Council (AEAC), with Zubrzycki as chairman, supported the notion of cultural pluralism. It concluded:

> We believe, therefore, that *our goal in Australia should be to create a society in which people of non-Anglo-Australian origin are given the opportunity, as individuals or groups, to choose to preserve and develop their culture* — their languages, traditions and arts — *so that these can become living elements in the diverse culture of the total society, while at the same time they enjoy effective and respected places within one Australian society, with equal access to the rights and opportunities that society provides and accepting responsibilities towards it.*[20]

The AEAC argued that the three key principles of a multicultural society were social cohesion, cultural identity and equality of opportunity and access.

Five years later, the Australian Council on Population and Ethnic Affairs (ACPEA), a merger of the AEAC and the Australian Population and Immigration Council (APIC), reaffirmed multiculturalism as "the most suitable model for relations between all ethnic groups in Australia and as the preferred basis for government ethnic policies".[21] The ACPEA extended the three principles of multiculturalism adopted in 1977. It suggested that Australian institutions should adapt to reflect the diverse composition of the Australian population and so ensure social cohesion; it supported the retention of cultural heritage, including minority languages, in order to maintain cultural identity, and stressed that equality of opportunity in the spheres of work and politics was an essential part of multiculturalism. Acknowledging that government assistance was necessary in achieving a multicultural society in Australia, the ACPEA favoured "an emphasis on the use of mainstream services by minority groups, wherever practicable, rather than the creation of a separate network of services".[22] The ACPEA also added a fourth principle to multiculturalism: equal responsibility for, commitment to and participation in society. It advocated that the majority of Australians should accept minority groups, while minority groups must accept "a primary loyalty to Australia".

Since Al Grassby first floated the concept of the "family of the nation", political parties in government and opposition have embraced multiculturalism as official policy. Despite this level of formal bi-partisan agreement, there is still considerable debate about the theory and practice of multiculturalism. Much of this centres on cultural versus structural pluralism, which loosely translates in practice to emphasising either lifestyle or life chances. Zubrzycki and others have long championed cultural pluralism as the central aspect of multiculturalism, with its emphasis on maintaining ethnic identity and cultural practices. Others, including Jean Martin, have maintained that structural changes at the economic and political level are required if migrant disadvantage in the labour market and under-representation in the broad political structures are to be overcome. We will return to this debate after considering the practice of multiculturalism since the early 1970s.

The practice of multiculturalism

Committees of Inquiry. While multiculturalism emerged, and was rapidly accepted as a philosophy, governments have been much slower to develop a multicultural practice. The Fraser Government had re-established the Immigration Department which, under the Whitlam Government was subsumed under other departments as immigration intakes were reduced. It was renamed the Department of Immigration and Ethnic Affairs in July 1976. "Ethnic affairs" had asserted a legitimacy unknown decades earlier. However, when assessing migrant policy prior to 1977, Jean Martin concluded that the federal governments from Whitlam to Fraser were generally "non-committal", with no coherent policy.[23]

In 1977 the Fraser Government established an inquiry chaired by Melbourne lawyer Frank Galbally into post-arrival programs and services for migrants. The inquiry's findings, published in 1978 as the *Galbally Report*, were a landmark in multicultural practice, introducing a more systematic and diverse framework for migrant services. The four principles on which the Galbally committee based its policy recommendations were: equality of opportunity and equal access to programs and services for all; the right of all Australians to maintain their culture; the need for special programs and services for migrants to ensure equality of access and provision; and that these programs should be designed and operated in full consultation with migrants, emphasising self-help.[24]

The *Galbally Report* made 57 specific recommendations involving additional expenditure of $50 million over three years. These recommendations covered a broad range of areas, including aiding settlement ($12 million), improvement of English language tuition for adults and children ($10m), translation services and improved communication and information ($4m), establishment of multicultural resource centres ($1.34m), and grant-in-aid programs to ethnic communities and trade unions ($1.65m). The *Report* also recommended the establishment of an Institute of Multicultural Affairs ($1.8m), the extension of ethnic radio

($3.23m), and the establishment of an ethnic television task force ($7.13m).

In May 1978 the Fraser Government announced that it accepted the proposals of the *Galbally Report*. A review of the Galbally proposals by the Australian Institute of Multicultural Affairs (AIMA), published four years later, found "an impressive record of implementation", with expenditure matching the provisions of the *Report*. By June 1981, 112 grants had been made, including 49 to ethnic agencies, under the grant-in-aid scheme; 19 migrant resource centres had been established; and 146 "once-only" grants had been awarded under the Migrant Project Subsidy Scheme. The ethnic media had been enhanced particularly through the establishment of Channel 0/28, set up under the Special Broadcasting Service, which was praised by the *AIMA Review* as "a watershed in the development of Australian multiculturalism". The *AIMA Review* concluded that the implementation of the *Galbally Report*'s proposals had been of substantial benefit to newly-arrived and longer-established migrants, giving Australia "perhaps the most comprehensive system of migrant and multicultural services in the world".[25]

Despite this lavish praise the *AIMA Review*, which was established to monitor the progress of ethnic affairs policy, found a number of inadequacies in migrant programs and services. This was evident in the area of English language teaching, child care, occupational health and safety and the labour market, where migrant disadvantage persisted. The *AIMA Review* made a further 89 recommendations, at a net additional cost of $6 million.

Four years later, in 1986, the Hawke Labor Government initiated another review of multiculturalism. The 1986 Committee of Review, chaired by political scientist James Jupp, occurred after the Blainey debate, when multiculturalism was the subject of severe criticism.

The *Jupp Report* was stage one of a two-stage review, with stage one to "advise on the Federal Government's role in assisting overseas-born residents to achieve equitable participation in Australian society" and stage two to evaluate key programs and services already in place. Stage one of the review concentrated on developing principles for migrant policy until the end of the 20th century.[26] The *Jupp Report* comprehensively reaffirmed multiculturalism as the appropriate government philosophy for the next decade, refusing to accept the critique made by Professor Blainey. At the same time, multiculturalism was redefined as "equitable participation". In this sense the *Jupp Report* broke important ground, shifting the emphasis of multiculturalism policy away from lifestyle to life chances. The *Jupp Report* clearly outlined the persistent disadvantage many migrants still faced in Australia, despite more than a decade of multicultural policy, and argued for the removal of structural inequalities. Moreover, unlike the earlier *Galbally Report* and *AIMA Review* which largely ignored the labour market aspects of migrant disadvantage, the *Jupp Report* identified the labour market as "the major determinant of whether certain persons or groups will be disadvantaged".

Identifying four key principles, the *Jupp Report* argued that all Australians should have:

- equitable opportunity to participate in economic, social, cultural and political aspects of life;
- equitable access to and a share of government resources;
- the opportunity to participate in or influence government policies, programs and services;
- the right to maintain their religion, culture and language in Australia.

It also suggested the following strategy for the implementation of these principles:

- migrants should be equipped with the basic resources;
- government and non-government institutions should change their decision-making processes;
- a program of community relations which respects the rights of all should be adopted;
- measures should be introduced to enable people to maintain their cultural heritage and identity.

The 32 recommendations of the Jupp committee were mainly concerned with bureaucratic reshuffling and improvements to existing services. These included the improvement of translation facilities, the recruitment of bilingual staff, establishing mechanisms to enable migrant qualifications and skills to be assessed prior to arrival in Australia and the setting up of a Standing Committee on Ethnic Affairs and Multiculturalism. The *Jupp Report* also called for the establishment of an Office of Ethnic Affairs to coordinate and monitor progress in achieving equitable participation of migrants.

Institutional embodiments of multiculturalism. Multiculturalism has given birth to a number of institutions, often characterised by subsequent reformulation or ultimate abolition. The major postwar overseeing body on immigration matters, the Australian Population and Immigration Council (APIC) was reformed and a new organisation, the Australian Ethnic Affairs Council (AEAC), established in March 1977. In April 1981, the APIC, AEAC and the Australian Refugee Advisory Council were collapsed into one body, the Australian Council on Population and Ethnic Affairs (ACPEA). To facilitate the development of ethnic media in Australia, the Special Broadcasting Service (SBS) was established in August 1977, the Ethnic Television Review Panel in May 1978, and the Independent and Multicultural Broadcasting Corporation (IMBC) Implementation Committee in 1980. The Australian Institute of Multicultural Affairs (AIMA), established in 1979 by the Fraser Government after the *Galbally Report*, was disbanded in 1987 by the Hawke Government and replaced by the office of Multicultural Affairs (OMA).

Paralleling the emergence of these institutional embodiments of multiculturalism by the federal government were developments from the state governments. The NSW Labor Government established the first State Ethnic Affairs Commission (EAC) in 1977. The NSW Premier is also Minister for Ethnic Affairs. This was followed by the South Australian EAC, set up by a Liberal government in 1979. In Victoria an Ethnic Affairs Commission was established by the Cain Labor Government in 1983, with a Minister for Ethnic Affairs also being appointed. The Burke Labor Government in Western Australia created the first Minister for Multicultural Affairs and established an EAC. Queensland is the only mainland state without an Ethnic Affairs Commission, although it established a Department of Ethnic Affairs in 1982.

The Ethnic Affairs Commissions, although varying from state to state, are generally involved in research, policy and relations with the ethnic communities and their organisations. The NSW EAC has recently initiated legislation requiring all state government departments and tertiary educational institutions to prepare annual Ethnic Affairs Policy statements. Other developments in federal and state legislation require attention to be paid to aspects of migrant employment and settlement. Since the late 1970s, anti-discrimination legislation has been adopted by the Commonwealth and several state governments. The Racial Discrimination Act was amended in 1975, the Human Rights Commission established in 1981, Equal Employment Opportunity provisions are becoming widespread and Affirmative Action legislation was passed by the federal government in 1987. Employers and governments are now compelled to address more formally the most blatant aspects of migrant disadvantage and prejudice.

In the last decade, a politically bi-partisan adoption of multiculturalism has spawned a multitude of inquiries and studies, institutions and legislative activity. Despite agreement between the major political parties and acceptance by many ethnic organisations, Australian multiculturalism has had its critics from both sides of the political spectrum. A review of the multiculturalism debate provides an opportunity to more acutely judge the success of a decade of multicultural theory and policy and its impact in practice on the lives of migrants.

The right-wing critique of multiculturalism

The Right found a champion in the guise of Melbourne historian, Professor Geoffrey Blainey. His views of multiculturalism can be gleaned from the following quotes:

Multiculturalism . . . is a recipe for trouble, but coated with platitudes and golden syrup. [Melbourne *Herald*, 30 August 1984]

The multicultural industry is divisive and parochial. [*Australian*, 20 September 1984]

Sadly, multiculturalism often means: "Australians come second". [Melbourne *Age*, 21 September 1984]

Our current emphasis on granting special rights to all kinds of minorities is threatening to cut this nation into many tribes. [*Sydney Morning Herald*, 25 January 1986]

With massive federal and state grants, the multicultural industry has become an ardent propagandist, pouring shame on Australia's past. [Melbourne *Herald*, 16 October 1986]

Blainey has found more support for his views on multiculturalism than he did for his assertions about Asian immigration. The political Right, whose views are expressed through journals like *Quadrant* and by commentators such as Frank Knopfelmacher and journalist Des Keegan, share Blainey's concerns. L.J.M. Cooray, in a *Quadrant* article entitled "Multiculturalism in Australia: Who needs it?" was disconcerted that there "are notions of multiculturalism which assert the right of each ethnic community to maintain its language and culture on Australian soil, if necessary with the assistance of public-funded programmes."[27] Cooray sees a clear choice between an Australian culture or a collection of distinct ethnic cultures. Frank Knopfelmacher, in an article in the Melbourne *Age* entitled "Save Australia's British culture", expressed a similar view. He supported Blainey's yearning for the old days of a British Australia and continued: "The most damaging aspect of the multiculturalism approach was the implicit, and sometimes explicit, insistence that Australia should be and will be disanglified. For this is what Australians do not want."[28] Des Keegan of *The Australian* wrote:

> Racial hatred has erupted everywhere the mixture has been too disparate . . . Why should Australia be flooded with people on the run from societies incapable of civilised behaviour, or of rational economics or of social harmony under common law.[29]

According to the Right, multiculturalism is costly and divisive. It has given the "ethnic industry" a position whereby it can influence government spending in favour of their minority interests and divert money away from other Australians, while at the same time antagonising the "Australian" people who strongly oppose such policies. Instead of this recipe for social tension and divisiveness the Right yearns for the "old days" of assimilation and a British Australia.

. . . The evidence of public opinion is not as strong as the Right would claim. Moreover, even if they were correct, it is questionable if an enlightened government should follow public opinion in perpetuating the material disadvantage and cultural isolation of NES migrants. To do so would entrench further NES migrants as inferior, second-class citizens. An Australian society based on such institutionalised inequality would be more likely to produce the divisiveness and conflict that the Right claims already exists. Multiculturalism's goal of equity and equality for all Australians, irrespective of their country of birth, in the economic, social, political and cultural spheres of life is a more likely path to tolerance and understanding.

The left-wing critique

Left-wing critiques of multiculturalism have persisted since the emergence of multiculturalism in the late 1970s. Unlike the right-wing critics, who question migrant access to special programs and services and the maintenance of ethnic cultural identity, the Left base their criticism on the failure of successive governments to extend multiculturalism from the cultural to the economic domain. In other words, the Left argues that multiculturalism has failed to fulfil its promise of equity and access for migrants. The other criticism from the Left relates to the conservative politics embodied in the operation of multicultural policy.

To date multicultural policy has tended to concentrate on the "cultural" aspects of life in Australia, such as dance, dress, food and language. While this makes daily life for migrants much more tolerable, the Left's concern is that it is vital to concentrate greater resources on migrant disadvantage in the labour market and in the other areas such as education. This is crucial to ensuring migrants have equal life chances. As Laksiri Jayasuriya wrote in 1984:

> Whereas the stress on "lifestyles", a concern for ethnicity and cultural maintenance, had merit in easing social adjustment for newcomers, the continued preoccupation with these issues through policies solely directed to preserving and sustaining cultural diversity and identity is misguided, irrelevant, and inimical to the best interests of ethnic minorities today.[30]

Nearly a decade of funding directed to multiculturalism has not, however, been able to overcome migrant disadvantage in terms of their standard of living. But of the three government inquiries into multicultural programs and services, only the *Jupp Report* explicitly addressed the need to reduce the structural inequality facing migrants in Australia, particularly in areas of the labour market and English language education. However, the *Jupp Report* did not recommend any specific initiatives to overcome this disadvantage. While government now pays lip-service to this area of multicultural policy, only a small proportion of the funds allocated to multicultural programs and services are di-

rected to labour market programs. The inability of multiculturalism to significantly reduce structural inequality is a serious short-
coming of Australian multiculturalism.

More controversial is the Left's critique of the "hidden political agenda" of multiculturalism. Sociologist Andrew Jakubowicz
has been the most consistent critic in this regard. He argues that
multiculturalism is a clever strategy for containment of migrants
as a political force. In 1984 Jakubowicz said "It is essentially
about sustaining the existing social order and the existing core
values, however sexist or oppressive they may be."[31] This view is
supported by Marie de Lepervanche, who stated in her review of
ethnic policy published in 1984 that ethnicity, "When harnessed
by the state and promoted as multiculturalism, gave priority to
ethnic rather than class differences, and thus provided an effective
means of social control."[32]

Jakubowicz's argument is that when ethnic organisations
began to demand attention be paid to migrant problems, and
when migrant workers, particularly in the car industry, demonstrated a militancy which went beyond the control of their union
leaders, multiculturalism was used to create federal and state institutions (an ethnic industry) which by concentrating on the non-
class cultural aspects of reform could contain and defuse
legitimate working class migrant demands and militancy. To
quote Jakubowicz:

> In the Australian context, state action began at the Federal level in sup-
> port for the cultural liberation of ethnic minorities. Over time such
> concerns were submerged in politically astute analyses of the changing
> base of Australian political life, and in a period of heightened class
> struggle and economic restructuring, the opportunity to use ethnicity
> to mediate and defuse class conflict.[33]

There is some evidence to support this view. Since the *Galbally Report*, multicultural funds for programs and services have been directed to ethnic groups and associations. However, since all the
communities have a variety of associations representing different
regional, political or religious differences, governments have to
choose which ethnic groups to fund. It is here that politics enter
the domain. As Jakubowicz argues, post-Galbally multiculturalism led to "the reinforcement of the client-patron relationship between politically acceptable ethnic organisations and the state."[34]

The ethnic media under the Fraser Government provides an interesting example of conservative politics influencing the shape of multiculturalism in practice. In 1974 a sub-committee of the Migrant Task Force, set up by Al Grassby, reported on the desirability of introducing community language broadcasting. Radio 2EA in Sydney and 3EA in Melbourne began broadcasting in June 1975, the same year in which the ABC introduced a new multilingual access radio station, 3ZZZ in Melbourne. In the words of one foundation staff member, "We hoped that 3ZZZ might not only reflect the diversity of Melbourne, but act as a catalyst in building a multicultural society."[35]

3ZZZ posed a particular problem for the Fraser Government, since as an experimental access radio station, it was open to less direct editorial control than 2EA and 3EA. As an access station, 3ZZZ allowed various ethnic groups editorial control over their programs, leading to sustained political in-fighting within ethnic groups and between the government, the ABC and 3ZZZ management. Right-wing ethnic groups protested loudly to the government over what they saw as a left-wing bias in programs broadcast by Palestinians. In June 1977, the Fraser Government forced the ABC to close 3ZZZ. As Joan Dugdale argued, the closure was for political reasons, with open access for ethnic groups regarded as a dangerous experiment:

> 3ZZZ gave people the opportunity to speak across social and ethnic barriers and to share with politicians and experts the right to broadcast an opinion. It allowed an injustice done in one area to be communicated rapidly in many languages to other possible victims; it allowed rights, which are often buried in fine print, to be publicised. At 3ZZZ people who thought they had nothing in common discovered they shared a valuable asset in a radio station. They were beginning to learn that they also shared a city and a future which, together, they could influence. Such political activity was not welcomed by either a Labor or a Liberal Government.[36]

Another criticism of multiculturalism in practice relates to the growing "ethnic industry" and the ethnic leaders who have emerged as spokespeople. It is claimed that a "bureaucratic aristocracy" has been created by the state as a means to introduce conservative ethnic leaders into the mainstream of political life and block those who represent working class migrant interests, even though most migrants in Australia are working class. Marie de Lepervanche, for example, has argued that "Most ethnic leaders and spokespeople are men, and they represent male and bourgeois interests rather than those of women or the working class majority."[37] Similarly, Jakubowicz suggests that conservative politicians have cultivated ethnic leaders who are reluctant to publicly criticise the actions of government.[38]

W(h)ither multiculturalism?

The history of the state's policy relating to migrant settlers is one of decades of neglect. Migrant disadvantage was simply not acknowledged by successive post-war governments until the mid-1970s when the state adequately acknowledged its responsibilities. Despite a decade of multiculturalism, the most enlightened government philosophy of migrant settlement, migrant disadvantage persists. The hypothesis that the success of Australian post-war immigration is due to enlightened government policy fails dismally.

Nevertheless, via multiculturalism, governments do have the potential to redress the major areas of disadvantage experienced by many migrants, particularly newly-arrived NES migrants. Unless migrant disadvantage is more systematically challenged, many NES migrants will be entrenched further as second-class citizens in Australia, which will be a recipe not only for individual hardship, but also for the escalation of racial unrest and prejudice. Multiculturalism, in its latest version in the *Jupp Report*, stresses the importance of aiming to achieve equitable participation of migrants in Australian life. This is an important principle, even if its implementation has been inadequate. The critics of the Right would, if heeded, throw back the cause of migrant rights to the days of assimilation and the attendant personal hardship, prejudice and institutionalised inequality that this embodied decades ago.

Multiculturalism does have a hidden class agenda, despite its positive contribution in areas of cultural pluralism. However, multiculturalism is essentially contradictory, a fact not always appreciated by the most prominent left-wing critics. It has positive and negative benefits for the majority of working class migrants.

Ethnic affairs policy in the post-war period began with decades of assimilationist ideology which denied migrants their past, implicitly condoning racist prejudice and intolerance from the British-Australian population. In the last decade of multiculturalism, important advances have been achieved and can be seen as significant influences in the dilution of prejudice in Australia. However, multiculturalism has not paid sufficient attention to migrant disadvantage in the labour market and education system and further efforts must be made to redress the unequal life chances of migrants. The *Jupp Report* acknowledges this point, and made an important advance in the theory of multiculturalism by stressing structural, as well as cultural, pluralism. But if multiculturalism does not extend its brief to empowering the disadvantaged, working class majorities of the migrant population it will be open to charges of elitism and conservatism.

In the changing economic and political climate of the past few years some positive aspects of multiculturalism practice have been questioned and undermined. Professor Blainey and his cohorts challenged the very validity of programs and services for migrants, and it has been necessary to defend multiculturalism from such critics who do not even recognise the importance of cultural pluralism, let alone structural pluralism. Moreover, the economic recession of the early 1980s, and the subsequent conservative economic strategy of the Hawke Government, has led to cutbacks in the already inadequately funded areas of migrant education and English language tuition. The high cost of teaching migrants English is an anathema to the budget-cutting Hawke-Keating economic strategy. "Holding the line", rather than extending inadequate services, has become the key political fight.

One tempting solution for government and treasury officials is to press for the rapid "mainstreaming" of multicultural programs and services. Since the emergence of multiculturalism it has been argued that special migrant programs and services are a temporary second best. The *Galbally Report*, for example, proposed the view that "services to migrants should as far as possible be through general reforms directed at the whole community."[39]

This view was endorsed by the *AIMA Review*, while the *Jupp Report* remained largely agnostic on the question. In an ideal world, all government departments would embody a recognition of the special disadvantage of migrants and adopt appropriate policies and programs. However, the attraction of "mainstreaming" in today's economic and political climate seems to lie with the short-term cost savings rather than any long-term policy focussing on the best interests of migrants. This view is taken by researchers at the University of Wollongong's Centre for Multicultural Studies, who see "mainstreaming" as a possible "fourth phase" in state/migrant relations in post-war Australia. After outlining the cuts to NES migrants in the 1986 federal budget, Stephen Castles, Mary Kalantzis and Bill Cope argued, in an article entitled "W(h)ither multiculturalism?", that "mainstreaming" might simply come to mean cutting multiculturalism:

> Mainstreaming represents a fourth phase. Although mainstreaming aims to strengthen multiculturalism — and, if sensitively handled, would have that effect — it could become a pretext for dismantling the capacity of services and programs to meet special needs.[40]

Today it is important to defend multiculturalism from its rightwing critics and treasury officials aiming to trim government expenditure. Defending and extending multiculturalism must be a central part of government immigration policy in the coming years. If the Australian government is not prepared to meet the responsibilities of past and present immigration policy through an adequate provision of programs and services, the case for increased immigration intake, a path being followed by the Hawke Government, is severely undermined.

Mistaken Identity

Stephen Castles, Mary Kalantzis, Bill Cope, Michael Morrissey

A Nation without Nationalism?

According to Benedict Anderson, 1987 was the 200th anniversary of the birth of the nation state. The "extraordinary invention" which was to become an "unproblematic planetary norm" came to the world, says Anderson, in the shape of the Constitution of the United States of America.[1] The nation whose 200th anniversary we are called upon to celebrate in 1988 was founded just one year later. That would make it the first completely modern nation.

This view of Australia may put quite a strain on our credulity: did the convicts know they were coming to found a nation? Did they want to? Do the descendants of the Aborigines who saw the First Fleet land see things that way? Was a nation founded at all? After all, our monarch still lives overseas; many of our basic institutions are imported from our former Imperial ruler. If so, when was it founded? In 1788, in 1901, with the Statute of Westminster in 1928, or when appeals to the Privy council were abolished in the mid-1980s? But what is a nation anyway in a world in which crucial economic and political decisions are no longer made at the national level, especially for the smaller states?

This book will attempt to grapple with some of the more significant recent attempts at making nationhood. In particular, it will focus on the conscious attempt to define the Australian nation as multicultural. The expression was first used in a public and official way by Al Grassby, as Immigration Minister of the Whitlam Government in 1973. The policy was elaborated by various government advisory bodies, in which the sociologist Jerzy Zubrzycki played a leading role, and was adopted by the Fraser Government. Its social policy consequences were mapped out in the Galbally Report of 1978. By the end of the 1970s multiculturalism had become not only a new Australian word, but also a full-blown "ism": a comprehensive ideology of what Australia was supposed to be and to become. The policy was taken over by the Hawke

Government and the state governments, and continues, despite some controversy, to enjoy the support of all major political forces.

Multiculturalism as an ideology calls for a celebration of cultural diversity as a continuing feature of Australian society. It thus appears as a departure from previously prevailing racist and nationalistic stereotypes of the nation. But this progressive move bears problems: how is the tension between ethnic pluralism and the cohesiveness of society as a whole to be resolved? How can a nation be defined, if not in terms of ethnic identity: shared history, traditions, culture and language? How are core values and acceptable behavioural forms to be laid down, if the dominance of Anglo-Australian culture is no longer accepted? The problems of a multi-ethnic state are neither new nor unique in the world, but the response of multiculturalism is certainly a new departure in the history of Australia. So we must ask what multiculturalism means, and if it is a viable way of defining the nation.

But we must also ask if it is to be taken at face value. Has it really changed the ethnocentric structures which are so entrenched in every area of Australian life? Is it even meant to? It is also seen by some as a form of social control, a way of incorporating ethnic middle classes into the Australian political system, and using them to control their less successful compatriots, at a low cost to the state.[2]

*   *   *

Richard White has documented the changing attempts to define the "Australian type": the muscular sunburnt bushman, the "Coming Man", whose self-reliance and physical prowess would renew the British race, the Digger, who proved himself at Gallipoli, the Bondi lifesaver:

> The emphasis was on masculinity, and on masculine friendships and team-work, or "mateship" in Australia. All the clichés — man of action, white man, manliness, the common man, war as a test of manhood — were not sexist for nothing. Women were excluded from the image of the "Coming Man", and so were excluded from the image of the Australian type as well.[3]

Being Australian has always been defined in sexist terms. It has also been defined in racist terms. In the early days, the pioneers' battle against the hard land was also seen as a struggle against the "dangerous and wily" blacks. Later the fight was against migrants who would dilute the British character of the nation, and undermine the race. The main threat was the "yellow peril" and above all the Chinese who started coming in the mid-nineteenth century. But there was hostility towards all "non-Britishers". One of the first Acts of the new parliament in 1901 was to pass the Immigration Restriction Act, designed to keep out non-European immigrants, and popularly known as the White Australia Policy. Humphrey McQueen has drawn attention to the role of racism in the construction of the Australian labour movement.[4] The restriction of immigration and the call for a white Australia were themes which had mobilised workers and their organisations — the unions and the Australian Labor Party in the latter half of the nineteenth century and which would continue to do so until the Second World War.

The Immigration Restriction Act was not generally used to keep out European settlers, although they were relatively few in number until 1947. Those who did come encountered considerable hostility. Australian workers were often unwilling to work with them. In the isolationist mood of the Depression era, attempts were made to exclude non-British migrants, and to combat their influence on other cultures within Australia. At Kalgoorlie in 1934 several people were killed in "anti-dago" riots.[5] Attempts by employers to employ new migrants at low wages or to recruit them as strikebreakers did not help.

So the Australian type was constructed in terms of the white, masculine, outdoor person originating from the British Isles. Even that was contradictory enough in the light of the struggles between English and Irish. These came to a head during the First World War in the context of the Irish fight for independence and the conflict on conscription in Australia. The concept "Anglo-Celtic", commonly used in debates on multiculturalism today, is an ill-conceived monstrosity, which can only partially paper over the gulf. One of the problems of defining the Australian nation is that its supposed substratum — the British nation — does not exist either. There is indeed a British nation-state, but it uneasily embraces four nations (or principal ethnic groups).[6]

* * *

Australia's self-image, therefore, has always been problematic. It has been racist, justifying genocide and exclusionism, and denying the role of non-British migrants. It has been sexist, ignoring the role of women in national development, and justifying their subordinate position. It has idealised the role of the "common man" in a situation of growing inequality and increasingly rigid class divisions. It has been misleading in its attempts to create a British/Australian ethnicity while ignoring the divisions within the British nation-state, and its Australian off-shoot.

But for all that the image might have been maintained had it not been for Australia's post-war immigration programme. We will argue in this book that the mass settlement of migrants from a wide range of countries has made the overt maintenance of a racist definition of the nation and of the Australian type impossible. Today an attempt is being made to re-interpret the immigration programme as a deliberate move towards a multi-ethnic society. That is far from the truth: immigration was seen in the mid-1940s as a strategic necessity to make the country economically and militarily strong enough to repel the "yellow peril". No ethnic diversity was intended: British migrants were wanted, and when they could not be obtained in adequate numbers, the call was for "assimilable types" who would rapidly become indistinguishable from other Australians.

But, as will be shown below, cultural assimilation did not take place. Australia became a country with at least eighty different ethnic groups. Non-English speaking migrants and their children make up about one-fifth of the population. If the idea of a nation and of a national type is needed to secure social cohesion, then Australia is faced with a new problem: how to define these in a non-racist and non-monocultural way.

According to Ernest Gellner:

> . . . nationalism is a theory of political legitimacy, which requires that ethnic boundaries should not cut across political ones, and in particular, that ethnic boundaries within a given state . . . should not separate the power-holders from the rest.[7]

In other words, nationalism is based on the idea that every ethnic group or nation should have its own state, with all the appropriate trappings: flag, army, Olympic team and postage stamps. People relate to these symbols. A feeling of nation-ness is an integral part of their lived experience. But what happens when the people of a nation-state consist of more than one ethnic group, with different symbols and lived experiences? This is a common enough situation, but in the nationalist view of the world, it is likely to lead to conflict. As soon as people become conscious of their destiny as a nation they will either subjugate the other ethnic groups within the state boundaries, or, if they belong to a minority, they will fight for their own state.

* * *

But what is a nation? It is not identical with a "race" (whatever that is), nor simply reducible to an ethnic group. Yet the distinction is not clear:

> . . . Communities which have been called national at one point of time or in one country, have been called ethnic and/or racial at others. While each collectivity has to be analysed in an historically specific manner, what is common to them all, in all their diversity, is that all are forms of ideological constructs which divide people into collectivities or communities . . . This involves exclusionary/inclusionary boundaries which form the collectivity, dividing the world into "Us" and "Them". Although the constructs are ideological, they involve real material practices and therefore have material origins and effects. The boundaries of such collectivities tend to focus around a myth . . . of a common origin or a common fate, so that membership of the collectivity is normally obtained through birth. The boundaries of such collectivities can shift — they can cross-cut, expand or shrink in specific historical and socio-psychological situations, nor are they always symmetrical . . . [8]

In fact there are very few countries today which are ethnically homogeneous. The process of industrialisation and modernisation leads to larger state units, embracing a variety of ethnic groups. There are few advanced countries without their "old" minorities such as the Bretons in France, the Basques and Catalans in Spain. Sometimes this develops into serious cleavage as in Italy and, increasingly, in Britain. Moreover, the process of development almost always involves rural-urban migrations which quickly transcend national boundaries: in the nineteenth century the Irish went to Britain, the Poles to Germany, the Italians to France and Switzerland, and people from all over Europe to the USA, Canada, and some South American countries. Since 1945 there has been large-scale labour migration to most Western European countries, to North America and Australia, leading to the development of significant new ethnic minorities throughout the First World.

In encouraging labour migration, the states concerned followed short-term labour market interests, with little consideration of the long-term consequences. There was certainly no desire to create multi-ethnic societies. Now that this has happened, there are various responses: *laisser-faire,* state racism or exclusionism, assimilationism, and multiculturalism. Whatever policy is followed, a new situation has to be dealt with: membership of the collectivity is no longer simply a result of birth; the boundary of the collectivity cannot easily be defined according to a myth of common origin or fate. If nationalism is a crucial social ideology then a new way must be found to define the nation. Nowhere is this problem more pressing than in Australia where the post-war migrations have been so large in scale that they have transformed the ethnic composition of the population. Forty per cent of the Australian people today are immigrants or children of immigrants. Half of these are of non-British origin.

Sixty years ago, J. Lyng could write:

> The position can be compared with that of a river, started by a small spring in the mountains, winding its way through unknown country, gaining in volume and importance as it flows along, till, at the end of its course, it has become a mighty stream with incalculable potentialities. Here and there the river is made slightly bigger by tributaries.[9]

The river was "English language", "English culture" and "British stock" (an interesting juxtaposition). The tributaries were the most "modest contributions" of "non-Britishers". Even in the 1950s it was possible to assert:

> Our life is still British wholecloth, so to speak, and though the warp-threads may have turned a little, they are still strong; we have only coloured and arranged the weft-threads a little differently.[10]

With hindsight, we can say that such a view of the world was ethnocentric and mistaken even then. But it did provide a workable basis for a national ideology.

That ideology could not survive the fundamental changes resulting from the crumbling of the British Empire, the post-war immigration programme and increasing vocal claims by Aboriginal groups. What were the alternatives? . . . As Richard White has pointed out, in the 1950s attempts to define the nation focused on "the Australian way of life". The image was one of a prosperous suburban society, in which every man had his house and garden, his Holden and his hobby. Again, it was a sexist image, centred around the man as bread winner for a neat and happy nuclear family.[11]

It was a new image, that could compete with increasingly irrelevant Anglocentric traditions. And it could draw in the New Australians: you did not have to come from Britain to want a Holden and a house, to be a good worker and trade unionist, and to support the idea of a fair go. Consumerism matched the idea of assimilationism: to be Australian meant simply to conform in terms of work and lifestyle. The ideology of "the Australian way of life" appeared as the pinnacle of modernism: pride in economic progress, technical advance and a high standard of living was to make differences in origin, race and ethnic background meaningless.

But by the 1970s, this approach was failing, and there was a need for a new national ideology. There were several reasons for this. First, the modernist, assimilationist principle had only scratched the surface of a society still highly elitist and dominated by Anglocentric values. Second, the onset of recession and restructuring of the world economy was making Australian living standards vulnerable. Third, trends towards economic and social segmentation linked to race, ethnicity and gender were making the whole concept of the "Australian way of life" questionable. The idea of "multiculturalism" was an attempt to modify existing concepts of the nation to match up to the new realities.

Whitlam's Minister of Immigration, Al Grassby, announced his version of a "multi-cultural society of the future" in 1973. The ALP Government made efforts to take account of "migrant needs" in its social policies. Fraser's neo-conservative Government took up the slogan, and by the end of the decade had worked multiculturalism up into a full-blown ideology for the Australian nation. Multiculturalism has been embraced by the Hawke Government and the various state governments, and remains a multi-party consensus. It has been questioned, recently, both through the old-style racist populism of Geoffrey Blainey and Bruce Ruxton, and through the strange New Right slogan of

"Anglomorphy". But multiculturalism retains considerable power as an ideology because it does reflect important realities in Australia's social and cultural situation. For all its problems and contradictions it is unlikely that multiculturalism will be abandoned in favour of a return to Anglo-Australian ethnocentrism. It is currently the dominant discourse in the attempt to define the nation, and is likely to remain so for some time. Multiculturalism has become a necessary ideology.

Multiculturalism is progressive because it attempts to define the nation in non-nationalistic, non-ethnocentric terms. It is regressive because in some of its guises it often trivialises more serious social issues of inequality, founded in socio-economic structures, gender relations and structural racism. Its affirmative celebration of being colourfully different is a frequent cloak for deep-seated racism, for the continuing exclusion of Aborigines from Australian society, for the hardships of immigration, for the virtual exclusion of women from structures of economic and political power.

Multiculturalism is regressive for a second reason: it does not question the need to define the nation and to draw boundaries of inclusion and exclusion. By celebrating diversity within the nation, it reaffirms, even if often only in a perfunctory way, the need for a national cohesion which is more than that of the face-to-face community and less than that of all humanity. The step beyond multiculturalism is the transcending of national identity, the denial of its necessity, the recognition that through the crisis of modernity we are now all in the same boat — economically, ecologically and politically. Human identity must become transnational.

* * *

Community without nation?

What about racism as an instrument for securing social solidarity? By drawing the boundaries of the nation in an exclusionary way, racism creates an "imagined community", drawing people together through affective links which transcend conflicting socioeconomic interests. Racism has had this function for most of Australian history. The White Australia Policy was a central element of Australian history. The White Australia Policy was a central element of Australian nationhood from the late nineteenth century right through to the 1960s. If we look overseas, we see that racism has been a traditional and frequent instrument for constructing national solidarity in crisis situations. It currently plays this role in several advanced industrial countries, particularly in Western Europe.

Racism no longer works that way in contemporary Australia. It does exist in several forms: first, racism towards Aborigines has been continuous and intense throughout Australian history. At present, anti-Aboriginal racism takes the form of prejudiced attitudes, and of economic and social marginalisation. Second, some migrant groups are victims of structural racism, through mechanisms of labour market segmentation. Third, the Blainey Debate of 1984, as an attempt to develop an embracing racist ideology, did point to the existence of racist attitudes which could be articulated and mobilised.

Yet the fact that the Blainey Debate did not lead to a substantial and lasting racist mobilisation points to the non-viability of racism as an ideology of the Australian nation today. Anti-Aboriginal racism persists because of the structural marginality of black Australians. An ideology based on anti-migrant racism is a non-starter just because migrants are structurally incorporated: as workers, small business owners, professionals and as citizens with civil and political rights. There is no significant social grouping which has a material interest in their dis-integration. And even if there were, there is no conceivable mechanism to achieve this. Blainey and Ruxton were aware enough of this not to direct their campaign against immigrants in general, but against Asians (and, later, Africans). The difference of skin-colour seemed to offer a chance for exclusionary policies (as the example of Britain indicated). It did indeed prove possible to mobilise anti-Asian feeling, but only on the streets and in the pubs. There was no significant political force or interest group willing to take it up for their own ends; it corresponded with nobody's interests.

The material reason for the non-viability of anti-migrant racism in Australia is the sheer size of their contribution to society and the economy, together with their incorporation into the people as voting citizens. The ideological reason is the existence of the doctrine of multiculturalism, as a reasonably successful way of managing the potential conflicts of a multi-ethnic society. Multiculturalism does bear racist elements: the recourse to primordiality as a basis for ethnic identity; the acceptance of ethnic chauvinisms (and sexism) as acceptable elements of cultures. The neo-conservative project of multiculturalism (of the Fraser-Zubrzycki-Galbally type) trades on such regressive elements as aspects of a divide-and-rule strategy for social control in a multi-ethnic society. The social democratic variant of multiculturalism is open to this critique too, despite its generalist social policy aims, for it cannot manage without recourse to culturalism in the final analysis. Multiculturalism is based on a construction of community through a celebration and fossilisation of differences, which are then subsumed into an imagined community of national cohesion. It is a necessary project for the contemporary Australian-state, and one which makes an overt return to a racist definition of the nation impossible.

But that does not necessarily mean that the multicultural project can succeed. We argue that it is too contradictory and limited an ideology to gain wide and enduring support. To start with, multiculturalism is not an accurate statement of power relations in Australia, where there is still a clear link between ethnicity (or more accurately, migrant worker status) and socio-economic life chances. Second, multiculturalism postulates at best an equal chance to be unequal, in a society where inequality is growing and welfare declining. It fails to address the fundamental dimensions of inequality: the ways in which ethnicity overlays class and gender. Third, cultural pluralism can actually preserve and deepen inequality, by creating separate and inferior educational and social systems for different groups. Fourthly, multiculturalism, despite the declarations on its relevance to all Australians, is not an ideology that has much attraction for the Anglo majority. The constant changes and re-evaluations of multicultural policies indicates how contradictory and ephemeral the ideology is.

The answer to this dilemma is not to abandon multiculturalism, but to concentrate our efforts on combatting the structural factors which maintain inequality. In the context of a struggle against economic and social marginalisation, it will be possible to resolve the issue of ethnic separatism: all individuals and communities should have the right to cultural autonomy in a society based on equal social, economic and political rights for everyone irrespective of gender, race, ethnicity or class background. This implies combatting racist and sexist attitudes and institutions, both in Australian society, and in all of its subcultures. Our society will continue to be made up of communities of varying character, but such variation must cease to be a focus for discrimination or disadvantage.

Options for Australia

What possibilities are available to Australia as we enter the third century of white settlement? We see four options.

Inequality plus imagined community. This means the continued integration of the economy as part of the world market, but with the development of a firm ideological basis for national identity, leading to a strong commitment to the Australian nation-state. This option, as spelt out by the New Right, seems highly unlikely to succeed, given the problems of Australian national identity described in this book. Attempts to create a general "we-feeling" through sport, life-style symbols or indeed through the Bicentenary, have had no enduring success.

Inequality plus state repression. This is the "Latin American" model, in which social and political divisions become too sharp to be accommodated in consensus-type parliamentary politics. If the Australian economy really moves into the "Banana Republic" mode envisaged by Keating in 1986, and no equitable way of sharing the burden can be found, so that the billionaires get richer and the number of people in poverty grows, then a peaceful solution may not be possible. Under similar pressures, formally democratic states in Latin America (Chile, Uruguay) succumbed to military dictatorships in the 1970s. This option seems possible, but not likely, for consensus politics have certainly not broken down here yet.

Inequality plus fragmentation and quiescence. In this option the breakdown of social solidarity takes the form not of polarisation, but of fragmentation. Politics becomes increasingly meaningless, as the lack of real power of parliaments can no longer be concealed. Since the decisions are made in the stock exchanges of Tokyo, London and New York, and in the international corporate bureaucracies, why bother anyway? The result is hopelessness, hedonism and retreat into the private sphere. Protest takes the form of life-styles and sub-cultural pressure groups, and can easily be co-opted by the leisure industries. Increasing drug and alcohol addiction, fundamentalist religion, mental illness and violence are products of the real powerlessness of the social being. Politics shift from interests to values, providing a focus for New Right ideologies of family, individuality and competition. This seems the most likely scenario of all, for it is simply an extrapolation of existing trends.

Equality plus real communality. An alternative to these less than inspiring possibilities is a society based on the best elements of national Australian tradition, the most important postulates of multiculturalism, and the needs and interests of the broad majority of the population. Such a political and cultural reorientation would transcend any idea of nationalism, nation-state or simply imagined community.

The Australian traditions which should be reasserted are not those of colonisation or war, but those of the "fair go", that is, of social justice for all. The image of Australia which should be brought back is that of the "workingman's paradise", though the racist and sexist aspects of this ideal would need to be worked through and modified.

The aspects of multiculturalism worth maintaining are the principles of cultural self-determination and of cosmopolitan identity. They must be linked to measures to meet the specific needs of discriminated and disadvantaged groups, and include policies to overcome structural marginalisation and labour market segmentation, and to combat racism and prejudice.

Above all, the history of white racism and genocide against the Aborigines must become a central theme of education and public debate, and an accommodation with the Aborigines must be achieved through payment of reparations and Land Rights legislation. Steps must be taken to improve dramatically the economic and social situation of the Aboriginal population, not through welfare measures, but through making adequate resources available to Aboriginal communities and these being placed under their own control.

Any such strategy must be based on an attempt to redefine the basis of social organization, and to move away from a political emphasis on the nation-state. Australian life today is determined as much by events on the local level, as by those on the level of world politics and economics. In Britain, it has been local politics which have provided hope in the wasteland of Thatcherism. There is no contradiction between attempts to build community and bring about change at the local level, political work in the national arena, and participation in world politics.

The Bicentenary could have been an occasion for celebration. The opportunity was thrown away by Australian political leaders' unwillingness to face up to the real issues and problems. Once the decision was taken to ignore Aboriginal demands for real expiation, the Bicentenary became a lost cause. It changed from something with potential social meaning to a public relations exercise. Bicentennial Authority propaganda let the cat out of the bag, by calling for the inclusion of youth, women, ethnic groups, Aborigines and the handicapped in the celebrations. The conclusion was inescapable: only white Anglo middle-class men really had anything to celebrate in Australia; the inclusion of the rest was tokenism. If the Bicentenary had been concerned with helping to create an all-embracing society, it would have been based on real changes, designed not only to secure equality for the groups mentioned, but also to bring in others, whose marginalisation makes them invisible for those in power: the unemployed, those living below the poverty line, the industrial casualties, the financially, culturally and socially deprived.

The Bicentenary is yet another indication of how the concept of the nation has become ideological and exclusionary, failing to embrace most of the population. The group which wields power and benefits from it gets ever smaller. More and more of us are members of minorities. Building communality means taking the real situation in our cities, suburbs and country areas as a starting point, adopting political and economic forms which correspond with the needs and interests of many groups who are voiceless at present, and working for change everywhere. We do not need a new ideology of nationhood. We need to transcend the nation, as an increasingly obsolete relic of early industrialism. Our aim must be community without nation.

Part Four
Identifying Women

Women have been systematically excluded from myths of national identity in Australia. Where do women figure in the parade of bushmen, Anzacs, lifesavers, "ordinary blokes", even poets and painters? Feminist analyses of the presence (and absence) of women in Australian culture and history began to make an impact in the 1970s. These interests have now expanded to a more wide-ranging set of concerns, not only with women, feminism and femininity, but also with masculinism and the masculine assumptions around which images of the nation are invented.

In Reading 8, Gail Reekie examines feminist challenges to constructions of Australian history and identity. She identifies three characteristic features of recent feminist history writing in Australia: its interest in processes of reproduction; its rejection of "progression" as the model for historical argument; and its attention to the specificity of women's experiences.

Marilyn Lake, in Reading 9, argues that gender must become a central category of historical analysis. Her interpretation of "the Australian legend" does this by focussing on the masculinism of the bushman as a cultural icon.

The final reading is a short story by Barbara Jefferis, "The Drover's Wife". As a feminist re-writing of Henry Lawson's famous story of the same name, it "sets the record straight" by allowing the woman to speak for herself about birth and death in the bush. Jefferis's story also makes reference to the painting of the same name by Russell Drysdale, and stories by Murray Bail and Frank Moorhouse ("Franco Casamaggiore") — both also called "The Drover's Wife"!

Further reading

Daniels, K., and Murnane, M., *Uphill All the Way: A Documentary History of Women in Australia*. St Lucia: University of Queensland Press, 1980.

Dixson, M., *The Real Matilda: Women and Identity in Australia 1788-1975*. Ringwood: Penguin, 1976.

Grieve, N., and Burns, A., *Australian Women: New Feminist Perspectives*. Melbourne: Oxford University Press, 1986.

Matthews, J.J., *Good and Mad Women: The Historical Construction of Femininity in Twentieth Century Australia*. Sydney: Allen & Unwin, 1984.

Modjeska, D., *Exiles at Home: Australian Women Writers 1925-1945*. Sydney: Angus & Robertson, 1981.

Schaffer, K., *Women and the Bush: Forces of Desire in the Australian Cultural Tradition*. Cambridge: Cambridge University Press, 1988.

Spender, D., *Heroines: A Contemporary Anthology of Australian Women Writers*. Ringwood: Penguin, 1991.

Contesting Australia: Feminism and Histories of the Nation

Gail Reekie

The history of post-war feminism in Australia has been marked by the persistence of a critical engagement with history. In Australia the maleness of Australian history was the initial impetus for the production of feminist scholarship, and history continues to be one of the most frequently targetted masculinist areas of knowledge. For two decades, Australian feminist scholars have located male historians as their primary adversaries in a struggle for a definition of nation that included women and their experiences. The first major works of Australian feminist scholarship — Ann Summers' *Damned Whores and God's Police* (1975), Beverly Kingston's *My Wife, My Daughter and Poor Mary Ann* (1975) and Miriam Dixon's *The Real Matilda* (1976) — were primarily arguments about Australian history. In contrast to the findings of Canadian feminists such as Susan Mann Trofimenkoff, which suggest a convergence of interest between feminism and nationalism, Australian feminism has been fundamentally opposed to nationalism since at least the late nineteenth century.

This article charts the antagonistic relationship between Australian feminism and histories of the nation. The nation is here assumed to be a cultural construction or imagined fraternal community which has retained its masculinist integrity through the exclusion of female lived experience. A survey of the feminist historical literature produced since 1970 reveals the ways in which the findings of feminist historians fundamentally challenge, contradict or explicitly deny most of the myths of nationalist history.[1] These traditional "Australias" have been constructed through positively-inflected accounts of the workingman's paradise, the social laboratory, pioneers and settlers, Anzac heroes, egalitarianism, social harmony, manliness and the bush.

There are a number of common themes in this diverse scholarship: the significance of reproduction to Australian women's experiences; the difficulty of accommodating women within the traditional historical narrative dominated by linear progression: the acknowledgment of the specific nature of women's experience; and the significance of the private sphere — all of which histories of the nation must submerge and transcend. Despite its necessity to the construction of the nation in material terms, women's work in both reproductive and productive realms has had to be silenced in historical constructions of the nation. I conclude therefore that women have, symbolically and materially, carried the burden of an essentially sacrificial relationship to the "nation" in Australia.

What makes Australian history "Australian"? Historians, overwhelmingly male, have long been preoccupied with the Australianness of Australia's history and its distinctiveness as a nation. As generations of schoolchildren can attest, the traditional panorama of Australia's past has given pride of place to convicts, colonial governors, explorers, settlers, gold diggers, bush workers and bushrangers, socialists and soldiers. The country's penal origins, the battle against the land, and the struggle to achieve independence from imperialist masters assumed centre stage in a national narrative that relied on a public (that is, diplomatic, political, military and economic) definition of historical significance and progress.

The radical nationalist school of historians of the post-war period challenged this orthodoxy by revealing the socialist principles underlying a more proletarian nationalism. Their picture of Australian history, however, was no less masculine. Russel Ward's *Australian Legend* has since its publication in 1958 constituted an almost irresistible magnetic pole of historical debate about the nature of Australia's difference. Recent general histories tread a circumspect path between the whig and radical versions of Australia's past but, despite two decades of feminist scholarship, fail to challenge the maleness of the national vision. As feminist reviewers of the recent crop of bicentennial histories of Australia have observed, even the most gender-sensitive national histories either omit crucial dimensions of women's experiences or grant class primacy over sex as their major analytical category. Jill Julius Matthews notes that the bicentennial historians of the nation find it almost impossible to accommodate women or admit their own (gendered) subjectivity within their conceptual frameworks.[2] Survey courses in Australian history currently being taught in some universities are still, like the bush of the Australian Legend, no place for a woman.[3]

The question arises, then, as to the reasons for this apparent exclusion of women from histories of the nation and images of national identity. Part of the solution certainly lies, as feminist historians have been arguing since 1970, in the need to rigorously and systematically incorporate women, gender and feminism into mainstream history. There is evidence to suggest, however, that historical accounts of the nation can not *by definition* accommodate feminism. Feminism and nationalism as it has been represented in historical writing continue to operate as opposed and mutually exclusive categories. The evidence from feminism suggests that histories of the nation are *necessarily* predicated on, and only made possible through their refusal of the feminine.

The nation as a fraternal community

That we now feel obliged to talk of the "nation" with inverted commas is largely the achievement of historians who have disputed the conception of nations as material and geographical realities. Studies by Benedict Anderson and Richard White in particular have considerably facilitated our rethinking of the nation: Anderson by positing nations as imagined political communities, and White by demonstrating the ways in which Australia has been invented and re-invented by the intelligentsia to meet the needs of powerful social groups.[4] Their work now enables a re-vision of the nation as a cultural artefact which has been manufactured and maintained by particular people for particular psychological and political motives. Historians have been fully engaged with the project of invention: war historian C.W. Bean, for example, actively elevated the Anzac soldier into a distinctively Australian hero of legendary proportions.[5]

White's invention theory and Anderson's imagination thesis are of only limited utility, however, in explaining the inherent contradiction between the nation and the feminine. Certainly, as White acknowledges, women were rarely if ever present as actual inventors of Australia, and as a result images of the nation were incapable of incorporating the female experience. Women were excluded from cultural production, hence invented Australias were inevitably masculine. By implication, there is little point in feminists attempting to reconcile the history of women's actions, thoughts and experiences in Australia with histories of the "nation", because the invented nation simply reflects male interests. White's flat assertion of the masculinity of "Australia" leads to a theoretical dead end for feminism, because it discourages scrutiny of the closures and silences which have enabled and sustained the nation. While the nature and intellectual foundations of the masculine nation remain unexamined, the work of feminist historians risks being relegated to the periphery of Australian historical writing.

How, then, are we to interrogate the nation in such a way that men, women and gender become visible and central? One route would be to show the ways in which women have been actively involved, perhaps complicit, in the material processes which contribute to nation-formation. Many women have undeniably been just as enthusiastic nationalists as men. Women's patriotic activities, however, were enlisted to service a national vision that denied the feminine. *Women* may have been active in constructing, defending and celebrating the nation, but *woman* and her world was excluded from "Australia". Anderson directs our attention to the significance of the nation imagined as a fraternal community. The nation is more than a community: it is a community of brothers. It is the imagined bond of brotherhood that enables females as well as male citizens to overcome their everyday knowledge of social and sexual differences, their individual identity and their attachment to life itself. Seeing the nation as a fraternal community opens up interesting possibilities, fraternity implying as it does rigorous exclusion of women and non-masculine men, rituals of male bonding and homosocial forms of behaviour, and demands on brothers to prove their masculinity by renouncing civilising, domestic or feminine influences.

Recent feminist analyses of social and political thought shed considerable light on this unacknowledged maleness of the public sphere and the inherent masculinity of citizenship. Carole Pateman finds in this recent critique a dominant theme: the masculine and public world is defined only in contrast or in opposition to the private world of women.[6] The private (female) sphere is that realm of social life against which the public (male) sphere can be made known and understood by social theory.

History is a similarly phallocentric discourse whose practitioners have adhered to a positivism which effectively renders mute the specificity of women's experiences. Histories of the nation have silenced the female voice by using the alibi of "no evidence" and thereby given the impression that the nation was an autonomous and self-sustaining social reality. With an apologetic shrug as if to say "we did our best, but we couldn't find the evidence", historians have maintained the fiction that the fraternal nation was not only parthenogenic but self-cleaning and celibate.

The feminist challenge to "Australia"

The cumulative work of feminist historians over the last fifteen years provides abundant evidence of women's contribution to production, reproduction, domestic labour, social reform and other nationally useful activities. This contribution may have been consistent with an allegiance to the fraternal community, but did not necessarily grant women access to the brotherhood of the nation. On the contrary: the history of women in Australia appears to run counter to, and directly contradict many of the shibboleths of the history of Australia. Australian historians working from oppositional political positions — especially those who draw attention to inequalities of class, race and ethnicity — have also contested Australia, and shown how a range of social groupings have been left out of its conceptualisation. Feminism, however, mounts a qualitatively different and arguably more theoretically subversive challenge to histories of the nation. In exposing its conceptual substructure, feminism reveals the nation to be something of an intellectual charlatan, a "sexually particular theory that masquerades as universalism".[7]

The evidence from feminist historiography of this radical challenge to the nation contradicts some of the truisms of Australian history. The portrayal of Australia as a paradise for the working man, for example, was one of the dominant nineteenth century inventions of Australia. White has shown how emigration agents, employers and government officials promoted a vision of Australia as a place of unusually high wages, unequaled opportunities for social advancement, the possibility of home ownership, a plentiful supply of fresh meat and high quality food, and a generally superior standard of living. Many historians have accepted these contemporary perceptions that the Australian worker (sex unspecified but assumed to be male) was comparatively better off than his counterpart in Europe.

This rosy picture of the workingman's paradise has been challenged from several quarters. Women were heavily represented among the many casual and seasonal workers who did not benefit from improvements in the national economy. Shirley Fitzgerald's study of Sydney's working class men and women between 1870 and 1890 shows the uneven effects of economic development and the detrimental consequences of unregulated industrialisation and urban expansion.[8] Beverley Kingston's demographic analysis of the age differential between wives and husbands between 1860 and 1900 adds a further dimension to this inequality. Men who married, many of them single immigrants, were on average about four years older than their native-born wives. Age and experience may have reinforced the socially sanctioned patriarchal authority of the husband and probably contributed to the low esteem and relative powerlessness of younger, "mere colonial" women.[9] The work of Kingston and Fitzgerald places women's working environment — the home — alongside man's in importance, with the result that their servicing of the workingman's paradise is revealed and "the notion of an egalitarian society in which anyone could make a comfortable living lies now in tatters".[10]

Feminism has not, of course, been the only politics to engage with and dispute the assumption of colonial peace, prosperity and a "fair go" for all. The effectiveness of the marxist challenge to a classless and egalitarian Australia is suggested by its incorporation into mainstream accounts of the history of the nation. The feminist challenge to the national myth of egalitarianism, while still marginal, is no less damaging.

Penny Russell has developed the theme of women's particular contribution to class difference in her study of upper class women in nineteenth century Melbourne. She argues that historians have until recently denied the existence of an Australian upper class in their desire to regard Australia as an egalitarian society. Feminist history, however, undermines this view:

> Belief in the egalitarian nature of Australian society can only be sustained while historians look at what have been traditionally regarded by men as the only important realities — namely economics, politics,

and affairs of state. Once you begin to incorporate women into your analytic framework, the myth of egalitarian society vanishes — and not only because of the obvious inequalities of opportunity between men and women.[11]

Russell's work, like that of many feminist historians, shows how "the nation" was only made possible by the work of women. This female labour, however, had to be hidden and denied in order for the fraternal community to retain its hold over the national imagination.

Like the workingman's paradise and the egalitarian nation, Australia's designation as a "social laboratory" has marked its history as distinctive. Australia acquired a favourable reputation among overseas social reformers and radicals between the late nineteenth century and the 1920s for its relatively progressive adoption of protective labour legislation, various forms of state arbitration and the establishment of minimum and basic wages. In pointing out the inequities of the social laboratory, feminist labour historians have revealed the extent to which Australia's international reputation as a progressive liberal democracy with a relatively high standard of living was only made possible by women's labour, paid and unpaid. The social laboratory, then, not only had little to offer women but was sustained as a national vision only by denying their economic contribution and silencing their political voice. The image of the social laboratory, moreover, failed to encompass aspects of Australian society which made it a "working model of comparative development" immediately relevant to women's domestic lives, such as the management of sexuality in a masculine culture in which women were in short supply.[12]

The pioneer legend has similarly been maintained by the silent presence of women. Although the nationalist category of pioneer is one of the few that has readily admitted women, those women who failed to conform to what Judith Godden has called the "virtuous woman" model of pioneer womanhood were excluded from legendary status.[13] The pioneer woman was defined in opposition to her real life counterparts who refused to be or were incapable of being middle class, respectable, moral, domestic, feminine, compassionate or self-sacrificing. As Marilyn Lake's reassessment of pioneer women shows, rural women working in small scale family enterprises comprised a psychologically oppressed, physically overburdened and economically dependent class.[14] The heroic stature of Australia's returned soldiers who were given small grants of land from state governments in the inter-war period, the soldier settlers, was equally achieved at the expense of the health and material well-being of their wives and children. In detailing the reality behind the myth of the digger, Lake also contributes to a feminist reassessment of the Anzac soldier as a dominant representative of the nation.[15] She points out that soldier settlement schemes were designed to "tame" unruly and disruptive returned soldiers whose drunken and violent behaviour was not only disturbingly unpatriotic but a threat to social order.

We can see in First World War Australia how critical was a sexually differentiated heroic status to the preservation of the nation as a public, male sphere.[16] Women's national duty was to overcome her maternal attachment to her own particular sons in order to sacrifice them to the greater brotherhood of the nation. Loyalty to the nation was only possible if loyalty to the family, to the personal and to the individual was overcome. War, and by extension the making and defending of nations, was a man's game. The nation, citizenship and selfhood could only be sustained if women were kept away from the battlefield; the fraternal community of the Anzac could only be glorified if the private world of women was kept separate and subordinate. It is then not surprising that historians equated the attainment of manhood at Gallipoli with the achievement of nationhood. They have failed to point out, however, that this nationhood was achieved at the expense of women.

The view held with some tenacity by historians that Australia has been fortunately free from major internal strife or war on her [sic] own shores could similarly only be maintained by turning a blind eye to the many forms of domestic conflict. "Domestic" here denotes not only "local", that which is internal to the nation, but also the private and personal forms of conflict within families, between parents and children, between mistresses and servants and between men and women. Feminist historians have recently begun to document, often with great ingenuity given the paucity of sources, the extent and nature of this intra-national conflict in a "peaceful" nation.

This challenge has been taken up by feminist scholars working within cultural and literary studies as well as history. Kay Schaffer's *Women and the Bush* critiques the conventional place of the bush in accounts of national identity, including those constructed by historians.[17] She argues that white anglo-saxon men have invented the nation through phallocentric language structured on systems of difference that oppose male and female. The bush and the Australian landscape have constituted a focal point of this project to define the nation. The bush, according to Schaffer, functioned as a metaphor for woman, a feminine "other" to the masculine subject of the nationalist discourse. Schaffer shows, for example, how the text of Keith Hancock's 1930 history, still influential in popular notions of "Australia", reveals a preoccupation with the land personified as woman and avenging mother: something to be assaulted, possessed, tamed, and dominated by Man. The value of Schaffer's work to feminist historians lies not only in her deconstruction of the male Australian legend, but also in revealing the place of woman in nationalist discourse. The feminine is not simply absent, as White argues, but is present as that *against which* the male national character defines himself. Feminism reveals a submerged but necessary feminine counterpoint to dominant, masculinist histories of the nation.

The nation in chaos

Other feminist historians have less explicitly engaged with the history of the nation by investigating, for example, the colonial family; women's fertility control; marriage, divorce and motherhood; meanings of the female body; the regulation of family life and reproduction; feminist campaigns around sexuality; population ideologies; rape, sexual and domestic violence. Much of this work reveals the hidden human substructure of the nation, a foundation built and maintained at considerable personal and economic cost by women. Women were blamed at the turn of the century for jeopardising the nation by refusing to personally increase the national birthrate and in subsequent decades by resisting the new scientific and "rational" methods of parenting.[18] The urgent need for women's co-operation suggests that nations cannot be sustained without the reproductive and productive labour of women, or without their complicity (enforced or otherwise) in the ordering of society.[19]

Just as significantly, the kinds of history written by feminists about Australian women is qualitatively different from "Australian history". Julia Kristeva's discussion of the problematic of women in Europe, "Women's Time", helps illuminate the major themes of this Australian feminist historiography. First, feminist history investigates the material and bodily processes of reproduction (sexuality, childbirth and childcare, fertility, family formation, mothering, contraception) as well as, or instead of, the more abstract history of production and economic development.

Secondly, feminist histories of Australia reveal a different relationship with time. Kristeva suggests that "when evoking the name and destiny of women, one thinks more of the space generating and forming the human species than of time, becoming, or history". Repetition and eternity (cyclical time and monumental time) are more appropriate to female subjectivity than "time as project, teleology, linear and prospective unfolding; time as departure, progression, and arrival — in other words, the time of history".[20] . . . The work of Australian feminists indicates precisely this suspicion of the linear temporality of histories of the nation which rely on beginnings, endings, developments and directions, if not achievements and progress. In the light of feminism's distrust of linear temporality, it is perhaps not surprising that, apart from the early attempts of Summers and Dixson and one project in progress, we have no feminist history of Australia.

A third feature of feminist historiography in Australia is its attention to the specificity of women's experiences. Historians of Australian women almost without exception begin their investigations from a position defined in relation to dominant representations of Australian history which have falsely assumed a unified and non-sexually specific human experience which is on closer examination male experience. Feminist historiography not only points to the particularity of women as a sex but is, through the work of Lake and others, revealing the history of men as a sex.[21] It is this attention to the specificity of the female and that of each individual woman that is feminism's particular contribution to debates around the nation, a specificity that renders extremely problematic any unitary concept of community.

The work of Australian feminist historians shows how women have repeatedly been sacrificed to the nation: as bearers of class distinction, as wartime heroines, as workers worth two-thirds of a man's wage, as the unpaid housekeepers of the workingman's paradise and the liberal democratic society, as helpmate and slave to the pioneer settler, as the silent victims of domestic conflict, as mothers of the nation responsible for national prosperity and security, and as a metaphor for an Australian landscape that constituted the object of men's desire.

The work of feminist theorists and historians therefore demands a radical appraisal of national histories. It suggests that it is only possible to write the history of the nation if the (masculinist) historian effaces or mutes the sexually-specific experiences of women and their sphere. The nation is predicated on the validation of the public sphere of human (that is, predominantly male) action over the private. It is, moreover, defined as that which transcends the private: loyalty to the nation must take precedence over family, emotional or self-interested concerns. War is a moment in the history of the nation in which the feminine and private sphere is most nakedly denied and the expectation of women's sacrifice most insistent. The masculinity of nationhood, like the masculinity of war, "consists in the capacity to rise above what femaleness symbolically represents: attachment to private concerns, to 'mere life' ".[22] The nation represents community in opposition to family, unity in opposition to specificity, citizenship in opposition to individualism, ethics and ideals (mind) in opposition to hedonism and corporeality (body), linear temporality in opposition to repetition or eternity.

The feminist challenge to histories of the nation, then, lies in its fracturing of a false unity and in its revelation of the hidden masculine assumptions around which the nation is invented. We stand at a critical moment in the feminist contestation of nation. If, as Yeates argues for sociology, the private sphere is reinstated into history and histories of the nation become self-consciously dualistic, can the nation retain its coherence as a theoretical unity? To use Marilyn Frye's analogy, once the stagehands (women) begin to encroach on the stage of phallocratic History, the reality of the nation risks disintegration into chaos.[23]

The Politics of Respectability

Marilyn Lake

The history of womanhood has now been much studied, here and abroad, yet historians have been slow to recognise "manhood", "manliness" and "masculinity" as social constructions requiring historical investigation and elucidation.[1] This is all the more remarkable in Australia as for men in this country their "manhood" has so often seemed their chief source of pride and identity.

The men in most Australian history books are sex-less: they appear in most accounts as neutered and neutral historical agents. Men become universalised Man: White Man, Working Man, Nineteenth-Century Man, the Coming Man. Male historians have been blinded to the problematic nature of the sex of their subjects by their own sex-centredness. It is time that we started treating men, historically, as men, socialised into "masculinity" (whose meanings have changed from one age to another, one society to another) and pursuing their "masculinist" interests as men, as well as the interests of their class and race. In other words, it is time for historians interested in gender to move beyond "women's history" — beyond the static conception of "woman's role" which lies at the heart of "contribution history".[2] It is time that gender became a central category of all historical analysis. For just as women's history cannot be fruitfully written without reference to men, neither can men's history be properly written without reference to men's relations with women.

The gender factor has been obscured in Australian historical writing by a number of phenomena: by the dominance of a narrowly defined political history, by the sex-blind nature of much of what passes as class analysis and by the centrality in our historiography of organising concepts such as "national character" and "national tradition" and the dichotomy of "respectability" and "unrespectability". I wish to suggest that the adoption of such conceptual frameworks has served to obscure one of the greatest political struggles in Australian history: the contest between men and women at the end of the nineteenth century for the control of the national culture. To cast the struggle in terms of respectability and unrespectability is to miss the sexual dynamic in history. An examination of this battle of the sexes suggests that its resolution involved the resolution of another, related, conflict: that between competing ideals of masculinity.

In his study of the national ethos in *The Australian Legend*, Russel Ward identified the pastoral workers as Australia's cultural heroes. The stockman and the shearer are represented as the supreme embodiments of the "national character". Although, like many analysts of the national character, he conflated a distinct set of male cultural practices with a "national tradition", in identifying the emergence of a particular masculine ideal in Australia, Ward has unwittingly made a significant contribution to our understanding of gender relations in Australia. In a review of Ward's thesis, Graeme Davison argued the importance of relating the Australian legend to "the ideas and situation of those who created it".[3] He pointed to the urban sources of the legend and demonstrated that it was an urban malaise which served as the springboard of the idealisation of the bush. But there is a further dimension to the "ideas and situation" of the legendmakers which Davison only hints at. In a later study of "national identity", Richard White stressed the "masculine exclusiveness" of the bush ethos and pointed to the continuities between the culture of the bushworkers and that of the men who, in the 1880s and 1890s, celebrated them in literature.[4] White cites the evidence of Arthur Jose who, in his memoir of "the romantic nineties" had noted that "the romance . . . was singularly devoid of feminine interest . . . It was not that kind of romance. There were a few girls among the Boy Authors, but they were tolerated there mainly because they made tea and organised refreshments".[5] Richard White's analysis can be pushed further.

The Australian legend was a celebration of the "one powerful and unique national type yet produced in the new land" — the Bushman.[6] It represented the promotion of a particular model of masculinity — the Lone Hand — by men with firm views about gender relations and who, whether married or not, enjoyed the pleasures of "bachelordom". Most importantly, the idealisation of the Lone Hand represented a rejection of the idealisation of Domestic Man which was integral to the cult of domesticity, imported to Australia in the cultural baggage of English immigrants.

The cult of domesticity in England, Catherine Hall has pointed out, was vitally linked to the rise of Evangelicalism: "Between 1780 and 1820, in the Evangelical struggle over anti-slavery and over the reform of manners and morals, a new view of the nation, of political power and of family life was forged. This view was to become a dominant one in the 1830s and 1840s".[7] The Evangelicals were champions of married life and the joys of domesticity. W. Cowper, the "poet of domesticity", eulogised:

> Domestic happiness, thou only bliss of paradise that has survived the Fall.[8]

For ideologues of domesticity in the colonies, the truly noble man was the one "whose affections lure[d] him to the serene enjoyments of Domestic Life". Men were promised that those prepared to find happiness at home could expect the status of "Serene Highness". The "abandoned man" was defined as the one who had "abandoned the joys of domestic life".[9] The ideal of Domestic Man was actively fostered in Victoria by such evangelical groups as the Young Men's Christian Association (YMCA), founded in Melbourne in 1871 for the purpose of improving the moral, intellectual and social conditions of all within its reach. The object of the YMCA was a missionary one — to extend "home influence" to all the boys in the colony.[10]

To the militants of the emergent men's press, "home influence" was emasculating. The Sydney *Bulletin* liked to believe that in "virile cultures" where "home-life [had] not become so all absorbing":

> men live and struggle and fight out in the open most of the time. When they go to their homes they go to beat their wives. We live in the home. All our real life is home life. All our moral and mental life is the moral and mental life of men who are half women in their habits, men breathing always a domestic atmosphere . . .[11]

According to the *Bulletin*, home life trammelled a man's spirit and sapped his masculinity. And it robbed him of his independence. Randolph Bedford, prominent Bohemian and *Bulletin* contributor, recalled how his father had encouraged him to "go bush" with the words:

> You're me all over again, lad. There's only one thing that will tie you down, and that's responsibility. A wife and children will put the hob-

bles on you. You'll look over the fence at the horses who are going somewhere; but you'll have to stay in the paddock.[12]

The *Bulletin* was the most influential exponent of the separatist model of masculinity which lay at the heart of the eulogies to the Bushman. From its establishment in 1880 until 1902, this flamboyant magazine was edited by J.F. Archibald, described by Francis Adams as "the most fascinating personality in Australia" and the "one Australian journalist of genius".[13] Archibald was an unhappily married, childless misogynist. His jaundiced views about the relations between men and women formed a major strand of the *Bulletin*'s message.

*   *   *

When the "nationalist" school of writers represented the pastoral workers as cultural heroes, they did so because in their apparent freedom from the ties of family and in their "independence", these bushmen most closely approximated to their masculinist ideal. The pastoral industry provided the perfect subjects on which they could project their attitudes and values. They were Lone Hands and their much vaunted "independence" was equated with mobility, the freedom to move. This "nomad tribe" inhabited a world without families, though not without women. As Russel Ward points out, sexual relations between pastoral workers and Aboriginal women were common.[14] Indeed from the bushworker's view, Aboriginal women were the perfect sexual partners, affording the men sexual pleasure without burdening them with family responsibility. As Henry Reynolds has noted, for "most frontiersmen an encounter ended abruptly with ejaculation and withdrawal".[15] The uses of white women were similarly episodic; many were abandoned in huts and homesteads. The bushman's heart, like the Bohemian's, had learnt to "love and roam".[16] . . .

These were city men who promoted Bushmen as cultural heroes, but it is important to note that not all rural men qualified for heroic status. From the 1860s a new class of rural worker had moved across the colonies — the agriculturalists put on the land by the Selection Acts. The supporters of land reform had invoked the model of the yeoman: selectors were to be neither employers nor employees, but independent freeholders. In the event their lack of capital drove them into a network of dependencies. Unable to afford hired labour, most relied heavily on the unpaid work of their wives and children and unlike the roving men in the saddle, the selectors, as men bogged down in family life, could not be admitted to the pantheon of heroes. The "smiling homesteads" envisaged by land reformers were replaced by images of "sordid farms". Indeed, "by about 1890", according to Ward, "the 'cocky' had become, at least in the mythology of the migratory bushmen, a byword for meanness and stupidity".[17] By 1900 the family men, Dad and Dave, had emerged as embodiments of everything unheroic, national objects of pity or mockery.

Henry Lawson, unhappily married, returned again and again in his verse to the pleasures of the "careless, roaming life" and the nobility of the love between men encountered on the track, a love named mateship. In "The Vagabond" he represented the family as a tyranny and the family man as a fool:

> Sacrifice all for the family's sake,
> Bow to their selfish rule.
> Slave till your big, soft heart, they break.
> The heart of the "family fool".[18]

The lone bushman was these writers' love object. In 1888 Francis Adams gushed:

> Yonder the band is playing
> and fine young people walk.
> They are envying each other and talking
> their pretty empty talk.
> There, in the shade on the outskirts,
> stretched on the grass, I see
> a man with a slouch hat, smoking.
> That is the man for me![19]

It is little wonder that the nationalist writers of the men's press greeted the advance of the "new" trade unionism so warmly: for them it represented a great fraternity. The Labor movement was men's movement. As Labor stalwart W.G. Spence later claimed, it "had in it that feeling of mateship which [the bushman] understood already". Or as William Lane so nicely put it, "socialism . . . is the desire to be mates, is the ideal of living together in harmony and brotherhood and loving kindness".[20] One of the chief objects of the labour movement in Australia was the exclusion of "cheap labour" in the form of Chinese, children and women. Independence was considered the privilege of the white man. Unless women were to remain economically dependent, observed the *Bulletin*, the labour market would be ruined for white men no less than by Asian competition.[21]

By the late nineteenth century the gulf between the experience of manhood and womanhood, even allowing for class differences, was large. The separation of work from home, which occurred with industrialisation, gained an added dimension in Australia from the dominance of the pastoral industry in the Australian economy. The Drover's Wife and her kind were left alone with the children because their husbands were away at work, droving, shearing or boundary riding. In the towns and cities this sexual apartheid was reinforced by the casual nature of much employment, the consequent mobility of labour and the acute segregation of the labour market. When women joined the paid workforce, they usually worked in different jobs than men, and when in the same occupations, such as teaching, they worked at different levels of the hierarchy. After work, the separation often continued, with men seeking a haven away from their home in the public house or their private club.

Although men and women inhabited different worlds, they were bound together by economics. Denied access to a living wage on the assumption that they were supported by men, women were thus forced into relations of dependence. The prescription became self-fulfilling. Locked into economic dependency, women's material (and often emotional) fate thus depended on men's circumstances and predilections. In this situation, men's cultural pratices could have profound implications for women and children; and there were particularly injurious consequences of the style of masculinity propagated by the champions of the Bushman.

Given the demographic imbalances of nineteenth century Australia — with men outnumbering women — the promotion of the Lone Hand as the ideal Australian was in some ways making a virtue out of necessity. Large numbers of men were compelled to be bachelors for life whether they liked it or not. By the 1880s, however, the excess of males was declining and the proportion of men marrying in Australia beginning to increase. Significantly, large numbers of men were of quite an advanced age, with habits already set, when they embarked on marriage.[22]

Just as the independent, free-wheeling Bushman was being enshrined as Australia's cultural hero, the balancing of the sexes was resulting in more men entering wedlock. But while these men were willing to try the anticipated comforts of a marriage, many, like Randolph Bedford, were not so willing to forgo the traditional pleasures of Australian masculinity. And within a family context, masculinist cultural practices could take on dramatically new meanings. If men chose to spend a large proportion of their earnings on drinking, tobacco and gambling, the result well might be a deprived diet for their family and barefooted children. Drinking bouts could exacerbate domestic tensions and precipitate wife beating and child abuse. Men exercising their presumed right of access to women's bodies could produce unwanted children and spread venereal disease. Encouraged to roam the country in search of work and freedom, men's departures could render their families destitute. As Kay Daniels has noted, "women often paid for the 'mobility' of the nomad tribe"; the prevalence of desertion as a factor in pauperism is documented in government records and in legislation.[23]

* * *

The response to the women's movement in Australia, both friendly and hostile, can only be understood, I suggest, in its relationship to the ascendancy of the masculinist culture outlined earlier. The women's movement aimed at dethroning the style of masculinity championed by the men's press — a style of masculinity that had deleterious consequences for the lives of women. "Whisky, Seduction, Gambling and Cruelty" — these were the targets of the Women's Sphere.[24] To depict women's concerns with temperance and social purity in terms of "respectability" is to ignore the sexual politics; to describe the campaigners as Wowsers is to stigmatise them in the language of their masculinist enemies. The women's movements in Britain and the United States shared similar concerns but in Australia, where masculinist values had been elevated to the status of national traditions, feminist activism acquired a particularly subversive, counter-cultural dimension. These women's aims were limited but they were no less threatening for that. They sought to curtail masculine privilege and those practices most injurious to women and children — notably drinking, smoking, gambling and male sexual indulgence. They did not seek a total independence for women, but to make their dependence a happier and more secure state. They sought to change mankind — to make men more considerate and responsible fathers, more companionable husbands. Recognising their lack of power to effect radical change, all campaigns converged in the demand for female suffrage.

The women's temperance campaigns were of course part of a wider crusade initiated by the Protestant churches against social evil, but as J.D. Bollen has commented, on the Drink issue, "churchmen were joined as never before in public life by women".[25] Not surprisingly, the masculinist press responded venomously to what they perceived, rightly, to be a female project of cultural reconstruction. Feminists were mocked, abused and insulted. They were "officious busybodies" and "leathery social interferists". When a woman became interested in political rights she became "hoarse and hysterical".

> She neglects her hair, and allows her stockings to fall into holes; she wears her hat with a sort of reckless abandon, and takes no more pride in complexion pastes and remedies for wrinkles, warts and outstanding freckles; she becomes an ache and an aggravation, and a thorn planted in the side of man.[26]

The response of the men's press, threatened and abusive as it was, shows more insight into the significance and meaning of the women's movement than many historians have recognised. A whole way of life was at risk.

* * *

The outcome of this struggle for cultural control between masculinists and feminists involved a complicated set of compromises. Shortage of space permits only the briefest sketch. The first point is that the feminist demands for men's reform coincided with the increasing need of an urbanised, industrialising society for a disciplined, sober and efficient workforce. Women's objectives and those of employers and the State were differently motivated but they converged and triumphed. A classic instance of this was the introduction of six o'clock closing of hotels in 1916.

"Honest, sober and industrious" became the standard terms of recommendation for the post-war working man.[27]

Secondly, the emergent labour movement, welcomed so effusively by the *Bulletin*, was in fact a bearer of mixed messages for men. While placing great emphasis on mateship, some in the movement argued that women could be mates too — albeit in their different spheres. William Lane, perhaps the most charismatic Labor leader of the late 1880s, promoted a style of masculinity the exact opposite of that idealised by the *Bulletin*. For Lane the "manly" man was straight, temperate and monogamistic. Whereas the *Bulletin* depicted the nomadic bushman in heroic terms, Lane described a pathetic figure deprived of family: "aged too soon, wifeless and childless, racked with rheumatism". The New Australia Cooperative Settlement Association promised to "secure the most complete homelife to its members". Significantly, one of the major issues to cause disaffection in Paraguay was the refusal of some colonists to abide by Lane's injunctions to temperance, a fact which gave rise to much malicious mirth in the *Bulletin* office. Although Lane left Australia in 1893, his vision of a new society whose economic arrangements would permit men to be sober and responsible breadwinners and women, the "weary sex", relieved of the necessity to support a family, could be free to care for home and family, was shared by many in the Labor movement.[28]

By the 1920s misogynists were in retreat; the culture had been, to a degree, "feminised". Whereas the 1880s and 1890s had been the great years of the men's press in Australia, by the 1920s *Woman's World, Everylady's Journal* and *The Woman* were in the ascendant. Masculinity was defined in terms of responsible breadwinning. When Justice Higgins decreed in the Harvester Judgment of 1907 that a man should be paid sufficient to keep a wife and three children in "frugal comfort", he was locking men into breadwinning just as surely as he was confirming women in dependency. By 1918 Judge Heydon, president of the Board of Trade, was sure that "A boy knows from birth he will be a breadwinner; this is his lot in life." Two years later the Royal Commission into the Basic Wage could stigmatise some men's distaste for the national obligations of husbandhood and fatherhood "unmanly". "Single life" was to be discouraged.[29] A decade later a woman's contempt for a husband who had beaten and humiliated her found expression in the charge that he was not "man enough to support his wife and little ones".[30]

In the light of the challenge of men's autonomy and independence which these various developments posed, it is tempting to see the celebration of Australian masculinity under the banner of Anzac as a mythic reparation to "hobbled" men.

The Drover's Wife

Barbara Jefferis

It ought to be set straight. All very well for them to spin yarns and make jokes but nobody has written any sense about me. Nobody has even given me a name except one and he got it wrong and said I was called Hazel. The drover's wife, the doctor's wife, the butcher's wife. You wouldn't think of all the countries the one where women are the fewest would be the one where they don't exist, where men'll say "the missus" sooner than give a name. Small wonder the Eyetalian got his facts wrong and said there weren't any women in the country for the first hundred years. I had to laugh. I don't know why; it isn't funny when you think about it.

I better say first who I am. I'm forty-six years old. I have four children, all of them boys. My womb has fallen, so've most of my teeth, but I've got a straight back and a good head of hair and I can match anyone on a hard day's work. I know seventy-three poems off by heart and I'm not afraid of the dark.

I was born somewhere on the stock route between Tibooburra and Broken Hill; nobody ever told me exactly where.

My father was a drover. Times there was no stock to be moved he dug dams or went fencing — hard grafting for very little money. He died quietly one night by his campfire without saying a word to anyone. I was twelve.

We weren't on the road with him. We had a shack out of Nyngan — my mother, my two brothers, my sister Bessie and me. Ma was a hard-handed woman. I never saw her after I cleared out with the dentist but sometimes still I dream I run into her. I'm glad to wake up.

The boys cleared out as soon as the first was old enough. We never did hear what became of them. We had a few acres and three cows and some pigs and fowls. It wasn't much of a life. Ma took up with a shearer when I was fourteen and *she* cleared out for six months. It was better there without her than with her. Then they both came back and the next thing was Bessie ran off with a Bananalander. I'd like to see old Bess again; I really would, but she was never much for writing letters so there wasn't anything I could do, not knowing where she was. She's forty-nine now, if she's alive.

That left me stuck there two years with them, like a bandicoot on a burnt ridge. I gave as good as I got but I took the first chance that offered to get out of it.

Now it's a matter of what each of them had to say — answering it. Take them as they came. Mr Lawson first. He didn't mean me any harm, far from it. But men can only see women as being heroines when they do something a decent man would do for them if he happened to be around, like killing a snake or an injured calf, or hauling a rotting sheep carcass out of the well.

He was a nice little bloke, Mr Lawson. No bother to anyone, quiet, deaf; drank too much. Every man I've had to do with from my own dad down to the drover drank too much on occasions, but very little was too much for Mr Lawson and it didn't seem to make him happier any longer than the time it took to get it down his gullet. He was a good listener — the best I ever knew in those dry times when there wasn't much listening going begging for ones like me who'd spend weeks talking to the flies on the wall. And he really listened. You could tell because he'd ask things, wanting more.

So I told him a lot. Talked too much — must've — because some of it he took and turned into that story about the snake, as though what I'd really told him wasn't true or wasn't fit. His snake story was true enough. Nobody goes to sleep with a black snake under a floor that's got gaps in it in a room that's full of children. Yes, I watched; I had a candle going and a green sapling close at hand and Alligator in with me because he was a champion snake-dog all his life till a big brown brute got him down at the dam. Mr Lawson made it a great and terrible night. It wasn't. I've spent great and terrible nights.

Like the one I told him about. Joe was droving and the baby was ten months old the time it happened. He was the one Mr Lawson mentioned that I had without anyone with me, only the old black woman, Mary. I was into my time and Tommy and Billy both in the cot together and me blind silly with the pain and the fear of what'd happen to them if I died, which can happen. And her ugly face came in at the doorway. I screamed, and that set the two kids screaming. Next thing I knew she had her hands on me, and she knew what she was doing.

Only time I worried was when she went off down the cowyard with the bucket to get some milk for the kids. I thought she mightn't come back, being who she was. It made me feel a bit different about the blacks and Reg was as fine a baby as the others had been, and fatter.

Until he was ten months old. One moment he was as bonny as usual, the next he was screaming and going into a fit. I got the tub and the hot water the way I'd been told but had never needed before. It was no good. I got the dog in and threw the tub of water on the fire and banged the door and left the kids yelling in the dark hut with only Alligator to mind them.

He took another fit in my arms while I was catching Roley, and another on the ground while I was saddling up. Then I don't know how many more there were. Roley wasn't a fast horse but he was a stayer and we would have made the nineteen miles in an hour and a half. We'd gone maybe ten miles, perhaps eleven, when the baby had another fit and right at the height of it everything stopped. I knew he'd gone.

I got down, holding him, and lay down with him behind some bushes. I don't know how long I was there. When I do remember again there was enough light, starlight I suppose, to see Roley, off a hundred yards grazing. I was lucky he'd been trained not to light out for home.

But I wasn't thinking of home. I could only think of the baby. I was hugging him, crying and talking, kissing him, closing his eyelids and then opening them up again, trying to push my tit into his mouth. You do strange things when you're by yourself at a death. I must have been there a long time. He began to get cold. I put him inside my clothes and caught Roley and went home.

The dog got up when I opened the door, but the boys were asleep with their arms round each other. It was near dawn. I got the spade and went out. It took me a long time to dig deep enough, being a dry year and my head full of strange fears out of things I'd read about vampires and wolves' claws digging him up. It was when I had finished and was making it all tidy that I suddenly felt the pains, and there was no mistaking what they were. I could have gone back, but what was the point? The kids would have woke and asked about their brother. All I could do was what the black gins do — scrape a hole in the ground and squat over it, waiting for what was to come to come. I would have given Roley and his saddle and bridle then for a sight of Black Mary, but there was nothing there but small trees and the dry ground and the grey light that said it was nearly sun-up.

It hurt me a lot for a little thing no bigger than a small peach with the stone out of it. I covered it up and went back, gathering sticks on the way, knowing I'd have a wet stove to work at before I could boil the kettle and start the day. But later, when I had the fire going and the children were fed and playing round the woodheap, what with the sadness and no sleep and the sick fancies I had about wolves and that, I went back and scratched the soil off the hole and took the thing back with me and lifted the lid of the stove and dropped it into the heart of the fire. I don't know why I did that.

That was the story I told Mr Lawson a long time afterwards, or at least the parts of it that were all right to tell to a man. Funny the way he was more taken by a snake story, the sort that happens to everyone two or three times in a year. But that was the thing about him. Nervous. A nervous man who could never write about things as they really were but only about how they would have seemed to be if he'd been what he would have liked to be.

Gloomy, that, but I wanted to tell it just to show how wrong they are when they write about us. They don't understand the strength women have — won't see it, because they think it takes away from them. Not that I'm gloomy much, far from it. Wasn't it the dentist said I had a silly streak? Well, fair enough, if that's his name for someone who laughs a lot and can see the funny side.

Mr Lawson could laugh himself when he felt at his ease and had half a pint of tanglefoot under his belt, but it's a funny thing about humorous men — they don't go much on other people's jokes, only liking to work them over into something funnier for themselves.

He said another thing that wasn't right; he said "As a girl she built the usual air-castles, but all her girlish hopes and aspirations are dead. She finds all the excitement and recreation she needs in the *Young Ladies' Journal*, and, Heaven help her, takes a pleasure in the fashion-plates."

Who says they're dead? Who thinks that hopes and aspirations have anything much to do with expectations? Even the hardest times don't stop your fancies, don't stop a woman being broody, trying to hatch out stones like an old hen we had when I was a kid. And times haven't all been hard, not by a long chalk.

Hardest thing of all for women is that everything they do is for un-doing. It's not like sinking fence-posts or putting up a shed. *They'll* last, maybe fifty years if they don't get burnt. But the work a woman does hardly lasts a minute — if it's not mouths today it's moths or mould tomorrow, and the whole lot's got to be done over again. You have to laugh sometimes at the way your hard work goes down people's throats or under their dirty boots. Either that, or lash out with the copper stick. Best to laugh if you can and get on with it.

Another thing; didn't he notice the hut was papered floor to roof with pages from the Bushman's Bible? Perhaps he thought I put them up and never looked at them again. I put them up for two reasons — they were all pieces that were worth keeping to read again, and because they were the best thing I had for teaching the boys something a bit better than the simple rubbish out of school readers. Well, for three reasons, the third being that the walls looked better covered than bare.

If he'd looked he would have seen one of his own *Bulletin* stories. There was *Telling Mrs Baker* stuck right along under the shelf we kept the plates on. His idea of a good woman — a fool who'd believe anything she was told even when the truth was plain in front of her face. But I had it up there for the words, and the beautiful way he had of using them.

That's something I got from my dad. He had a way with words and a great belief in them. He used to say, "No one knows what's coming after you die, or if anything's coming at all. Best you can do is stuff your head with words and poems and things to think about, just in case that's all you're going to have to keep you happy for ever and ever." Well, he's gone now, so he knows what the answer is. It makes me laugh to think of him up there somewhere, spouting all those verses from the *Bulletin*, loud-voiced.

Come to think of it, if you could count hymns I know a lot more than seventy-three poems. Some of them must be by poets. Only a poet could have thought of "blinded sight". It doesn't make any sense but it's beautiful enough for me to think of it six times a day. And the one that says "Before the hills in order stood." I like that. I suppose it's because all around here it's so flat and there's no hills to make you lift up your eyes. I suppose the best thing you could take with you when you die is some words you've put together yourself into a poem. But you try it; it's not as easy as it looks.

I wish they had more poems from women. I don't mean I like them just because they're women's poems, but some of them really get into the heart of things. Everyone says Mrs Browning but for me they're like men's poems, written on ruled lines. Christina Rossetti — there's a name. I wonder if it's made up, like The Banjo and The Breaker and Ironbark and the rest of them. Not that she's in the *Bulletin*, but I bought a fourpenny *Goblin Market* once in Sydney. Something to think about in the next world, if my dad's right. And I know some others of hers, too. "Sing no sad songs for me." That's a fine poem, sad and funny too, if it means what I think it does.

The next one was Mr Drysdale. He did no harm, except to my vanity, which I wouldn't have if all my hopes and aspirations were dead. He knew the place, give him his due. He didn't sit down in George Street and try to imagine it. You can smell the dust and the ants squashed under your feet, and you can hear the crows when you look at it, even though they're not there. He made me into a black dress over a big belly. And the feet! Could have been size eleven. And a soft look like butter wouldn't melt to my face. But he knew it; he knew how the ground reaches up into you.

Then there was Murray Bail. I never remember seeing him, though he may have called himself something different then. He doesn't sound like one from our part of the country — more like a cow cocky, from the river areas. He must've known the dentist, but.

He never could tell the truth, the dentist. He'd never come right out and tell an honest lie, just say enough to give the wrong idea and then never a word to put it right. Like him saying about me, "How can you tell by a face? That a woman has left a husband and two children." I'd left a husband, all right, and *his* children, which is a different thing. Isn't anything a woman can do blacker than leaving her own kids, and that's what he was trying to make you believe.

He was a dirty man, the dentist — I didn't like him. I could tell what the night would be like by the way he came home. If his patients had been men, he'd come home wanting his tea. If they'd been women he'd come home with spit in the corners of his mouth and some of the things he wanted, in the dark with the blinds down, would've fetched him a bullet if he'd been an animal wanting them in the farmyard. Should've known, since that's the way I met him, over a rotten tooth that had to come out. Should have had more sense.

People said I'd never last, shut up in a backyard in a town. He had these two kids, poor little buggers. I was sixteen. Did what I could for them, them having no mother and him what he was. There were times I thought he was more than a bit mad — forever looking out to see who was looking in. He was very ignorant for all he had letters after his name and a brass plate. He couldn't read more than half a page of a book without getting bored and coming on words that were too big for him. I never knew him read anything much except for the racing pages in the paper and the labels on bottles, to see whether they'd thought up a better germ-killer than the one before.

All my life I never knew anyone who worried so much about germs. He was frightened of flies the way most people are of crocodiles, and a bit of fruit that hadn't been washed or a moth falling into his soup would give him something to talk about for half an hour. He says I was quiet. Well, I was while I was with him. Day to day things are for doing, not talking about, and he had nothing else.

He couldn't abide to see me chop wood or dig a hole to bury a bit of rubbish or a runover dog from the street. He'd do it himself in his good clothes and his white shirt with the sleeves rolled up and his chin stuck up on his starched collar like a sick calf trying to look over a paling fence. Poor job he'd make of it. I never knew him ever put on old clothes for a bit of hard yakka. Too afraid people would see him and think he was used to it.

That he was no bushman you could tell from the stupid thing he said, when he used a magnifying glass on Mr Drysdale's picture to see if he could tell who it was I'd gone off with. He said, "It's my

opinion, however, that he's a small character. See his size in relation to the horse, to the wheels of the cart. Either that, or it's a
ruddy big horse." Any fool could see there were two horses, and
that the waggon had a centre pole, not shafts. But that was him —
couldn't see what didn't interest him.

That holiday he talks about, up over Port Augusta, that was a
disaster. It was supposed to be for me. He never for a moment
stopped grousing — the heat, the flies, the dust, the snakes, the
flies, the blacks, the cattle, the flies. Frightened. His kids liked it
though. He says we only saw the drover once, boiling up on one
side of the track. Gordon wanted to know where his cattle were.
The drover just waved his arm, gave a grin. He was half-miling
them and the grin meant the half-mile had got stretched and they'd
be eating someone's good grass four days or more before anyone
could cut the travelling brands out from those that belonged to the
place.

We'd seen him five days before, a few miles up, and that day
too I'd had a mug of tea from his billy with Gordon wandering
off, too afraid of germs and the look of the thing. We didn't say
much — just enough for him to know the two kids weren't mine
and me to know he'd make it into Adelaide in a month with the
cattle. It was how he looked — I knew he'd find me.

It's no surprise the dentist can't understand it. He could never
see what it was about the country, so dry that days you could sit
looking at it and your mouth would melt for the thought of a
peach, maybe, or a tomato. He couldn't understand you could
give up a board floor and a bit of carpet and some wax fruit under
a glass bell for a shack with no floor at all in the kitchen and water
that had to be carried half a mile when the tank ran dry. Lonely at
times, yes, but it's quiet, and that's something.

There's more to a man than trimmed nails and a dark suit, and
I'd rather have beer fumes breathed in my face than fancy pink
mouth-wash.

He's never going to understand it, how I could find the drover
superior. Put it down to my silly streak if you like, but we could
laugh. We used to laugh over something or nothing, it didn't matter, just laughing because we felt good, because our skins liked
each other, and our hair and teeth. Laughter doesn't last for ever
any more than hair or teeth. But what I'm saying, when it all boils

down and you've stopped laughing, he was a good man. Still is, even though his back's gone. And anyway, there are our kids, and bringing them up to know there are two or three more things in the world than how to break a horse and bring down a tree without smashing your fences.

Another thing he said, how a dentist can't afford to have shaky hands and how after I left him he sat for nights in the lounge with the lights out. Heart-rending, that is. Makes me laugh. The lights out and the blinds down too, I'll be bound, so's nobody passing could see the bottle on the table.

There's nothing better than rot-gut to give you a shaky hand next day, particularly if you're not eating right, and he'd never learn to do for himself the way men learn in the bush. Truth is I worried about those kids of his when I'd left. Kay'd have been all right, but young Kev was a picky little kid, had a weak stomach.

After him, I thought I'd done with them talking about me, but then this Eyetie bloke. Dirty-minded. Hard to tell whether he's had his leg pulled or is trying to pull ours. I'll thank him all the same not to call me a sheep. You have to laugh, though. He's fallen for one of those stories they tell, round the fire. Voices carry a long way at night. I've heard worse than that. You can tell he's a foreigner by the words he uses, like "inter-species reciprocity." I had to first look it up and then sit and puzzle it out to mean taking a poke at a sheep. Any backblocker would have come right out with it, in four letters.

But once you've puzzled it out all you've got is the old story about someone off on his own having to do with a sheep or a pig or a cow. Only when they tell it here it's not a drover, not one of their mates, it's a half-mad manager or some rotten overseer. I don't say it never happened; they say everything you can think of happened somewhere or some time. So they say. But it's not the drovers' way. I don't have to spell it out, do I, more than that he can count on his five fingers?

It's funny to think this Eyetie chap, Franco Casamaggiore, isn't really different from any of the rest of them. Truth is there are many sorts of men, all the same; only one sort of woman, all different. We could be a lot fonder of them if only they'd admit how scared they are. Having their sex on the outside leads to a lot of boasting and worrying.

A lot of them cover it up by telling yarns. With our men it's some trollopy girl or a flash barmaid they took up with. With the Eyetalians it's animals. Same difference with the Greeks. It's rams with golden fleeces or it's white bulls or it's swans having their way with young girls. Our fellows don't go as far as that but often enough they talk about women as though they were animals — "She's in pup", they'll say, or "She's running round Bourke like a slut on heat", or "Got to get home to the missus, she's due to drop her foal any minute." Reason's plain enough; these are things you can own, use, brand — better or worse, batter and curse.

I'll say that for the drover; he doesn't talk about me as though I've got four legs and he doesn't think the way to praise a woman is to say she thinks like a man, acts like a man. Perhaps it's why I'm still with him, after so long. That, and the kids.

Worst thing ever happened to me was the day the baby died, losing two of them at once. And never knowing what it was I lost. Mary's black face came in at the door about a week later. I asked her about the thing I'd put in the fire. "Inside . . . little man . . . all curled up," she said. I'd never thought to look.

That started me dreaming. Dreams all mixed up with *Goblin Market* — golden head and long neck, dimples and pink nails. Laura like a leaping flame. One may lead a horse to water, twenty cannot make him drink. I would have called her Laura. More sensible to have called her Lizzie, for the sober sister. Put it down to my silly streak, if you like, but I would have called her Laura, and hoped she'd have some wildness and wisdom, like Miss C. Rossetti. I suppose I dreamed that dream twenty times before I wore it out. Oh well, dreams go by opposites, they say. Chances are it would have been another boy.

What I meant was to tell not so much about me and the drover and the dentist and the rest of them but about how women have a history, too, and about how the Bushman's Bible and the other papers only tell how half the world lives. You ought to be able to put it down in two words, or twelve, so people could remember. Women have a different history. Someone ought to write it down. We're not sheep or shadows, or silly saints the way Mr Lawson would have. There's more to us. More to me than any of them have written, if it comes to that.

The dentist was right about one thing, though. I'm not the drover's wife. Or only in the eyes of God if he's got any, if he's not another one with blinded sight.

Part Five
A Country Practice?

The bush, the outback, pioneers, stockmen, shearers, drovers and drovers' wives, even bushrangers — these images have been plundered again and again for representations of who Australians really are or where the true Australia can be found. After having read the previous sections, though, you will immediately be aware of which groups in society get left out of such definitions of Australia. Yet even in the 1990s they continue to work — in advertising, cinema, fashion, journalism and political debate — as powerful images of Australian identity.

How can this be so? Russel Ward provided one of the earliest and most influential accounts of what he called "the Australian legend". Ward argues that a particular ethos of egalitarian values grew up among the nomadic bush workers in nineteenth-century Australia, and this ethos later came to define the values associated with the "typical" Australian. An excerpt from Ward's opening chapter supplies our first Reading.

Ward's thesis has provoked an enormous amount of commentary and criticism, some of which you will already have encountered in Readings 1, 2 and 9. Graeme Davison, in Reading 12 below, attacks from another angle, arguing that the bush legend was largely a by-product of the urban milieu of writers, artists and intellectuals in late nineteenth century Sydney and Melbourne. In Richard White's terms, it was an "invention".

J. B. Hirst, in Reading 13, examines the literature and art of this period and discovers an alternative set of values, the "pioneer legend", which he argues has also been influential right up to the present. (One might think of the Stockman's Hall of Fame in Longreach, Queensland.) The "bush" does not have a single meaning but is a cultural symbol which has been used by many different individuals and social groups for a wide variety of diverse, sometimes contradictory, purposes.

Further reading

Alomes, S., *A Nation at Last? The Changing Character of Australian Nationalism 1880-1988*. Sydney: Angus & Robertson, 1988.

Astbury, L., *City Bushmen*. Melbourne: Oxford University Press, 1985.

Carroll, J., ed., *Intruders in the Bush: The Australian Quest for Identity*. Melbourne: Oxford University Press, 1989 (2nd ed.).

Docker, J., *The Nervous Nineties: Australian Cultural Life in the 1890s*. Melbourne: Oxford University Press, 1991.

Hodge, B., and Mishra, V., *The Dark Side of the Dream: Australian Literature and the Postcolonial Mind*. Sydney: Allen & Unwin, 1990.

Schaffer, K., *Women and the Bush: Forces of Desire in the Australian Cultural Tradition*. Cambridge: Cambridge University Press, 1988.

The Australian Legend

Russel Ward

> For I'm a ramble-eer, a rollicking ramble-eer,
> I'm a roving rake of poverty, and a son of a gun for beer.

In the last seventy-odd years millions of words have been written about Australian nationalism and the "Australian character". Most writers seem to have felt strongly that the "Australian spirit" is somehow intimately connected with the bush and that it derives rather from the common folk than from the more respectable and cultivated sections of society. This book seeks, not to give yet another cosily impressionistic sketch of what wild boys we Australians are — or like to consider ourselves — but rather to trace and explain the development of this national *mystique*.

Nearly all legends have some basis in historical fact. We shall find that the Australian legend has, perhaps, a more solid substratum of fact than most, but this does not mean that it comprises all, or even most, of what we need to know to understand Australia and Australian history. It may be, however, a very important means to this end, if only because we shall certainly be wrong if we either romanticise its influence or deny it.

National character is not, as was once held, something inherited; nor is it, on the other hand, entirely a figment of the imagination of poets, publicists and other feckless dreamers. It is rather a people's idea of itself and this stereotype, though often absurdly romanticised and exaggerated, is always connected with reality in two ways. It springs largely from a people's past experiences, and it often modifies current events by colouring men's ideas of how they ought "typically" to behave.

According to the myth the "typical Australian" is a practical man, rough and ready in his manners and quick to decry any appearance of affectation in others. He is a great improviser, ever willing "to have a go" at anything, but willing too to be content with a task done in a way that is "near enough". Though capable of great exertion in an emergency, he normally feels no impulse to work hard without good cause. He swears hard and consistently, gambles heavily and often, and drinks deeply on occasion. Though he is "the world's best confidence man", he is usually taciturn rather than talkative, one who endures stoically rather than one who acts busily. He is a "hard case", sceptical about the value of religion and of intellectual and cultural pursuits generally. He believes that Jack is not only as good as his master but, at least in principle, probably a good deal better, and so he is a great "knocker" of eminent people unless, as in the case of his sporting heroes, they are distinguished by physical prowess. He is a fiercely independent person who hates officiousness and authority, especially when these qualities are embodied in military officers and policemen. Yet he is very hospitable and, above all, will stick to his mates through thick and thin, even if he thinks they may be in the wrong. No epithet in his vocabulary is more completely damning than "scab", unless it be "pimp" used in its peculiarly Australasian slang meaning of "informer". He tends to be a rolling stone, highly suspect if he should chance to gather much moss.

In the following pages we shall find that all these characteristics were widely attributed to the bushmen of the last century, not, primarily, to Australians in general or even to country people in general, so much as to the outback employees, the semi-nomadic drovers, shepherds, shearers, bullock-drivers, stockmen, boundary-riders, station-hands and others of the pastoral industry.

This was so partly because the material conditions of outback life were such as to evoke these qualities in pastoral workers, but partly too because the first and most influential bush-workers were convicts or ex-convicts, the conditions of whose lives were such that they brought with them to the bush the same, or very similar, attitudes.

In nineteenth-century Australia this particular social group developed a surprisingly high degree of cohesion and self-consciousness but, in isolating it for the purposes of study, some distortion may be inevitable. In fact, of course, pastoral workers were constantly influencing, and being influenced by, other sections of colonial society. A convict often spent months or years on government constructional work in the city before being assigned to the service of a country settler, or he might be returned to the city after some years "up the country". Small farmers and selectors often sought work as shearers on the western runs to supplement their incomes, and many a city wage-earner did the same for a few seasons, especially during bad times when work was scarce on the sea-board. Bullock-drivers, especially before railways began to creep farther and farther into the interior after about 1870, regularly flogged their teams from the colonial capitals and coastal ports to outback stations and back again. They carried news, gossip, manners and songs, as well as stores, wool and hides. One of them, Charles Macalister, wrote of Sydney in the 1840s:

> A chief house of call for us country folk then was the old Blackboy Hotel, at the corner of George and King Streets. A kind of theatre or people's music-hall was kept in connection with this Hotel, where the leading comedians and singers were Jim Brown and "Micky" Drew; but, as the platform of the Blackboy "theatre" was somewhat free and easy, sometimes a strong sailorman, just off a six months cruise, would favour us with "Nancy Lee" or other jolly sea-song; or an ambitious carrier or drover would "rouse the possum" by giving some long-winded ditty of the time.

Drovers brought not only cattle and sheep to the city markets but also exotic styles of dress, speech and behaviour, wherewith to impress respectable citizens and newly arrived immigrants. And many a bushman from the interior settled down in the agricultural areas or the city, after a happy marriage or old age had terminated his roving habits. As Alan Marshall wrote, in 1955, of his father:

> After he started work he drifted round from station to station horsebreaking or droving. His youth and early manhood were spent in the outback areas of New South Wales and Queensland, and it was these areas that furnished the material for all his yarns. Because of his tales, the saltbush plains and the red sand-hills of the outback were closer to me than the green country where I was born and grew to manhood.

In some ways it is difficult to consider the pastoral workers apart from their employers, those who came to be known in and after the late 1830s as squatters. Right through the nineteenth century there is abundant evidence of class hostility between pastoral employers and employees. It culminated in the disastrous and bitter strikes between 1890 and 1894. This hostility was itself a very important factor in shaping the distinctive ideology of the pastoral employees and yet, except towards the absentee landlords who multiplied exceedingly towards the end of the period,[1] the hostility was always qualified and conditional. The differences between master and man were economic and often political, but not social in some cases. In the 1840s one squatter wrote of a neighbour:

> He was a native-born white, and had been a stockowner all his life. His parents had given him a few cows and brood-mares at his birth, and he was now, by dint of time and industry, the owner of many thousands of cattle. But though fully possessed of the means, he had no wish to alter his style of living for the better, or to rest in any way from his hard and laborious employment . . .[2]

At least in the earliest pioneering stage, before the squatter's wife arrived to define more rigidly the barrier between "the house" and "the huts", conditions forced a certain degree of understanding between the occupants of both. As Samuel Sidney wrote in 1854: "Now, living in the Bush, and especially while travelling, there is not the same distance between a master and a well-behaved man, although a prisoner, as in towns . . ."[3]

Moreover, although climate, economic factors and the effects of land legislation[4] generally combined to make it difficult for a poor man to become a squatter, it was by no means impossible. An occasional unknown workman like James Tyson or Sidney Kidman, by superior industry, temperance, or skill in cattle-duffing, became a "shepherd king" and, especially in times of drought or depression like the early 1840s or 1890s, many a squatter was reduced to working for wages at one of the bush trades.[5] The truth seems to be that the working hands, while feeling strongly opposed to their masters in general and in principle, were prepared to take each individual squatter as they found him.[6] Also, as the work of the dispossessed squatter's son, A.B. Paterson, no less than that of Furphy shows, "there was a region, or so it seemed, where the thought and feeling of the station was identical with that of the shed."[7] The region was that in which the interests of both conflicted with those of absentee squatters, pastoral companies, banks, and other institutions domiciled in the cities or in Great Britain. The rather complex relationship between masters and men was thus described by an English visitor in 1903:

> It is sometimes said that in Australia there are no class distinctions. It would probably be truer to say that in no country in the world are there such strong class-distinctions in proportion to the actual amount of difference between the "classes" . . . The "classes" collectively distrust and fear the "masses" collectively far more than is the case at

home . . . Individually, it is true, relations are for the most part amicable enough between capitalists and workmen; and the lack of deference in the tone of employees, their employers, being unable to resent, have grown to tolerate, and even perhaps in some cases secretly rather to like . . .[8]

Up to about 1900 the prestige of the bushman seems to have been greater than that of the townsman. In life as in folklore the man from "up the country" was usually regarded as a romantic and admirable figure. The attitude towards him was reminiscent, in some interesting ways, of that towards the "noble savage" in the eighteenth century. We shall see that, in general, he had more influence on the manner and *mores* of the city-dweller than the latter had on his. The tide turned somewhere between 1900 and 1918. Even today the tradition of the "noble bushman" is still very strong in both literature and folklore, but, at least since the publication in 1899 of *On Our Selection*, it has been counterpoised by the opposing tradition of "Dad and Mum, Dave and Mabel". True, Dad and Dave were not pastoral workers, bushmen proper,[9] but poor selectors, "stringybark cockatoos", who were sneered at by the men from farther out long before it became fashionable for townsmen to regard them as figures of fun. It is also true that the original creations of A.H. Davis ("Steele Rudd") were real comic characters and not the semi-moronic, burlesque puppets which they have since become in popular imagination. Nevertheless their appearance in literature fifty years ago was symptomatic of a real change in Australian attitudes towards the "bush". Since the early days of federation the capital cities have grown rapidly both in prestige and in their relative share of state populations, and bushmen are now usually willing to be taken for city-dwellers where formerly the reverse was the case.

In making generalisations about the bush-worker a difficulty springs from the fact of separate origins of the colonies which later became the federated states of the Commonwealth. There have always been, and still are, differences between them in speech, manners, tradition and outlook. But compared with similar differences in, say, Canada or the USA, they are slight indeed, tending to be differences of degree and emphasis rather than of substance. They are more noticeable among middle-class than among working-class people, and in and near the state capitals than in the back country. We shall see that the convict-derived bush ethos grew first and flourished in its most unadulterated form in the mother colony of New South Wales, but that it early spread thence, by osmosis as it were, to become the most important basic component of the national *mystique*.

* * *

The fact that no convicts and relatively few Irishmen emigrated directly to South Australia explains some real differences in outlook which are still discernible, especially in Adelaide and the thickly-settled agricultural districts near it.[10] But the dry, pastoral interior of the state is separated from the station country of New South Wales and Queensland by nothing but a line on the map. Since occupation of the interior began a hundred and fifty years ago almost every observer of outback life has been forcibly struck by the extreme mobility of the pastoral population, and especially of the wage-earning part of it in which we are interested. This mobility has naturally resulted in a diffusing of attitudes and values throughout the interior regardless of state boundaries . . . The songs of the bushmen graphically reflect both their nomadic habits and their disrespect for policemen and the law they were employed to enforce. As one version of *The Overlander* has it:

> No bounds have we to our estates
> From Normanton to Bass's Straits;
> We're not fenced in with walls or gates —
>   No monarch's realms are grander.
> Our sheep and cattle eat their fill,
> And wander blithely at their will
> O'er forest, valley, plain or hill,
>   Free as an Overlander.
>
> We pay no licence or assess,
> Our flocks — they never grow much less —
> But gather on the road I guess,
>   As onward still we wander.
> We vote assessments all a sham,
> Nor care for licences a flam,
> For free selectors, not a d—n,
>   Says every Overlander.[11]

South Australia and Western Australia were most completely insulated, by distance as well as their lack of convict origins, from the social attitudes emanating from "Botany Bay". Yet, even in these colonies, almost from the moments of their founding, the manners and *mores* reflected in the convicts' and pastoral workers' ballads rapidly gained strength among the lower orders.

In part this was no doubt due to like conditions having like effects. The early labour shortage in Western Australia, for example, unalleviated by convicts, would alone have been enough to evoke in working men the saucy and independent attitude so much deplored by their masters on the other side of the continent. The Advocate General and Judge of the Colony's first Civil Court complained constantly that masters there were such only in name, being actually "the slaves of their indentured servants". He wrote:

> In my absence, — does nothing, and if I speak to him — exit in a rage. I could send him to gaol, but I do not like this extremity, and yet I cannot afford to lose the advantage of his time, and pay £30, besides diet, to another in his place.[12]

But when we hear that, within two years of the first landing at Fremantle, workmen had "got into the habit of demanding" a daily rum ration, we may suspect that manners were being directly influenced by those of early New South Wales and Van Diemen's Land. At the end of the following year, 1831, the Judge Advocate noticed:

> Great visitings among the neighbouring servants; seven or eight of them patrolling about; and all this is sure to end in drunkenness and mischief — they talk of forming a *club*! They have too much control over their masters already; and club-law would be a terrible exercise and increase of their power.[12]

And "a man who had come from Van Diemen's Land" seems to have been largely responsible for "trouble" with the Aborigines. Relations had been fairly good until early in 1833 when this man saw some unoffending natives in the way: " 'Damn the rascals,' said he, 'I'll show you how we treat them in Van Diemen's Land,' and immediately fired on them."[12]

Samuel Sidney recorded in 1852:

> The timber of Australia is so different from that of Europe that English workmen are very helpless until instructed by bush hands. The first South Australian colonists could not even put up a fence until the overlanders and Tasmanians taught them how.[13]

Even before they set foot on the mainland some South Australian pioneers were taught, in 1836, how to bake a damper by two "frontiersmen" — sealers named Whalley and Day who had lived with kidnapped Aboriginal women on Kangaroo Island since 1818.[14] In the early 1840s George French Angas found that bush men to the south-east of Adelaide and, even more surprisingly, in the doubly isolated wilderness of Eyre's Peninsula, had already acquired a perfect familiarity with Australian slang, which was largely convict-derived, and with the art and terminology of bush cooking. Bush slang was also established, at the same early date on the then pastoral frontier of Western Australia south of York.[15]

Nineteenth-century observers were no less struck by the essential mobility of the outback pastoral workers than they were by their unity. Anthony Trollope travelled extensively in the outback and spent some months in 1871 and again in 1875 staying on sheep stations, including that of his son Frederick, in western New South Wales. To him it seemed that:

> . . . the nomad tribe of pastoral labourer — of men who profess to be shepherds, boundary-riders, sheep-washers, shearers and the like — form altogether one of the strangest institutions ever known in a land, and one which to my eyes is more degrading and more injurious even than that other institution of sheep-stealing. It is common to all the Australian colonies . . .[16]

Trollope thought that these itinerant workmen were degraded by their customary right to receive free rations and shelter for the night in station "huts", but he was not blind to their virtues. As Harris had noted of them half a century earlier when the convict element still predominated among them, though they might cheat and rob respectable people, they were honest and loyal to each other.[17] Also they were still, as in the time of Harris, very capable at performing practical bush tasks, and very prone to vary long periods of hard work by short bouts of tremendous drunkenness. As Trollope further wrote:

> The bulk of the labour is performed by a nomad tribe, who wander in quest of their work, and are hired only for a time. This is of course the case in regard to washing sheep and shearing them. It is equally so when fences are to be made, or ground to be cleared, or trees to be "rung" . . . For all these operations temporary work is of course required, and the squatter seldom knows whether the man he employs be married or single. They come and go, and are known by queer nick-

names or are known by no names at all. They probably have their wives elsewhere, and return to them for a season. They are rough to look at, dirty in appearance, shaggy, with long hair, men who, when they are in the bush, live in huts, and hardly know what a bed is. But they work hard, and are both honest and civil. Theft among them is almost unknown. Men are constantly hired without any character but that which they give themselves; and the squatters find from experience that the men are able to do that which they declare themselves capable of performing. There will be exceptions, but such is the rule. Their one great fault is drunkenness — and yet they are sober to a marvel. As I have said before, they will work for months without touching spirits, but their very abstinence creates a craving desire which, when it is satisfied, will satisfy itself with nothing short of brutal excess.[18]

A just understanding of the distinctive ethos of the "nomad tribesmen" is of cardinal importance for the understanding of many aspects of Australian history, both in the last century and subsequently. The pastoral industry was, and still is, the country's staple. Its nature, the nature of Australian geography, and the great though decreasing scarcity of white women in the outback, brought into being an itinerant rural proletariat, overwhelmingly masculine in composition and outlook. In the United States the cattle industry, during the stage of "the open range", produced in the cowboys a not dissimilar social group, but its existence was brief[19] and, relative to the total population, its numbers were small. Throughout the nineteenth century as a whole the typical American frontiersman was a small individualist agricultural proprietor or farm labourer, not a cowboy or ranch-hand. In Canada and New Zealand, too, the farmer was the typical frontiersman . . . For these reasons it is not too much to say that those whom Trollope designated the "nomad tribe" constituted a singular social group possessing an ethos which, though similar to those of certain other communities distant in time and place, was in some ways unique.

Among the influences which shaped the life of the outback community the brute facts of Australian geography were probably most important. Scanty rainfall and great distances ensured that most of the habitable land could be occupied only sparsely and by pastoralists. In combination with nineteenth-century economic conditions, climatic factors ensured too that the typical station should be a very large unit employing many casual "hands", but owned by a single man or company of substantial capital. If Australia had been occupied by the French or any other western European people, it is likely that somewhat the same kind of pastoral proletariat would have been shaped by the geographical and economic conditions. Still, there would have been important differences.

As it happened, the interior was occupied by British people who naturally brought with them much cultural luggage. Moreover, in the early period of the "squatting rush", when the nomad tribe was forming, the vast majority of its members were British people of a certain type. At first convicts and ex-convicts tended the flocks of the advancing "shepherd-kings", and at least until 1851 these pioneers predominated in influence and prestige, if not in numbers. But the germ of the distinctive "outback" ethos was not simply the result of climatic and economic conditions, nor of national and social traditions brought with them by the "government men" who first opened up the "new country" beyond the Great Divide. It sprang rather from their struggle to assimilate themselves and their *mores* to the strange environment. We shall find much evidence to suggest that the main features of the new tradition were already fixed before 1851. A considerable number of the gold-seekers and of the later immigrants who found their way to the western plains differed from most of their predecessors in having a middle-class background. They influenced the "bush" outlook in certain ways, but in the upshot its main features were strengthened, modified in certain directions perhaps, but not fundamentally changed.

Although the pastoral proletariat formed a recognisably distinct social group it was obviously not, as has been said, completely isolated from the rest of colonial society. From 1813 when Blaxland, Lawson, young Wentworth and their convict "hands" struggled back across the Blue Mountains, there was a constant coming and going of men, and resulting exchange of manners and ideas, between the coastal cities and the hinterland. But the strength of outback influence is indicated by the very phrase used, in the first half of the nineteenth century, to describe Sydney roughs. These rowdy, "flash" plebeians took some pains to stress the differences between themselves and respectable immigrants. Many were Australian born and all liked to behave in what they considered truly "Currency" or colonial ways. This involved their imitating "up-country" manners, for the bushman was axiomatically more "Australian", and hence differed more from the Simon Pure Briton, than the flashest Currency Lad in the whole of Sydney Town. Life in a bark hut on the Bogan necessarily changed a newcomer's manners and ideas more rapidly than life in a George Street cottage. Hence the roughs of early Sydney, affecting outback styles of dress and behaviour, were known as the "Cabbage-tree Hat Mob".

The cabbage-tree palm (*Livistona australis*) grew only in the rain-forests between the Great Dividing Range and the Pacific, being very common in the Illawarra district which was one of the earliest "frontier" areas. The heart or bud at the growing tip of the palm was a substitute for cabbage among the early settlers and cedar-getters, and the pinnate fronds were woven into broad-brimmed, flat-crowned, "cabbage-tree hats". When the "squatting rush" to the interior began in the late 1820s, this indigenous hat had already become standard wear among bushmen and, like the stockwhip, a potent symbol of outback values. Thus the cabbage-tree hat migrated with the frontier to the western plains, many hundreds of miles from the nearest source of the raw material from which it was made. Plaiting these hats was a favourite pastime among shepherds, whose occupation was an extraordinarily lazy and lonely one. They remained standard wear for stockmen and others until nearly the end of the nineteenth century, though by about 1880 a cabbage-tree hat might cost up to five pounds.[20]

From the beginning, then, outback manners and *mores*, working upwards from the lowest strata of society and outwards from the interior, subtly influenced those of the whole population. Yet for long this was largely an unconscious process recorded in folk-lore and to some extent in popular speech, but largely unreflected in formal literature. Towards the end of the nineteenth century, when the occupation of the interior had been virtually completed, it was possible to look back and sense what had been happening. Australians generally became actively conscious, not to say self-conscious, of the distinctive "bush" ethos, and of its value as an expression and symbol of nationalism. Through the trade union movement, through such periodicals as the Sydney *Bulletin*, the *Lone Hand*, or the Queensland *Worker*, and through the work of literary men like Furphy, Lawson or Paterson, the attitudes and values of the nomad tribe were made the principal ingredient of a national *mystique*. Just when the results of public education acts, improved communications, and innumerable other factors were administering the *coup de grâce* to the actual bushman of the nineteenth century, his idealised shade became the national culture-hero of the twentieth. Though some shearers are now said to drive to their work in wireless-equipped motor-cars, the influence of the "noble bushman" on Australian life and literature is still strong.

Sydney and the Bush: An Urban Context for the Australian Legend

Graeme Davison

"It was I," recalled Henry Lawson in his years of fame, "who insisted on the capital B for 'Bush' ".[1] Lawson, as it happened, was not the first writer to adopt the convention and his pursuit of the bush idea was only one strand in a broader movement during the 1890s to make the rural interior a focus of Australian ideals. Though the bush, with and without a capital B, had figured in earlier writing, it remained for an expatriate Englishman, Francis Adams, in his book *The Australians* (1893), to identify the "bushman" as a distinct national type. It is interesting, in view of the significance that the "bush" was later to acquire, that Adams and Lawson should also have promoted the matching terms "city" and "cityman". "Bush" and "city" were plainly important literary touchstones to the writers of the 1890s and their symbolic counterpoint provides a vital clue to the sources of the "Australian Legend".

Historians of Australian cultural origins have generally sought the explanation of the "bush" myth in the social context of the bush itself. Russel Ward, its most influential interpreter, has traced the "Australian Legend" to a popular tradition of ballad and yarn that developed first among the convict settlers and itinerant workers of the pastoral frontier. Invoking the "frontier hypothesis" of Frederick Jackson Turner, Ward argued that while America, a small man's frontier, had produced a national ethos of individualism and privatism, Australia, as a big man's frontier, created a tradition of egalitarianism and collectivism, of "mateship". Towards the end of the nineteenth century, through the powerful influence of the Sydney *Bulletin* and the "new unionism" these traditions were imported from the pastoral frontier to the coastal cities where they formed the basis of a national, rather than merely sectional, culture.[2] As the "bush" became the "Bush", folk tradition was transmuted into literature.

It is a tribute to Ward's persuasiveness that, through a new generation of historical writing, *The Australian Legend* remains the standard account of Australia's cultural origins. Even as he was writing in the late 1950s, the foundations of his interpretation — the rural-export model of the Australian economy, his simple two-class model of pastoral society, the Turnerian concept of the frontier — were under attack. American historians were tracing their legend back from the far West to the popular song and story-writers of the great cities. In the early 1960s, Norman Harper, re-viewing the history of the American and Australian frontiers, urged Australian historians to shift their vantage point "from back of Bourke to the coast" and Michael Roe reminded them that "whereas the appeal of the bush has been the great myth of Australian history the appeal of the city has been the great fact".[3] Yet "fact" and "myth" have remained strangely unrelated, not least because the few casual attempts at an urban interpretation of the "Australian Legend" have lacked a definite intellectual and social context.

A fundamental weakness of folk history — a genre of which Ward's book is a superior example — derives from its assumption that popular values may be abstracted from creative literature without direct reference to the ideas and special situation of those who created it. We are required to look beyond the mediating au-thor to divine the *conscience collective*. The hazards of this method are obvious even with an unselfconscious, traditional cul-ture, but they are greatly multiplied when we apply it to a post-in-dustrial, culturally derivative society like nineteenth-century Australia. In such a culture, I suggest, we do better to begin, as we would any other exercise in the history of ideas, with the collective experience and ideas of the poets and storywriters themselves.

This experience, it must be emphasised, was of an emerging urban intelligentsia rather than a dying rural folk culture. All but a few of the *Bulletin*'s staple contributors and most of its occa-sional "correspondents" lived in the coastal cities, especially Syd-ney and Melbourne. But only a handful had apparently grown up as city dwellers. The most outstanding group — Henry Lawson, Bernard O'Dowd, Edward Dyson, A.G. Stephens, the Lindsays — came as fortune-seekers from the declining goldfields, their in-tellectual interests already often kindled by small-town self-im-provement societies. "Banjo" Paterson was the one important figure with even fair "bush" credentials. Moreover, while it may be true, as Geoffrey Serle has claimed, that "there is hardly one major creative artist, after Marcus Clarke and Buvelot, who is not a native Australian",[4] a striking number of the *Bulletin*'s second rank — James Edmond, G.H. Gibson, Ernest Favenc, "Price Warung" (William Astley), Victor Daley, D.H. Souter, Will Ogilvie, Will Lawson, F.J. Broomfield and Albert Dorrington — had arrived in Australia from Britain as adolescents or young adults. Rather than bush — or Australian city — origins, the recurrent feature in the biographies of the *Bulletin* writers was their arrival in Sydney or Melbourne as lone, impressionable, ambitious young men.

In some, literary ambition had been fired by the frustrations of more conventional pursuits. Drop-outs from law or commerce, like Roderic Quinn; failed matriculation candidates like Lawson; disillusioned schoolteachers like Mary Cameron: all clamoured for a place in the one calling, open to talent, and consistent with literary aspirations, which a colonial city provided. "Journalism", G.B. Barton noted in 1890, "is at present the only field in which literary talent can find profitable occupation".[5] The 1880s were a prosperous time for the press. Expanding colonial trade and a growing urban reading public produced a rapid growth of newspapers and trade journals and, in turn, an encouraging stimulus to literary effort. The number of "authors, editors, writers, and reporters", counted by the census-taker in Melbourne more than quadrupled from 89 in 1881 to 359 in 1891. But even in these best of times a journalist's apprenticeship was hard and the long hours, low pay, and drudgery of police rounds weeded out all but the most determined. His work, by its very nature, put the young reporter constantly on call and this "enforced irregular life" and "weakening of domestic influences" were reckoned to confirm the "bohemian tastes" and lifestyle of the average journalist.[6]

Many would-be writers had already cut adrift from "domestic influences" when they came to the city and, like other young urban immigrants, lived alone in lodgings. In 1890 Sydney, with its large floating population of dock labourers, seamen, and seasonal workers, had over 300 listed boarding-houses, most of them crowded into a narrow "transitional zone" between the terminal areas around the waterfront and railway station and the central business district . . . Sydney's boarding-houses were more than twice as numerous as Melbourne's and, since they lay athwart the main transport arteries, they were also more conspicuous. By the late 1880s, rising unemployment and the city's chronic housing shortage had swollen their population to crisis point. High population densities and residential mobility, a preponderance of unattached men and the volatile mixing of the poor, the vicious, and the exotic gave the region a distinctive ethos.[7] These were the tidelands of the city: a staging point for immigrants; a haven for the drifter, the outcast, the man or woman with a past; a twilight zone of rootlessness and anomie.

This was the sleazy urban frontier which provided the social context for the *Bulletin* writers' confrontation with the city and from which, as we shall see, they fashioned reactively their conception of the "bush" . . .

Throughout their early stories and verses there are vivid glimpses of boarding-house life. We meet the landlady, blowzy and familiar, and drawn — as we might expect with young men away from home — affectionately and rather larger than life. James Edmond describes one such "wild" bohemian establishment:

> There were ten of us there . . . including Bem, the humorous Polish tailor, who was vaguely understood to have thrown bombs at all the royal families of Europe, and then gone into exile. We paid seventeen shillings a week each, not including washing; and we lived riotously on boiled mutton. There were more empty beer bottles in the bedrooms, and more laughter, and more grease slopped on the floor, and the candle-ends got in the soup oftener in that boarding house than in any other I ever heard of. Also the neighbours got less sleep than anybody ever did in the vicinity of any other boarding-house. The dining room had not been papered since the beginning of history, and the landlady had only one eye; also her daughter had recently eloped with a non-union printer. She, the landlady, was aged about 40, and wore a green dress, and in the evening she used to sing songs to us with her hair down.[8]

But beyond the rough good fellowship of the boarding-house, the city melted into the fleeting images of the twilight zone: Chinese opium dens and sixpenny restaurants, drunken youths swaying under gas lamps, painted women waiting on street corners and the ceaseless tidal flow of faces in the street. Henry Lawson, who traversed the region daily on his way from Phillip Street to Redfern Station, gave us the essential vision:

> They lie, the men who tell us for reasons of their own
> That want is here a stranger, and that misery's unknown;
> For *where the nearest suburb and the city proper meet,*
> My window sill is level with the faces of the street —
> Drifting past, drifting past
> To the beat of weary feet
> While I sorrow for the owners of those faces in the street.[9]

None of Lawson's early poems establishes so precisely his marginal urban situation or attests so poignantly to his legacy of loneliness.

* * *

The overlapping circles of secularists, republicans, land-reformers, feminists and socialists, which together comprised Sydney's infant "counter-culture", focussed their activities on a small triangle of the "transitional zone" between the Town Hall, Hyde Park, and Redfern Station.

Its nucleus was the Hall of Freedom in George Street where, under Thomas Walker and W.W. Collins, Sydney's freethinkers continued to preach the doctrines of Thomas Paine, just as their great contemporaries Charles Bradlaugh and F.W. Foote did in London. Many of the Association's stalwarts were themselves apparently refugees from London's declining trades: hardworking hatters, drapers, upholsterers, and compositors, whose secularism, crude and iconoclastic, had reflected the disappointments of their lot. But economic aspirations denied by Clerkenwell and Finsbury found more encouragement in Sydney and by the late 1880s many older secularists had left the mean environs of George Street for Woollahra and Paddington. With their dispersion something of the old militancy was lost, and in 1889, at the opening of a new Freethought Hall, these "sons of Albion" were ardent in praise of their "Southern Home". Indeed, it was not resentment of England or a peculiar sense of being Australian so much as fidelity to the Paineite tradition that made some of Sydney's leading freethinkers, like Thomas Walker and William Keep, theoretical republicans. For them, kings and princes, like bishops and priests, were part of an outworn fabric of medieval superstition and oppression. It was only among a smaller cadre of native-born secularists — including, notably, the Lawsons, mother and son — that republicanism became the basis of a more distinctive nationalism. Other *Bulletin* writers who may be numbered, formally or informally, as republicans in the late 1880s include George Black, E.J. Brady, J. le Gay Brereton, John Farrell, Roderic Quinn and, away from Sydney, Bernard O'Dowd and A.G. Stephens.

From the attack on priest-and-princecraft, it was only a step further to an attack on inheritance. Since the days of the Land and Labour League in the 1860s, the causes of republicanism and land nationalisation had been closely associated in London radical circles and during the 1870s Charles Bradlaugh had made land reform a main plank of his electoral platform. In Sydney, secularists and republicans appeared, with the *Bulletin*'s W.H. Traill, among the leaders of the New South Wales Land Nationalisation League. The radicals of the inner city had good reason to crave "the abolition of that poverty which manifests itself in all large cities of the world" and the *Bulletin* urged them on with slashing exposes of rack-renting in lower George Street. The scapegoats for the city's housing problem were the hated Chinese. The pressures created by redevelopment around Circular Quay had forced them to abandon their old haunts in lower George Street and move south to the new market area near Belmore Park, an area which, with its boarding-houses and bookshops, the radical intellectuals regarded as their own. Their champion, George Black MLA, led the anti-Chinese campaigns of the late 1880s and early 1890s while the *Bulletin*'s illustrators led by Phil May depicted the squalid interiors of Chinese gambling houses, brothels, and opium dens.

The outlook of Sydney's radical intellectuals was, therefore, a product of two mutually reinforcing influences: the transplanted artisan culture of late nineteenth century London and the pressures of day-to-day life in Sydney's transitional zone. One cannot but remark how closely their ideological preoccupations — secularism, republicanism, land reform, and anti-Chinese feeling — match the "anti-clericalism", "nationalism", bush sentiments and "race prejudice" which Ward has identified as the defining features of the "Australian" ethos. Indeed in this chapter I argue that the projection of these values, born of urban experience, onto

the "bush" must be understood in terms of a concurrent movement to establish the "city" as a symbol of their negation.

The city depicted in the writings of the *Bulletin* school is one that
a dispassionate historian would find hard to recognise in contemporary photographs of Sydney's dishevelled townscape. But their
lurid imagery, we must remember, was more symbolic than photo-
graphic, and owed less to observation of the Sydney scene than to
the rich stock of urban imagery which the *Bulletin*'s "hard-read-
ing crowd", along with other colonial city-dwellers, imported
from London. The primacy of London and their stereoscopic vision of the nearer urban scene is nicely suggested in a line of
Lawson's, written "to speed enthusiasm in favour of the London
poor".[10] "I looked o'er London's miles of slums," he wrote, "I
saw the horrors here/And swore to die a soldier in the Army of the
Rear".[11] (His first and only journey to London still lay fifteen
years in the future.)

For J.F. Archibald, founding editor of the *Bulletin*, the experience of London merely crystallised and reinforced an already dismal view of the colonial city. He had first come to Melbourne in
the 1870s as an apprentice journalist from the Western district and
for eighteen months scraped along as a part-time stone-hand, living alone and depressed in a South Melbourne boarding-house. A
few years later, after becoming well established in journalism,
Archibald arrived in Sydney. He was "ill and tired" at first but
gradually established himself and in 1880, with his partner John
Haynes, founded the *Bulletin*. But the metropolis continued to
exert its fatal attraction and in 1884 he arrived in London. Sick
and burdened with financial worries, he lived for almost two years
on the margins of Fleet Street, shut out from regular employment
but supplying the *Bulletin* with leaders and "pars" that reflected
his acquaintance with contemporary radical journalism and the
mounting sense of crisis in "Outcast London".[12] The experience
reinforced his distaste for the "selfish", "hysterical", and
"callous" ways of the city but, paradoxically, increased his reverence for London standards. Under his influence the *Bulletin* in the
later 1880s continued to project its view of local affairs onto a rolling backdrop of metropolitan events: the West End riots, the rise

of the Social Democratic Federation, the fortunes of Charles Bradlaugh, and the Dock Strike.

Among the paper's contributors over the following decade, it is possible to distinguish three main styles of urban writing, each firmly rooted in the London context. As bookish schoolboys in the 1860s and 1870s the *Bulletin*'s writers naturally fell under the pervasive influence of Charles Dickens's rich, but essentially segmental and antipathetic, view of London. Henry Lawson, for example, claimed that "every line that Dickens wrote/I've read and read again" while his friend Jack Brereton recalled how "Lawson and I used to wander into all sorts of queer corners and neglected backwaters of Sydney, and he pointed out to me the localities which he fancifully associated with the one novelist with whose work he was fairly familiar, Charles Dickens". Unhappily it was the weaker side of Dickens — the pathos of young Oliver and Little Nell — rather than his powerful vision of urban landscape which Lawson emulated in his 'Arvie Aspinall and Elderman's Lane stories.[13] But then the value of the London influence lay not in the quality of these imitations so much as the later, less obviously derivative, work for which they provided a scaffolding.

Archibald's stay in London had also coincided with the success of the journalist and light versifier, George Robert Sims. As a protege of Douglas Jerrold and G.A. Sala and a patron of the National Sunday League and the Hall of Science, Sims united the sympathetic, but otherwise separate, worlds of literary bohemia and militant secularism. Today he is remembered mainly for the impact of his book, *How the Poor Live and Horrible London* (1883), on the housing debate of the 1880s, but he was equally celebrated in his day as the author of *Dagonet Ballads*, a book of light verse dramatising the condition of the London poor. (It included "It is Christmas Day in the Workhouse" and "The Lights of London Town".) The *Bulletin* regarded Sims as "undoubtedly the most read light litterateur in the world" and reprinted his verse on several occasions.[14] With his use of colloquial speech and the ballad convention, and his theme of rural innocence and "urban degeneration", Sims may have excited a powerful influence on the style and anti-urban bias of Australian popular verse.

The third, and most seminal, influence on the *Bulletin* writers was the tradition of rhetorical, quasi-religious verse which descended from the late eighteenth century through Blake and Shelley, persisted in Chartism, and returned to fashion in the radical movements of the 1870s and 1880s. For Dickens, the city was mainly a *theatre* of human character; with Sims, it was a *cause* of human degeneration; but among the radical poets it became a gigantic *symbol* of corruption and exploitation invested with the apocalyptic shades of Sodom and Gomorrah. The most formative English exponent of the style was the "poet laureate of freethought", James Thomson, whose "City of Dreadful Night" first published in 1874 enjoyed a vogue during the 1880s. In Australia he was followed by the "Arnoldian Socialist" Francis Adams whose collected verse, published in Sydney in 1887, was, according to E.J. Brady, "a notable incident in the pre-socialist period". Adams's gloomy view of London, "the City of Wealth and Woe", reflected his deep hostility to the land and class of his birth but became, through its resonance with the marginal urban situation of the *Bulletin* poets, a pivotal image in the verse of J.A. Andrews, George Black, E.J. Brady, Edward Dyson, Henry Lawson, and Bernard O'Dowd, who all served for a time as poetic footsloggers in Adams's "Army of the Night".[15]

These three styles of urban image-making corresponded roughly with different kinds of social and political consciousness and the gradual predominance of the third over the first and second is one index of the deepening sense of urban alienation among *Bulletin* writers around 1890. Only careful attention to the chronology of their writings discloses the connection between their increasingly dismal view of the city and the rise of the bush ideal. Until about 1890, for example, Henry Lawson's writing had consisted mainly of republican "songs for the people", verses on urban themes ("Watch on the Kerb") and semi-autobiographical sketches on gold-fields and selection life. But in that year we find his interests moving further inland. In a series of newspaper articles he discussed the idea of decentralisation and land reform, arguing that "if some of the surplus suburbs of Sydney were shifted up country a few hundred miles, New South Wales would greatly benefit by the change". Almost simultaneously his verse leaps "Over the Ranges and into the West":

> We'll ride and we'll ride from the city afar
> To the plains where the cattle and sheep stations are.[16]

In the late 1880s "Banjo" Paterson may have stood closer to the rest of the *Bulletin* crowd than he did in later life. It is true that he joined few of their campaigns and lived in semi-rural seclusion across the Harbour at Gladesville, but his solicitor's office was within a block of the city's most sordid flophouses and in one of his first published pieces, a tract on land reform *Australia for the Australians* (1888), he invited his readers to

> take a night walk round the poorer quarters of any of our large colonial cities [where] they will see such things as they will never forget. They will see vice and sin in full development. They will see poor people herding in wretched little shanties, the tiny rooms fairly reeking like ovens with the heat of our tropical summer. I, the writer of this book, at one time proposed, in search of novelty, to go and live for a space in one of the lower class lodging houses in Sydney, to see what life was like under that aspect. I had "roughed it" in the bush a good deal . . . But after one night's experience of that lodging I dared not try a second . . . I fled.[17]

In his flight from the horrors of the city, Paterson retreated inland; his solution to urban ills was to open up "the rolling fertile plains" to closer settlement. The city and the country were established as separate moral universes: the poet worked in a "dingy little office" in a "dusty dirty city" but his better self, on permanent vacation, rode with the "western drovers", sharing the "pleasures that the townsfolk never know".[18]

* * *

The dream-like "Land of the West" which emerged in the late 1880s as an anti-type of the city began to acquire a more definite character during the urban conflicts of the early 1890s. With the Maritime Strike of 1890, the Sydney waterfront, already ridden with unemployment, overcrowding, and racial tension, became a frontier of class conflict. There was rioting on Circular Quay and unionists held almost daily meetings in the Haymarket. Battle lines were strictly drawn and the radical intellectuals, occupying the narrow divide between the eastern (middle-class) and western (working-class) sectors of the city, were bound to take sides. E.J. Brady refused his employer's instructions to enrol as a special constable and was dismissed without credentials. He was now a "marked man", shut out from regular employment and disowned by friends and relations. "I very shortly learned what it feels like to go without regular meals, and what it feels like when the soles of your boots preserve but a nodding acquaintance with your uppers and your only coat is out at elbows and turning a faded green.''[19] He tried to organise a clerks' union but his brother clerks, loyal to the white collar, held aloof. In 1891 he was appointed secretary of the Australian Socialist League whose members, for a brief moment of radical solidarity, spanned the range of anarchists, social democrats, Georgists, and labourites and extended from the intellectuals of the transitional zone to the working-class respectables of the western suburbs. Roderic Quinn wrote euphorically of a new unity of "Labour and Thought" and many of the *Bulletin* crowd — including Lawson, George Black, Mary Cameron, Con. Lindsay, and "Price Warung" — were active in socialist circles at the time. The engagement of their sympathies laid an ideological basis for the "egalitarian" and "collectivist" elements of the bush ethos and began the transformation of socialism into "being mates".

* * *

Writers, as a group, had experienced a sharp reversal of fortune. As a boom occupation, journalism was hard-hit by the depression. Full-time respectable reporters set up an Institute of Journalists to defend themselves, but the part-timers and free-lancers of the colonial Grubstreet had little collective strength left to exert.

* * *

During the depression the *Bulletin* became one of the chief sources of outdoor relief for unemployed journalists and it is no accident that older family men — "Price Warung", Edward Dyson, and Ernest Favenc — were its most prolific contributors during these years. The depression also took a heavy toll on writers' wives and saw the break-down of several marriages, including those of Brady, O'Dowd, Black and Becke.

For Melburnians especially the 1890s were a period of terrible disillusionment. Even with their ideological defences up, the city's radical intellectuals could not help sharing the optimism of the land boom era and the fall of "Marvellous Smellboom", as the *Bulletin* cruelly dubbed the scandal-ridden metropolis, destroyed the illusion of urban progress and brought them a step closer to the dark city of the revolutionary poets. During the good years Edward Dyson had migrated to "a very exclusive suburb, out at the far end of a methodical and cautious railway" but by the mid 1890s he had been forced back "In Town".[20] Bernard O'Dowd, who fled with his in-laws when their Carlton bootshop failed, looked down from its windswept northern perimeter on a city cursed — as he was himself — with disease and poverty.

> The City crowds our motley broods
> And plants its citadel
> Upon the delta where the floods
> Of evil plunge to hell.
>
> Through fogs retributive, that steam
> From ooze of stagnant wrongs
> The towers satanically gleam
> Defiance at our throngs.
>
> It nucleates the land's Deceit;
> Its slums our Lost decoy;
> It is the bawdy-house where meet
> Lewd wealth and venal Joy.[21]

O'Dowd's was possibly the most protracted and overwrought response to the depression crisis and it was more than a decade before his celebrative poem "The Bush" (1912) provided a symbolic counterweight to the despair of "The City".

Under the impact of the depression, Sydney's boarding-house zone had deteriorated almost to the level of "Outcast London". As well as the familiar "boozers", "loafers", and "spielers", hundreds of respectable working men were wandering aimlessly through Hyde Park, eating frugally in the "Full and Plenty Dining Rooms" and sleeping under newspapers near the old Fruit Market. Henry Lawson, who spent much of 1892 in doss-houses round Dawes Point, left a grim picture of boarding-house existence during the depression in his story "Board and Residence" (1894). He describes his hypocritical Welsh landlady, her uninviting board of warm grey tea and thin white bread, and the dumb resentment of her guests. "This", he reflects, "is the sort of life that gives a man a God-Almighty longing to break away and take to the Bush."[22]

At last, at the end of 1892, Lawson broke away from Sydney and made his famous journey out to Hungerford on the Queensland border — the brief, unhappy episode that was to be, as A.G.

Stephens noted, "his sole experience of the outback".[23] He had
gone prepared to be disillusioned for already, after a less arduous
trip "up-country" the *Bulletin* had published the verses which
sparked off his famous duel-in-doggerel with "Banjo" Paterson:

> I am back from up the country — very sorry that I went —
> Seeking for the Southern poets' land whereon to pitch my tent;
> I have lost a lot of idols, which were broken on the track,
> Burnt a lot of fancy verses, and I'm glad that I am back.
> Further out may be the pleasant scenes of which our poets boast
> But I think the country's rather more inviting round the coast.
> Anyway, I'll stay at present at a boarding house in town
> Drinking beer and lemon squashes, taking baths and cooling down.[24]

Hungerford confirmed his worst apprehensions about the county
"further out" and, in a letter to his "Aunt Emma", Lawson resolved "never to face the bush again". Even so, he was the exception among the *Bulletin* writers in testing experience against the
bush ideal, and though others came to his defence in the controversy with Paterson, few in practice adopted as sardonic a view of
outback life.[25] After Hungerford, even Lawson remained in two
minds on the question, for the savage realism of his best stories depended for its effect on the continued cultivation of a bush ideal,
a process which Lawson the poet himself assisted by his adoption,
in the mid 1890s, of the "capital B for Bush".

The 1890s have been rightly interpreted by Russel Ward, Vance
Palmer, and others, as a watershed in the creation of an "Australian Legend". But that "apotheosis", as Ward calls it, was not the
transmission to the city of values nurtured on the bush frontier, so
much as the projection onto the outback of values revered by an
alienated urban intelligentsia. How far itinerant bush workers absorbed these values, or shared them already, remains very much
an open question. The most, perhaps, one could say is that urban
experiences, intensified by the economic crash, might almost suf-
fice in themselves to explain the value-structure, if not the mytho-
logical setting, of the bush legend. With anti-urban sentiment
flowing strongly in the wider community, the depression years
fixed the rural ideal, and by the end of the decade the original negative image of the city had slid silently away, leaving the bush to
acquire a new reality of its own.

As the depression lifted, the *Bulletin* writers made their belated escape from the inner city. Most moved back into regular journalism and under A.G. Stephens, fresh back from London, were drilled into a self-conscious literary school. Stephens was convinced that "it was in the cities, not the bush, that the national fibre [was] being . . . slackened and destroyed" and the collected editions of *Bulletin* material he published around the turn of the century omit most of the writers' earlier city-influenced verse and prose.[26] By now most had dropped their old radical associations. The scandal of George Black's "domestic infelicity", blazoned forth in John Norton's *Truth* in 1891, sowed the first seeds of suspicion between the "intellectuals" and the "horny-handed sons of toil".[27] Con. Lindsay was expelled by the socialists and Brady by the Redfern Electoral League, while Lawson passed from socialism to anarchism and on to alcohol. Most of the *Bulletin*'s young radicals had forsaken their old haunts in the twilight zone for the pleasanter pastures of Darlinghurst and Paddington. "Banjo" Paterson married and moved to a big house in Roslyn Gardens; Rod Quinn, Victor Daley, F.J. Broomfield, "Price Warung" all lived in the vicinity of Glenmore Road, Paddington; while several of Stephens's newer discoveries, Alex Montgomery and D.H. Souter, moved further out along the Bondi Road.[28] Their association was more convivial and artistic than ideological, their one common cause the defence of "art for art's sake". They gathered, now, only in the boozy fellowship of the Dawn and Dusk Club, affecting the strenuous bohemianism that was their last defence against the encroachment of suburbia.

The Pioneer Legend

J.B. Hirst

Schools have been the most influential purveyors of the pioneer legend and in literature for children it occurs in its purest form. The first item in the Fifth Grade *Victorian School Reader*, in use for two generations or more earlier this century, was the poem "Pioneers" by Frank Hudson:

> We are the old world people,
>   Ours were the hearts to dare;
> But our youth is spent, and our backs are bent,
>   And the snow is on our hair . . .
>
> We wrought with a will unceasing,
>   We moulded, and fashioned, and planned,
> And we fought with the black, and we blazed the track,
>   That ye might inherit the land . . .
>
> Take now the fruit of our labour,
>   Nourish and guard it with care,
> For our youth is spent, and our backs are bent,
>   And the snow is on our hair.[1]

This legend, it need scarcely be said, is very different from the one discussed by Russel Ward. It celebrates courage, enterprise, hard work, and perseverance; it usually applies to the people who first settled the land, whether as pastoralists or farmers, and not to those they employed, although these were never specifically excluded. It is a nationalist legend which deals in an heroic way with the central experience of European settlement in Australia: the taming of the new environment to man's use. The qualities with which it invests the pioneers — courage, enterprise and so on — perhaps do not strain too much at the truth, although it assumes wrongly that owners always did their own pioneering. Its legendary aspect lies more clearly in the claim that these people were not working merely for themselves or their families, but for us, "That ye might inherit the land." The pioneer story can also be described as legendary because of what it leaves out: there is usually no mention of the social, legal or economic determinants of land settlement. The pioneers are depicted in a world limited by the boundaries of their properties, subduing the land, and battling the elements. Their enemies are drought, flood, fire, sometimes Aborigines; never low prices, middle-men, lack of capital, or other pioneers.

The pioneer legend can scarcely help being conservative in its political implications. It encourages reverence for the past, it celebrates individual rather than collective or state enterprise, and it provides a classless view of society since all social and economic differences are obliterated by the generous application of the "pioneer" label. In claiming that the pioneers were working for us, it puts on later generations a special obligation not to tamper with the world which the pioneers made. One of the first of the epic pioneer poems was written in 1898 by Robert Caldwell, a conservative politician in South Australia. It concluded with an attack on land reformers and socialists for wanting to deprive the pioneers of their rightful heritage.[2] During the 1890 Maritime Strike, the *Argus* declared "this country should remain what the pioneers intended it to be — a land free for every man who is willing to work, no matter whether he belongs to a union or not".[3] The travelling lecturer of the Victorian Employers Federation used the same theme to keep the country safe from socialism,[4] and it has remained a minor strand in conservative rhetoric since.

Although the pioneer legend is very different from the other legend, in its origins it is quite closely linked to it: it began at the same time — in the 1880s and 1890s — and was celebrated by the same people. It owes much to Paterson and Lawson.

The term "pioneer" came into common use in Victoria and South Australia sooner than in New South Wales.[5] It was applied to those immigrants who had come to the colonies in their early years and so was not limited to those who had settled and worked the land. These pioneers were much honoured at the jubilee of South Australia in 1886 and during the Melbourne Centennial Exhibition of 1888.[6] New South Wales could not look back with similar confidence to its origins or so readily identify its "pioneers". In Victoria the members of the Australian Natives Association, looking towards the future of the coming Australian race, showed only a formal respect for the pioneers and were seeking genuinely national symbols and causes.[7] The honouring of early colonists as pioneers reflected the growth of colonial and local patriotisms; they clearly could not serve as heroes for the new nation.

"Pioneers" acquired its present primary meaning — that is, those who first settled and worked the land — in the 1890s. The older meaning survived, and still survives, but it now took second place. The shifting of meaning is nicely illustrated in the special Old Colonist numbers of the Melbourne *Tatler* in 1898.[8] Under the heading "The Pioneers of Victoria" appeared biographies of many early colonists, including bishops, officials, merchants, professional men, as well as settlers on the land. These were pioneers according to the earlier meaning of the word. But the cover illustration depicted a settler pushing his way through the bush and carried two lines from a woeful poem, "The Pioneers", which appeared in full inside: "Can you not follow them forth/Through the black treacherous bush." This was the new meaning of the term, but it was not well deserved by many of the worthies featured inside who had moved straight from the ship to Melbourne and had never pioneered in the bush. The pioneers as settlers on the land were a much more anonymous group than pioneers as early colonists, who always had an establishment, who's-who air about them. They were not identified with a particular colony and were much more closely connected with the land itself. The pioneers as immigrants had been first identified and honoured by the old colonists themselves. Pioneers as settlers and national heroes were the creation of poets and writers. It is to their work we now turn.

Ken Inglis in *The Australian Colonists* has outlined the largely unsuccessful search for national heroes in the years before 1870. We can see the difficulties facing a nationalist writer of this period in the work of Henry Kendall, the native-born poet who, like his friend Harpur, knew that poets can make a nation, and saw that as one of his tasks, but who never found the words or the audience to succeed. At the last, however, he touched on the pioneer theme which was left to others to develop. Kendall's views of what a proper hero should be were heavily influenced by the classical tradition of Greece and Rome. Heroes had to be statesmen or soldiers, preferably those who died for their country. For statesmen Kendall offered Governor Phillip, Wentworth, Bland, Lang, and other politicians of the 1840s and 1850s. This civic theme was extended by the celebration of those who built the Australian cities; this rather than the settlement of the land was the great triumph of colonisation, and one that could be described in classical terms. Melbourne is "Like a dream of Athens, or of Rome"; Sydney is "this Troy". Australia had no great warriors, but the explorers in their bravery and in their deaths were acceptable substitutes. Kendall frequently celebrates Cook, Leichhardt, Burke and Wills. In a later poem "Blue Mountain Pioneers" (1880) he moves away from the more heroic big-name explorers and celebrates the work of Blaxland, Lawson, and Wentworth in crossing the Blue Mountains in 1817.[9] This was a short expedition and it didn't end in death, but it could be linked much more closely than other expeditions to the settlement of the land.

> Behind them were the conquered hills — they faced
> The vast green West, with glad, strange beauty graced;
> And every tone of every cave and tree
> Was a voice of splendid prophecy.

What that conquest foretold was the settlement of the western lands, but Kendall was tied so closely to the notion of the heroic as public and civic, that he never celebrated the coming of the settlers themselves. For him "pioneers" was reserved for the explorers.

This poem was published posthumously in collected editions of Kendall's work in 1886 and 1890. Paterson must have read it there for it forms the basis of the historical section in his poem "Song of the Future" which is the classic statement of the pioneer legend, frequently reproduced in anthologies and school magazines.[10] This poem is much more ambitious than his usual ballad or bush-yarn work. It calls for a new response to landscape and nature in Australia, and to the history of European man in the continent. Paterson begins by criticising Adam Lindsay Gordon, Marcus Clarke, and others who had written in gloomy terms about the Australian scene, and he rejects the stock claims that Australian birds were songless and its flowers scentless. On Australian history he acknowledges that there has been no "hot blood spilt" — a commonly held prerequisite for worthwhile history — but Australians do have something to celebrate: "honest toil and valiant life". This introduces the historical section of the poem. The treatment of the crossing of the Blue Mountains is more extensive than Kendall's, and it is told as a great saga of the people, rather than as a celebration of individual heroes. The names of the explorers, significantly, are not mentioned, and the poem is more concerned with the achievements of those who came after them.

> The mountains saw them marching by:
> They faced the all-consuming drought,
> They would not rest in settled land:
> But, taking each his life in hand,
> Their faces ever westward bent
> Beyond the farthest settlement,
> Responding to the challenge cry
> Of "better country farther out".

Paterson measures the extent of this achievement by dealing with a sceptic who declares "it was not much" since the resistance to expansion was slight and — the stock objection — "not much blood was spilt":

> It was not much! but we who know
> The strange capricious land they trod —
> At times a stricken, parching sod,
> At times with raging floods beset —
> Through which they found their lonely way,
> Are quite content that you should say
> It was not much, while we can feel
> That nothing in the ages old,
> In song or story written yet
> On Grecian urn or Roman arch,
> Though it should ring with clash of steel,
> Could braver histories unfold
> Than this bush story, yet untold —
> The story of their westward march.

This poem, more than any other single piece, did bring about that new perception of Australia's past which Paterson sought. He still had to defend his heroes against those of Greece and Rome, but soon the heroism of the pioneers was accepted without question, and the references to the classical tradition ceased.

Lawson was more consistently preoccupied with Australia's past than Paterson. In a contribution to the *Republican* in 1888, he called for much more Australian history to be taught in schools.[11] As a nationalist, he wanted to give his country a past to be proud of. In the early stories and poems Lawson follows the orthodox line of dating Australia's greatness from the gold rushes, and so he accords heroic status to the diggers. These were the men

"who gave our country birth".[12] He rates their achievements
higher than those of the explorers, the ranking heroes of the time:
"Talk about the heroic struggles of early explorers in a hostile
country; but for dogged determination and courage in the face of
poverty, illness, and distance, commend me to the old-time digger
— the truest soldier Hope ever had!"[13] For the settlers on the land
and particularly the selectors, Lawson in his early years had scant
respect. He criticises the selectors for their slovenliness, dirt, and
ignorance, and depicts settling on the land not as an heroic endeavour, but as a madness. But this attitude changed with time.
His early emphasis on the wretchedness of the selector's life had
had a political purpose, since he wanted to discredit those who saw
small holdings as the cure for Australia's social ills. He never
abandons the view that the life of small settlers could be wretched
and narrow, but he becomes more willing to celebrate their powers
of endurance and the co-operation between them and, in the Joe
Wilson series, the satisfactions and pleasures which their small
successes gave them, although here Mrs Spicer, "watering them
geraniums", is still present as counterpoint being worn literally to
death. In his verse, where he always wrote at a higher level of gen-
erality and usually with disastrous results, he came to see the settling of the land as the central theme of the nation's history, which
could comprehend much more than the coming of the diggers.
"How the land was won" (1899) is a complete statement of this
theme, and is the counterpart to Paterson's "Song of the
Future".[14] The settlers are described firstly as immigrants leaving
the old world, and the poem tells of the variety of hardship and de-
privations which they experienced in Australia. These two verses
give the flavour of the whole, perhaps too favourable a view, since
six verses of hardships become a little tedious, although the quality
of the verse is better than Lawson's average:

> With God, or a dog, to watch, they slept
>   By the camp-fires' ghastly glow,
> Where the scrubs were dark as the blacks that crept
>   With "nulla" and spear held low;
> Death was hidden amongst the trees,
>   And bare on the glaring sand
> They fought and perished by twos and threes —
>   And that's how they won the land!

> They toiled and they fought through the shame of it —
>   Through wilderness, flood and drought;
> They worked, in the struggles of early days,
>   Their sons' salvation out.
> The white girl — wife in the hut alone,
>   The man on the boundless run,
> The miseries suffered, unvoiced, unknown —
>   And that's how the land was won.

In the early twentieth century scores of pioneer poems by many hands rang the changes on these hardships. Two important aspects of the legend are embodied in "How the land was won": in the first verse (not quoted here) we are told that the land was won "for us"; secondly, there is no differentiation of the settlers — they are all simply "they". This conflation is the more noticeable in Lawson since elsewhere he gives such particular detail about social conflict on the land. Nor can the co-operation among the settlers — in the stories he describes young men putting in crops for sick men and widows, and women caring for bereaved neighbours — find a mention here, since the pioneer legend prefers to see hardships overcome, if at all, by further individual effort. It is a sign of the attractiveness of the pioneer legend to nationalists that Lawson was ready to abandon so much to produce his simple compelling saga. Of course the Lawson of 1899 had abandoned much of his early radicalism, and in his disillusionment the struggle on the land took on an elemental, purifying quality, but changing personal views will not wholly explain "How the land was won". The pioneer legend is a literary mode or a type of history which shapes material in its own way. Writing on a different assignment in the same year he composed "How the land was won", Lawson highlighted the gossip and bitchiness of country towns and hinted broadly that incest was frequently practised in the isolated selectors' huts.[15] That would never do for the pioneers.

In Lawson's prose there is little explicit glorification of the pioneers, but here Lawson made his most powerful contribution to the pioneer legend with his description of bush women. "The Drover's Wife" occupies an important place in the pioneer canon. There is a sense in which all his bush women are heroines because, as he insists time and again, the bush is no place for women. When her husband had money, the drover's wife was taken to the city by train — in a sleeping compartment — and put up at the best hotel.

For Lawson, women deserve the attention and comfort which this signifies, and which bush life denied them. While she waits for the snake, the drover's wife reads the *Young Ladies Journal*, but Lawson does not use the hard life of a country woman to deride the artificiality of the woman's journal world; rather, he accepts that as legitimate, and so emphasises the sacrifices of the women who are obliged to live a different life, and in many cases do the work of men. The theme of women as pioneers was taken up by G. Essex Evans, a Queensland poet of the nineties, in his "Women of the West". This, together with his other pioneer piece "The Nation Builders", have frequently been reprinted in children's literature and anthologies.[16]

The work of Paterson and Lawson is described by Ward as the chief vehicle for spreading a democratic, collectivist, national mystique. How was it that these writers also celebrated the pioneers which meant frequently the squatters, who had been, and were still, the enemy of democrats and radicals? In *The Australian Tradition*, A.A. Phillips has noted how sympathetic writers of the nineties were in their description of individual squatters, despite the squatters being the class enemy. Phillips offers a number of explanations for this. He wonders first whether "the triumph of human sympathy over social prejudice" reflected the breadth of feeling one would expect in any good writer. Scarcely so, he concludes, since in other areas, notably the description of Englishmen, the writers reveal severe limitations and create caricatures. The writers knew some squatters personally and this no doubt helped them to write individualised, sympathetic portraits. But more importantly, according to Phillips, the squatter was a bushman too, and had shared with his men "the pride and expansiveness" that came with the escape from "fetid slums and the tight little hedgerow squares" of the old world, into the vast spaces of the new continent where the strength of individual character as a man determined success or failure. He concludes that the democratic tradition embodied in the literature reaches deep back into the pastoral age.[17] But we must remember that what squatters had felt, or others had felt about them, may well be different from their depiction in imaginative literature. The tradition of the pastoral age did not flow automatically to the pages of Lawson and Paterson. The writers were making a tradition as well as reflecting one — how much they created and how much they reported has been one of the matters debated in the argument over *The Australian Legend*. We can extend Phillips's analysis and come closer to understanding these writers' attitude to the squatter-pioneer if we examine what influenced their view of the pastoral age.

Both men were disturbed and angry at the new harshness and poverty which drought, depression, and strikes brought to the colonies in the 1880s and 1890s. They were cast into a world they did not like and, like many others before and since in this predicament, they began to exaggerate the virtues of the world they had lost. Lawson's poem "Freedom on the Wallaby" is well known.[18] It was written in Brisbane in 1891 to support the shearers' strike, and its last verse contains the much-quoted threat of violence: "If blood should stain the wattle". Less well known is the previous verse:

> Our parents toiled to make a home,
>   Hard grubbin 'twas an' clearin',
> They wasn't troubled much with lords
>   When they was pioneerin'.
> But now that we have made the land
>   A garden full of promise,
> Old Greed must crook his dirty hand
>   And come ter take it from us.

Those who know Lawson's usual description of the Australian country — unyielding, desolate, drought-ridden — will scarcely credit that he could describe it as a garden: domestic, fruitful, a symbol of paradise. Lawson's explanation for the lowering of wages and the assault on the unions is that Greed has invaded this garden. It was a theme he used many times. Sometimes Greed had invaded the countryside from the cities; on other occasions it was an unwelcome import from the old world into the new. In the poems the particular forms which Greed assumed were not always defined. The stories identified the process more explicitly. In the countryside it meant the increasing ownership of pastoral properties by banks and companies, and the replacement of resident proprietors by managers. Before this process began were the good times, and squatters of that time, or who have survived from it, are described as squatters of the "old school". In describing Black, the squatter who employed Joe Wilson, Lawson outlines their virtues: "He was a good sort, was Black the squatter; a squatter of the old school, who'd shared the early hardships with his men, and couldn't see why he should not shake hands and have a smoke and a yarn over old times with any of his old station hands that happened to come along."[19] A.A. Phillips errs when he says Black is Lawson's only portrait in any detail of a squatter. There were several other good squatters — Baldy Thompson, Job Falconer, Jimmy's boss[20] — and their goodness is carefully explained: they are resident proprietors of long standing, not managers for absentees. Job Falconer, for instance, was "Boss of the Talbragar sheep station up country in New South Wales in the early Eighties — when there were still runs in the Dingo-Scrubs out of the hands of the banks, and yet squatters who lived on their stations". Lawson's one detailed portrait of a bad squatter is that of Wall, the man who, until it was almost too late, refused to send his employees to fight the fire on Ross's farm. Until this last-minute repentance, Wall was a hard man who had done all he could to make the selector Ross's life impossible. But he had not always been so: "Men remembered Wall as a grand boss and a good fellow, but that was in the days before rabbits and banks, and syndicates and 'pastoralists', or pastoral companies instead of good squatters."[21] The pattern is clear: it is not only that managers for absentees are mean: all resident proprietors of the old days were good.[22]

In Paterson's work there was much less overt social commentary than in Lawson's, but briefly around 1890 Paterson was a committed reformer, and in his poem "On Kiley's Run", published in December 1890, he gives a clear picture of the world which Greed had disrupted and the new world it was making.[23] The poem describes the "good old station life" on Kiley's run. The squatter was resident, swagmen were welcome, there was plenty of good fellowship and horse racing with neighbouring stations, and relations between squatter and his men were excellent.

> The station-hands were friends, I wot,
>   On Kiley's Run,
> A reckless, merry-hearted lot —
> All splendid riders, and they knew
> The boss was kindness through and through.
> Old Kiley always stood their friend,

> And so they served him to the end
>> On Kiley's Run.

But droughts and losses forced the squatter into the hands of the bank, which finally took possession of the stock and sold the station. The new owner is an English absentee; a half-paid overseer runs the place, shearers' wages and all other expenses are cut, swagmen and drovers receive short-shrift — and the name of the run has been changed to Chandos Park Estate. Paterson felt this transformation very keenly, for at the end of the poem he adds, for him, a rare call to arms:

> I cannot guess what fate will bring
>> To Kiley's Run —
> For chances come and changes ring —
> I scarcely think 'twill always be
> Locked up to suit an absentee;
> And if he lets it out in farms
> His tenants soon will carry arms
>> On Kiley's run.

"The Song of the Future", Paterson's classic pioneer piece, in its last section contains a similar lament for the old bush life and urges that the land be thrown open to all to reduce poverty and unemployment.

Men live by myth, and golden ages have frequently been created. What is odd about this one is that it was placed in the very recent past. The democrats and land reformers of the 1850s had denounced the squatters as monopolists and tyrants: they were the lords who would make everyone else serfs if they could. In their defence the squatters had actually attempted, fruitlessly, to attach to themselves the name of "pioneers" and so justify their claim to retain their lands.[24] Thirty years after their political defeat, they were accorded that title, among others by the poets of democracy. How could they overlook the denunciations made so recently? A large part of the answer is simply that Lawson and Paterson, like most other people in the 1890s, knew very little of the struggles of the 1850s. John Robertson had given his name to the Selection Acts and had achieved legendary status, but he was not seen as part of a wider movement. The Australian-born certainly did not learn of the land reform movement in school. Those who had survived from that era, like Robertson himself and Parkes, did not talk freely of their early struggles, chiefly because, one supposes, the bitter social and economic divisions of those years and the whiff of republicanism which hung around the reform movement were no longer apt for their present political purposes.

The Sydney *Bulletin* was republican, a constant derider of British aristocrats and Australians who fawned on them, and it had no qualms about disturbing the liberal consensus over which Parkes and Robertson had presided, but it did too little to inform its readers — among whom were Paterson and Lawson — of the democratic movement of the 1850s or to celebrate its triumphs. The *Bulletin* ran a very crude line on New South Wales history: it insisted that very little had changed in the colony since the convict days.[25] The British had created an abomination in the convict system, and since its influence was still potent, New South Wales could never establish a truly democratic society until the British connection was severed. It wrongly attributed the flogging of criminals and other evils to the survival of the spirit of earlier times. Victoria, by contrast, had managed something of a fresh start with its gold rushes and the Eureka rebellion, whose anniversary the *Bulletin* wanted to celebrate as Australia's national day. Such a view of the past could not allow that there had been genuine and far-reaching reforms in New South Wales in the 1850s and 1860s. The history which the *Bulletin* promoted was Price Warung's *Tales of the Convict System*. This was the stick to beat the British with. The triumphs of Robertson over the landowners and squatters would not have suited its purpose.

We are now in a position to understand better why Paterson and Lawson were among the founders of the pioneer legend. Their work is suffused with a generalised nostalgia — "'Twas a better land to live in, in the days o' long ago"[26] — but they also created a highly specific past which was free from the social evils of the present. Before Greed invaded the land there were humane employers and decent class relations in Australia. Having made that past, and as they made it, they elevated the early settlers into pioneers. That they could create this past so freely gives new meaning to the dictum that Australia had no history. For Paterson and Lawson, the 1840s and 1850s, when the squatters were the popular political enemy, might never have existed. No democratic tradition had survived from these years.

In broad terms, the creation of the pioneer legend can be explained by the growth of nationalism in the 1880s and the 1890s and the need to find new national heroes and symbols. Paterson and Lawson were attracted to the pioneers as nationalists, but also as radicals. They used the past to condemn the present. However, the pioneer legend quickly shed its radical overtones. Paterson's classic statement ''Song of the Future'' is very simply rendered innocuous in anthologies and school readers by the omission of the last section which urges that the land be thrown open to all. In any case, the golden age of pioneering was, in some respects, rather uncertain in its political implications. Paterson's claim, though false, that there had been a time when land was freely available to all did relate clearly to the current radical demand for land taxes and breaking up of large estates. But the depiction of the old station life of hard work and mutuality between boss and men can serve the conservative cause, for clearly there were no unions or industrial arbitration or parliamentary limitations on hours worked on Kiley's Run. Reform movements which aim to purify and simplify government can appeal with some chance of success to golden ages; once radicalism is associated with state regulation and ownership, as it was in Australia from the 1890s, the ideal society needs to be placed in the future rather than the past. In finding a glorious past for Australia, Paterson and Lawson ultimately did more to help the conservative cause than their own. Once there is a valued past, the future is more confined. ''She is not yet'' Brunton Stephens had written of the Australian nation in 1877. Because we are nationalists as they made us, we still enjoy the celebrations of Lawson and Paterson, and we forget that as well as being an affirmation, their work marked also a retreat: the nation was no longer yet to be, it had arrived, and more amazing still, its best days were already passed.

In 1904 Frederick McCubbin painted ''The Pioneers'', a massive work in three panels which is the classic embodiment in art of the pioneer legend. The first panel shows a settler and his wife on first arriving at their selection in the forest; the second shows the selection established; and in the third, the ''triumphal stanza'' as the *Age* described it:

A country youth, with reverent fingers, clears away the undergrowth from the rough wooden cross marking the last resting place of the gallant couple. In the distance the spires and bridges of a glorious young city and the stocks of a rich harvest field tell of the joys that another generation is reaping from the toil of the once lusty pioneers now gone to dust.

The painting was, and is, enormously popular, and the *Age* successfully urged that it be purchased for the National Gallery. It described the work as a "poem of democracy".[27]

The conservative implications of the legend have already been noted; in what sense is the legend, nevertheless, a democratic one? In the first place it accords heroic status to the ordinary man — frequently the pioneers were squatters, but small settlers were also honoured with the title. The pioneer legend transforms the low-status selector of the nineteenth century into a nation builder. The legend also proclaims that success is open to all since all may possess the requisite qualities of diligence, courage, and perseverance. Secondly, the legend provides a simple, unofficial, popular history of all the nation. When it was formed the standard histories were still organised by the terms of office of the various governors to parallel the British histories which dealt with monarchs, the dates of their accession and death, and the chief events of their reign. Governors made some sense as organising principles for the period before responsible government, but in some works their comings and goings continued to be crucial events even after responsible government. In contrast to history as high politics and administration, the pioneer legend offered social (and economic) history and declared that the people had made the nation. The "people" in the pioneer legend have always included women. Feminists may object that too often they are seen merely as helpmeets for men, but their complaint that women have been omitted altogether from Australian history is not true of the popular history fostered by the pioneer legend. There are pioneer-women gardens and memorials in Melbourne, Adelaide, and Perth. In the celebration of state and national anniversaries, pioneer women have been honoured in special ceremonies and commemorative histories.[28] The pioneer legend is a people's legend; in this sense it is democratic. Its conservatism is not the conservatism of deference, but of communal pride in what the people have achieved.

Of democracy in the sense of a system of government, the legend has nothing to say, since it implies that politics were unnecessary or irrelevant to the work of pioneering. It is a further instance, then, of the Australian tendency to isolate politics from the heroic or the good. Paterson claimed his pioneers as worthy of Greece and Rome, but in fact he had abandoned the classical tradition which found its heroes in those who served the state. Kendall, true to that tradition, thought that an Australian democracy would want democratic statesmen for its heroes, but he was wrong, and he worked in vain on Deniehy and Lang.

The pioneer legend had a significant influence on the writing of formal history. It solved the problem which formal historians could never overcome satisfactorily: the embarrassment of the convict origins of the nation. The pioneer legend, by proclaiming the settlement of the land as the chief theme in Australia's history, found it easy not to mention the convicts at all. . . . The pioneer legend, having first excluded convicts, eventually enabled them to be rehabilitated and given a place in the nation's history. Convicts could be regarded as pioneers. In this role Mary Gilmore depicts them in "Old Botany Bay".[29]

> I was the conscript
>   Sent to hell
> To make in the desert
>   The living well;
>
> I split the rock;
>   I felled the tree:
> The nation was —
>   Because of me.

By the early twentieth century a new meaning of "pioneer" had come into common use. It was now also applied to people who were at present at work on the land, and particularly on new farms or at the edge of settlement. This extension of meaning occurred at a time of heightened concern for racial strength and purity and a new awareness of the vulnerability of the nation. Cities were now seen as dangers to national and racial health, and further development of the land was considered on all sides as essential for the nation's survival. The pioneer's struggle with the elements and the nation's struggle to survive in a more hostile world became fused. "The people in the bush were fighting the battle of Australia every day and every year", said George Reid in 1909 at the foundation of the Bush Nursing Association which was formed to bring medical help to remote country areas. "From a national point of view," the Association declared, "the lives of pioneers and their children are of the utmost value to the State."[30] G. Essex Evans, one of the important makers of the legend, caught these new concerns in "The Man Upon The Land".

> The City calls, its streets are gay,
>   Its pleasures well supplied,
> So of its life-blood every day
>   It robs the countryside.
>
> How shall we make Australia great
>   And strong when danger calls
> If half the people of the State
>   Are crammed in city walls . . .?[31]

The concluding lines of the poem are its refrain:

> And the men that made the Nation are
>   The men upon the land.

The change of tense here illustrates nicely how the men upon the land gained in glory from the heroic status of their predecessors. Well before the Country Party was formed, its ideology had been made — by no means solely by country people — and the pioneer legend gave it added force.

After the landing at Gallipoli, Australians acquired a legend more powerful than either those of the bushmen or the pioneers. In *The Australian Legend*, Russel Ward has outlined the way in which the legend of the digger embodied aspects of the bushmen's legend. A similar process occurred with the pioneer legend. *The Anzac Memorial*, published in 1917, carried a poem by Dorothy McCrae, "The First Brigade", reproduced subsequently in the Victorian *School Paper* with the sub-title "The Pioneers of Australia".

> They cleared the earth, and felled the trees,
> And built the towns and colonies;
> Then to their land, their sons they gave,
> And reared them hardy, pure, and brave.
>
> They made Australia's past: to them
> We owe the present diadem;
> For, in their sons, they fight again.
> And ANZAC proved their hero strain.[32]

The first celebration of Anzac Day in 1916 posed a problem for the compilers of the Victorian school calendar. Since 1911, 19 April had been set aside as Discovery Day. This was the anniversary of Cook's sighting of the Australian coast and was devoted to the celebration of explorers and pioneers. Since it fell so close to Anzac Day, it was suspended in 1916, but on Anzac Day teachers were encouraged to link diggers, explorers, and pioneers together: "The lessons and addresses on Anzac Day will, no doubt, include matter appropriate to Discovery Day, such as reference to the discovery, settlement, and development of Australia."[33] The connection between "settlement and development" and the Anzac spirit took substantial form after the war in the soldier settlement schemes. Diggers were to become pioneers.

The subsequent history of "pioneer" and the legend cannot be fully traced here. The legend still survives, although its foundations are not as firm as they were in the early twentieth century. It has suffered inevitably from the waning of faith in progress and the virtues of European civilisation. No one now writes of pioneers as Paterson did, although his pioneer verse is still collected in anthologies.[34] Historians have for a long time escaped the romanticism of Roberts's *Squatting Age* and have emphasised the clash between squatters' interests and those of the rest of the community. Paterson's golden age has received no help from them. The legend, which was made by creative writers, was eventually attacked by them. Brian Penton in *Landtakers* (1934) overturned the view that the squatter's life was exhilarating and free. His theme was the coarsening and hardening of a well-bred English emigrant as he coped with life in a "gaolyard" and then on the frontier, with "the grind and ugliness and shame of Australia". Xavier Herbert's *Capricornia* (1938) is still the most devastating anti-pioneer piece in our literature. It confronts the legend explicitly. Herbert's Northern Territory society is brutal, chaotic, hypocritical, and drunken. The book is an indictment of the white settlers of the Territory for the destruction which they brought to Aboriginal society and for their continuing exploitation of Aborigines and half-castes. "The Coming of the Dingoes" is how Herbert describes the arrival of the white man in the Territory. Herbert was the first to write black history in this country. Pioneers were the enemy to the original inhabitants of the land, and as sympathy with Aborigines grows and the brutalities of the frontier continues to be highlighted, the pioneers' reputation will suffer more. The growing concern with the environment will damage the pioneers still further as their ruthless exploitation of the land comes under closer scrutiny. And yet, sympathetic accounts of pioneering men and women continue to be written. Among the most notable are Margaret Kiddle's *Men of Yesterday*, Patrick White's *Tree of Man*, and Judith Wright's *Generations of Men*. While not endorsing the crudities of the pioneer legend, these works nevertheless depict the pioneers as a creative, ordering force, whose work gives their lives a certain nobility and completeness. *The Tree of Man* describes in its first pages the arrival of Stan Parker at his uncleared land in a forest, a similar scene to that McCubbin depicted in the first panel of "The Pioneers":

> Then the man took an axe and struck at the side of a hairy tree, more to hear the sound than for any other reason. And the sound was cold and loud. The man struck at the tree, and struck, till several white chips had fallen. He looked at the scar in the side of the tree. The silence was immense. It was the first time anything like this had happened in that part of the bush . . .
>   The man made a lean-to with bags and a few saplings. He built a fire. He sighed at last, because the lighting of his small fire had kindled in him the first warmth of content. Of being somewhere. That particular part of the bush had been made his by the entwining fire. It licked at and swallowed the loneliness.

We may come at last to see Stan Parker merely as a destroyer of the natural environment or as a labourer transforming himself into a small property holder, but so long as our spirit stirs in other ways at this scene, the pioneer legend will not be without its force.

Popular history is still very much pioneer history, embodied in new forms now in the reconstructed pioneer villages and settlements which have proliferated throughout the country in recent years. What is conveyed by these is in some ways rather different from the classic pioneer statements in literature. The concentration is much less on the struggle on the land, partly because the encounter with the elements, which was central to the drama, cannot be reproduced. But the buildings and their fittings strike the visitor with a sense of the pioneers' achievement, in making their homes or farms or businesses where nothing was before, and with a sense of the pioneers' hardships in contrast to his own life. We noted earlier how the legend confines pioneers to their land and ignores their wider society. The pioneer villages carry this tendency to its ultimate by leaving out people altogether. We are shown empty buildings, disembodied achievement, and are told nothing of the social and economic factors which determined who had the chance to achieve what. Buildings cannot speak readily of social conflict; these pioneer villages are powerful contributors to the consensus view of Australia's past.

Early immigrants generally, as distinct from the first settlers on the land, are still honoured as pioneers. In New South Wales there is a Pioneers' Club, formed in 1910, and in South Australia a Pioneers' Association, formed in 1935, to keep their memory alive.[35] These organisations define categories of membership by year of arrival of ancestor, construct genealogies and exercise a declining influence on the edge of the old state establishments. The pioneer-immigrants continued to be associated more with state than national loyalty. They were also honoured more frequently by those who wished to stress the British identity of Australia, and who saw its history as the winning of new areas for the Empire. The British heritage these pioneers brought with them was as important as their accomplishments here. At some times in the twentieth century — particularly in South Australia with its clear and clean foundation — pioneers as first immigrants may have had greater standing than pioneers as settlers on the land, but there is no doubt now of the latter's primacy. The two groups of pioneers are, of course, not totally distinct. The pioneer poem at the beginning of the Fifth Grade *Victorian Reader*, quoted earlier, is concerned chiefly with the struggle on the land, but the pioneers are identified clearly as British immigrants — "We are the old world people" — and this is part of their virtue — "Ours were the hearts to dare". The pioneer legend has served local, Australian, and imperial patriotisms.

The survival of the word "pioneer" itself means much. The word originally applied to those in an army who went as pioneers before the main body to prepare the way by clearing roads and making bridges and so on. It was then extended to the initiator of any new enterprise or new undertaking who "showed the way" for those who came after. In this sense it could well be used as Kendall used it in "Blue Mountain Pioneers" for the explorers. In

the new world, first in North America and then in Australia, the
meaning was again extended to refer to first settlers on the land.
But to whom or in what were the first settlers showing the way?
Their aim was to occupy the land for their own use and to keep
others out. The metaphor of showing or preparing the way was
now being stretched further to make them pioneers in a very general sense; they showed the way to the generations or the nation
which came after them, and benefited from their labours. In this
way the word itself obscures the private interests which they had in
acquiring the land and depicts it as a service, as something for
which we should be grateful, thus embodying a central concept of
the legend. Let any who doubt the significance of the word consider what would have to change before we consistently referred to
the first settlers as, say, landtakers, which was Penton's term.

I have shared here Russel Ward's assumption about the significance of a nation's legends, or its dreaming: "The dreams of nations, as of individuals, are important, because they not only
reflect, as in a distorting mirror, the real world, but may sometimes react upon and influence it".[36] That the legend which Ward
describes exists is unquestionable; he is misleading, however,
when he implies that this was the only national legend. Ward
claimed with very little analysis that Lawson and Paterson embodied the legend which he had described; what they embodied was a
great deal more complex and varied. We have already noted their
favourable view of the squatters, which A.A. Phillips identified.
Ward takes too little account of this in his attempt to stress the
radical collectivist aspect of the legend. Phillips is closer to the literature in writing of "The Democratic Theme". The anti-police
aspect of the legend is not well reflected in Lawson, who nearly always makes his policemen good cops, sympathetic to the poor and
outcast, and who wrote a poem celebrating the bravery of a police
trooper.[37] And both writers fostered the development of the pioneer legend.

Some of Ward's critics, over-reacting perhaps to his less-
guarded claims for the legend's influence, have attempted to deny
its existence or force by citing social behaviour which runs counter
to the legend. This is, of course, very easy to do, but when faced
with this criticism Ward can retreat to very safe ground and declare that he was merely tracing the origins of the national legend

which is not fully founded in fact, nor vastly influential.[38] Those who feel that Australia has not been made according to the legend would be better advised to establish the other legends, stereotypes, and symbols Australians have made or adopted. The pioneer legend is one such. It is a national rural myth, democratic in its social bearing, conservative in its political implications.

Part Six
Neighbours?

Commentators have frequently remarked that Australia is one of the most urban — or suburban — nations on earth. What is less clear is how this fact has had an impact on the way we conceive of Australia or "Australian-ness". Why has the bush continued to be such a powerful image? In what ways has "suburbia" been taken to define the essence of Australia? How have the patterns of suburban living affected men's and women's lives? How have attitudes changed over time?

In the final section of Reading 2, Richard White argues that the suburban life style was a key element in the notion of "the Australian way of life" that developed in the 1950s. Other writers have used their interpretation of the urban/suburban character of Australian life to intervene in on-going historical and social debates.

Sean Glynn, in Reading 14, considers Russel Ward's thesis (Reading 11) against the evidence of Australian urbanisation. He first details an alternative to the bush legend — a city legend of the larrikin. He concludes by questioning the process of seeing Australian history in terms of a national character, arguing instead for a view of Australia as a part of an international urban or suburban culture.

Tim Rowse, in Reading 15, examines the history of intellectual attitudes to suburbia in the twentieth century. Initially suburbia was a negative concept, opposed to the (bush) values of the "real" Australia; post-war, new ideas emerged which found more positive ways of talking about suburbia — even through Edna Everage! Rowse is critical of both the positive and negative arguments for ignoring social differences within suburban areas.

Further reading

Burgmann, V., and Lee, J., eds, *A People's History of Australia since 1788. Making a Life*. Ringwood: Penguin, 1988.

Curthoys, A., Martin, A.W., and Rowse, T., eds, *Australians: A Historical Library. Australians from 1939*. Sydney: Fairfax, Syme & Weldon, 1987.

Forsyth, A., "The Token Women: Hugh Stretton, Gender and the Suburbs". In L. Orchard and R. Dare, eds, *Markets, Morals and Public Policy*. Annandale: The Federation Press, 1989.

Frost, L., *Australian Cities in Comparative View*. Ringwood: Penguin, 1990.

Gilbert, A., "The Roots of Anti-Suburbanism in Australia". *Australian Cultural History*. 4 (1985): 54-70.

Modjeska, D., *Inner Cities: Australian Women's Memory of Place*. Ringwood: Penguin, 1989.

Rickard, J., *Australia: A Cultural History*. London: Longman, 1988.

Urbanisation in Australian History
Sean Glynn

Any historical quest for the Australian nation or national character should be extremely wary of contemporary definition and prejudice and should examine contrary, as well as supporting evidence for the existence of certain characteristics in the past.

In a brilliant pioneer work,[1] published in 1930, W.K. Hancock gathered together a number of generalisations and impressions relating to Australian society and character, and put forward a collection of hypotheses. Since that time, a long succession of writers — all of them lacking Hancock's historical insight and skill in presentation — have rendered these generalisations stale by frequent repetition, magnification and misuse. In popular mythology Australians are supposed to be identifiable by a set of characteristics, variously defined and sometimes contradictory which Russel Ward has outlined.[2]

* * *

In view of the hackneyed, ill-defined and untestable nature of the characteristics which are attributed to the national type, historians may perhaps be forgiven for not having taken them seriously, or for regarding them as being, very largely, a literary creation with little real historical basis. However, Russel Ward has shown that throughout the nineteenth century the characteristics *attributed* to bush workers add up, more or less, to his . . . definition of the traditional view of the national character. Thus he suggests a *real* historical basis for this character ("ethos", "mystique", "legend") in the behaviour and attitudes of bush workers from pre-goldrush times. What Ward does not attempt to explain is how, or why, the "bush virtues" came to be accepted by the nation as a whole. Why, paradoxically, did one of the most highly urbanised countries in the world seek its national inspiration in the bush?

The ideas of Russel Ward and his precursor, Vance Palmer,[3] rest heavily upon folksong and literary work published, particularly, by the *Bulletin* during the 1890s. The *Bulletin* romanticised

Australian rural character, with particular emphasis on "mateship", and argued the politics of nationalism and republicanism. In the opinion of some, "The symptoms of republicanism and extreme nationalism at this time have probably been dwelt upon since by historians to such an extent that they have loomed out of all proportion in our times".[4] Yet the literary search for distinct local character, which went hand in hand with chauvinism, was by no means entirely directed towards the bush, nor was it entirely a product of the 1890s.[5] Historians have largely ignored the substantial literary attention given to the urban larrikin — perhaps the closest city equivalent to the bush workers.

* * *

The term "larrikin" is of obscure origin and was used somewhat indiscriminately and applied equally to playful youths, teenagers, gangs, louts, loafers, rogues, thugs and tearaways. Certainly larrikins were drawn from the lowest social strata in Australian cities . . . As a literary and theatrical theme larrikinism rivalled the "bush hero" in attention. In poems, plays, novels and music hall productions, larrikin types were used to portray brutality, sex, crime and "low life" in general. At the same time there was an element of sympathy with the larrikin, and many productions featured a larrikin humour which has been compared with slum wit in the London cockney or costermonger tradition.

As a whole, the larrikin literature is highly imaginative rather than descriptive, and of doubtful worth as historical evidence. In *Bulletin* poems, by Lawson, Dennis and others, in Phil May's cartoons, and in poetic works and novels published elsewhere,[6] larrikins were used very largely as a convenient and colourful means of portraying social extremes of various kinds.

Australia's most widely read poet in the past was not Henry Lawson or A.B. ("Banjo") Paterson, but C.J. Dennis, whose most popular works dealt with larrikin types . . . Dennis's best known works had little literary merit and were written to meet popular taste rather than to express his own views on larrikins or life in general.[7] His portrayal of larrikin character owed more to imagination and the works of Louis Stone and others than to authenticity. In doggerel verse making use of stylised dialect, and in a highly sentimental and somewhat condescending fashion, Dennis presented his readers with a series of larrikin characters who were almost saintly by comparison with the types portrayed by other writers — including Lawson. Ginger Mick ("A rorty boy, a naughty boy, wiv rude ixpressions thick") was a rabbit hawker ("'e pencilled fer a bookie; an 'e 'awked a bit, did Mick") with a rough exterior which hid a soft heart.

The immense popularity of Dennis's larrikin poems (which were staged, filmed and recorded, as well as read) is attributable in part to the skill with which he was able to meet the demands of popular taste, and to the fact that during the 1914-18 war he had a captive and somewhat deprived market in the trenches. The decision to enlist Ginger Mick in the A.I.F. and send him to war, and the decision of his publishers to issue pocket editions for men in the trenches, added greatly to his success. In his portrayal of the courtship and marriage of "The Bloke" and Doreen, the army life and death of Ginger Mick, and the life of Digger Smith on his soldier settlement block, Dennis touched upon issues and sentiments which interested and appealed to the average Australian. In other works of greater literary merit, such as the *Glugs of Ghosh* (1917), where Dennis did not strike these chords, he met with little popular success.

Despite the undoubted appeal and success of Dennis's larrikin poems, they have been ignored by historians who give a good deal of attention to other literary works. Yet it could be argued that, as a social commentary, the work of a writer who has successfully catered for popular taste should, other things being equal, be more useful than a literary work which represents only the inner thoughts of a gifted individual. However, the temptation to use the work of Dennis and other writers in order to define an Australian urban character must be resisted. The use of literature as historical evidence (as opposed to illustration) is not an adequate substitute for lack of information. Would it be possible, for instance, to write an accurate social history of the English Industrial Revolution in terms of its contemporary poetry? Or a social history of the 1960s on the basis of the songs of the Beatles and other groups? Could we get a fair sample of Australian contemporary thought by taking a cross-section of the sentiments expressed in songs sung on the nation's most popular radio station? The Australian nineteenth-century bush songs and ballads collected by

Paterson and others may or may not represent Australian rural values. Paterson was interested primarily in "Australian" songs, yet it seems quite possible that English, Irish, Scottish and American songs, which Paterson did not collect, were much more widely known and sung. In fact many of the songs which are regarded as Australian were, in origin, neither Australian nor rural. The most popular songs of the early nineteenth century were "street-ballads" written by professional and semi-professional balladists in Dublin, London and other lesser cities including Sydney. Later in the century entertainment in taverns and "music hall" theatres in British, American and Australian cities became perhaps the major source of popular song. While some "street-ballads", sea shanties and music hall songs were adapted to suit bush settings and characters, their themes as well as melodies tended to remain intact. Where adaptation took place it seems not unreasonable to suspect that rhyme often took precedence over reason — particularly since the adaptors were not aware that they were writing social history!

Literary evidence of the emergence of national character is suspect and dangerous. While more reliable types of historical evidence exist, these too must be handled with extreme caution. For example, much has been made of the declining proportion of immigrants in Australian total population. By 1890 nearly three-quarters of the inhabitants of Australia were native-born Australians. In 1894, T.A. Coghlan pointed out that in New South Wales: "Not until the year 1861 did the Australian-born exceed those of British birth, and not until 1871 did the Australian-born exceed those of British and foreign birth together; but there is practically no such thing as yet as an Australian type, although there is one in the process of making".[8] At the 1891 census in New South Wales, 72 per cent of the population were native-born Australians, but the majority of these were children or minors, and in terms of influence the natives were easily outweighed by the overseas-born. Of people entitled to vote in 1891, only 36 per cent had been born in New South Wales; a further 8 per cent had been born in other parts of Australia and New Zealand; the rest were British or foreign-born. It should also be borne in mind that of the Australian-born a very large proportion were children of immigrants. Birthplace, of course, is not necessarily a good indicator of national sentiment — particularly in Australian circumstances. The national hero — Ned Kelly — was born in Australia yet in the "Jerilderie Letter" he speaks as an Irishman rather than an Australian; and in the present century at least two Australian-born Prime Ministers have been accused of being more English than Australian.

While we may question some of the inferences and methodology of Australian social historiography and commentary, and while we may remain a little sceptical of literary and statistical evidence as to the dominance of a particular type of national character by the 1890s, this does not detract from the great significance of that decade in Australian history. What emerged from the economic distress, droughts, industrial unrest and political flux of the 1890s was not republicanism, or even extreme nationalism, but the partial subjugation of inter-metropolitan rivalry and the emergence of a weak federal structure which still reflected this rivalry. The features of Australian settlement . . . gave rise to a series of widely dispersed coastal urban clusters which developed in relative isolation from each other. In a vast continent with inadequate transport facilities, this was perhaps the most efficient means of promoting rapid regional development. The metropolitan capitals looked to London rather than to each other and there was little functional specialisation between them. Yet, as development progressed, regional or metropolitan provincialism, while remaining basically viable and dominant, became increasingly inadequate and inefficient in certain areas of economic and political activity . . .

The assertion of Australian nationalism through urban literary media in the nineteenth century took place in two widely separated periods: the early 1840s and the 1890s. In each of these periods economic depression affected most of Australia. Deep and prolonged economic crisis sapped the confidence of colonial materialism particularly in the cities and gave rise to a temporary and introverted search for new values. In rural areas periods of drought and low prices were a fact of life and the attitude towards economic adversity was perhaps more philosophical.

* * *

During the long boom period between 1860 and 1890 the energies, aspirations and loyalties of colonial Australians were channelled into a system of metropolitan provincialism which in local Australian terms was largely self-sufficient. In the 1890s a second deep and prolonged depression and another intensive search for new values coincided with a radical change in the attitude towards capital cities. The pre-1890 boom reached its climax in the capital cities in the 1880s, with feverish speculation in urban buildings and land. In the collapse which followed Australians did not need "muckrakers"[9] or Henry Lawson to tell them that something had gone wrong with their cities in political and moral, as well as economic and financial, terms. The optimism and provincial metropolitan pride of the 1880s disintegrated during the scandals, hardships and uncertainties of the 1890s.[10]

Before 1890 the nearest approximation to nationalism in Australia took the form of metropolitanism, and Asa Briggs in *Victorian Cities* has made an interesting comparison between nineteenth-century Australia and provincial England. As Briggs points out:

> The feeling that there was a distinct Australian future was nurtured in the cities; culture not nature was to make it. At a time when the Australian landscape was felt to be greatly inferior to that of Britain, the cities were already believed to have a superiority of their own . . .[11]

This view is supported by the quantities of "booster" literature issued in praise of the various colonies and their capitals; by the attitude expressed, almost without exception, in the larger-circulation colonial newspapers; and in the opinions expressed by a succession of overseas visitors to Australia.

The proudest capital of all was, of course, Melbourne, which in terms of population size, functions and civic self-confidence outshone all other capitals. The confidence and bustle of "Marvellous Melbourne" of the 1880s was frequently contrasted with the staid languor of its nearest rival, Sydney: "If you wish to transact business well and quickly, to organise a new enterprise — in short, to estimate and understand the trade of Australia, you must go to Melbourne and not to Sydney . . ."[12] Since 1890 Melbourne and Sydney appear, in the popular imagination, to have changed roles and nowadays we hear much comment upon the "American" brashness of Sydney, and the "British" Victorian respectability of Melbourne. However, it might be argued that the character differences between Australian capital cities have been exaggerated out of all proportion. The similarities between capitals have been and are much more pronounced and significant than the differences — which reflect size rather than functional variations. Nevertheless, in order to understand Australian nineteenth-century attitudes we need to know much more about urban character — the character of the people who lived in towns and cities and the character of the towns and cities themselves. The key to the cultural changes of the 1890s lies in Australian urban mentality rather than in the views held beyond the ranges. As Asa Briggs has suggested:

> It is just as necessary to relate the new pattern of the 1890s to the eclipse of Melbourne in the years that follow the boom, to the increasing pull of Sydney as a "cultural centre", and to the changing images of Melbourne and Sydney, as it is to relate it to what was happening or what had happened in the outback.[13]

The nearest equivalent to the life of the two-thirds of Australians who, by 1890, lived in capital cities and larger country towns was to be found in provincial England rather than on the wheat frontiers of Canada and the United States. Up to that time the majority of adult Australians were British-born and in terms of culture, attitudes and institutions, Australian society was overwhelmingly British. Rather than seeking corroborating evidence of an assumed nascent Australian character or nationalism, it is much more rational for historians to assume that colonial Australians were Englishmen or Irishmen, unless they can find substantial evidence which contradicts this assumption. In Australian nineteenth-century circumstances it is easy to mistake provincialism for nationalism. It could be argued that the cultural differences between London and Cornwall, or London and Yorkshire, were greater than the differences between London and Australia. Yorkshire had its own distinctive dialect, stereotyped character (a taciturn, blunt, thrifty man with a dry sense of humour), local literature and xenophobia and it shared Australia's economic interest in a particular product — wool. In terms of this discussion, the only important differences between Australia and Yorkshire was distance from London. While Yorkshire could be efficiently governed from London, Australia could not. The emergence of Australia from colony to nation owes more to distance and regional provincialism than to the way of life in the bush.

Regional provincialism in England and Australia was closely related to urbanisation and the claims of particular cities to particular areas. Australian effort, talent and aspiration, instead of being united and made manifest on a national basis, was divided and spread between six rival provincial capitals which were relatively self-sufficient. In so far as these cities looked beyond themselves, they looked to London rather than to any other Australian city. No city was great enough to take precedence over all others, although Melbourne came close to doing so, and no city was willing to yield to any other. Whether or not this pattern meant a sacrifice of quality in favour of quantity in certain areas of activity (art, politics, overseas representation), it clearly delayed the desire for national unity and conditioned the eventual expression of it.

By 1890 urbanisation and, to a lesser extent, suburbanisation had begun to dominate the day-to-day life of a majority of Australians. Suburban life — conformist, rigid, materialistic, complacent, semi-puritan and withdrawn — had given rise to the ancestor of Barry Humphries's "Mrs Everage", with her monotonous daily routine in "Moonee Ponds". The "suburban pioneers" of the late nineteenth century developed into what J.D.B. Miller has described as:

> . . . a typically Australian middle income group, numerically vast, often socially indistinguishable, and displaying a character which is petty-bourgeois, self-centred, sectional, small-minded, but instinctively generous, mildly xenophobic, and attuned to prosperity and increasing opportunities for social mobility.[14]

While this may appear to be a far cry from the "noble bushman", one writer has dared to suggest that bush and suburbia may have had certain similarities in their influence upon attitudes and social patterns:

> In the atmosphere of suburbia, the unorthodox, let alone the eccentric, is frowned upon, and Australia is strikingly lacking in social "mavericks". Opportunities for the socially or intellectually deviant are limited; there is little inclination . . . to be different from the "mob". There is a shared and recognised pattern of behaviour.[15]

Whether or not we accept this view, the fact remains that the overwhelming majority of the inhabitants of Australia, both immigrant and native-born, have been "Australianised" in urban areas, and not in the bush.

Although Australia forged a national legend based in the bush, the acceptance of this legend must be related to the ideological needs of a highly urbanised population. As world urbanisation progressed in more affluent countries during the late nineteenth and early twentieth centuries, an increasing number of people found themselves living a somewhat monotonous, highly regulated way of life in an "unnatural" physical environment, subject to economic controls which they neither trusted nor understood. The emotional needs created by this environment were met in many ways: drink, evangelical religion, Marxism, aspirin tablets, and a variety of other means, provided emotional outlets or dulled the senses. Above all, however, there was a desire to escape. Urban escapism went hand in hand with a steady increase in nationalistic sentiment. In Britain (and other European countries) there were two obvious outlets for these feelings: the glories of the past were made known in popular histories and literary works; and for the present and the future Rudyard Kipling and others pointed to the far-flung Empire which offered salvation to the religious, death or glory to the adventurous, and economic gratification to the avaricious. The areas newly settled by Europeans — North and South America, South Africa, Australasia — had neither empire nor an heroic and glorious past. In Australia the convict past, far from being glorious, was, in the opinion of the *Bulletin* editors and other nationalists, best forgotten. In these areas the urban masses found their equivalent of Robin Hood, Marlborough or Robert Clive in the "noble frontiersman" — the cowboy, the gaucho, the trekker, and other, lesser, rural mortals.[16] In the United States the cowboy hero, laden with morals and physical prowess, was created by popular writers to meet popular demand.

In Australia there is not a great deal of evidence of demands of this kind being made or met before 1890, while civic pride and prosperity prevailed. At the same time, there was much more contact between Australian capitals and the bush than between American east-coast cities and the western frontier. The inhabitants of Australian towns and cities were well aware that the bush nomads, who periodically appeared to "blow their cheques", were far from being heroic or laden with morals. Nor did the city-dwellers envy them their way of life. Yet in the crisis of the 1890s drought, economic distress, industrial and political unrest and social changes (including decisions to have fewer children) gave rise to a changed Australian attitude towards urban life. The earlier pride and faith in cities, which was particularly apparent in the 1880s, gave way to feelings of insecurity and distrust. The reaction took the form of rural fundamentalism and nationalism. In the 1890s, small-farming developed more rapidly than in earlier decades; net population movement from urban to rural areas and from eastern capitals to Western Australia and Britain took place, but on a relatively small scale. The majority made do with a sustaining legend created by Lawson, Paterson and other writers. In their search for a contrast with the urban way of life and a distinct national type, these city-bred writers turned increasingly, although not exclusively, to the simple folk in the bush. The legend thus created met the emotional demands of urban escapism and the need for a distinct national identity which was apparently lacking amongst the urban majority. (At the same time the bush workers were flattered and confirmed in their belief that they were a superior type of "Australian" and they were, perhaps, the *Bulletin*'s most avid readers.)

The Australian legend — or the idea of a truly distinct and unique national character and culture — was created suddenly, at a critical time, on a somewhat flimsy and unrepresentative basis.

The attempt to see Australian history in terms of the evolution of a national character (distinct from British character) and the establishment of a culturally independent nation is a misleading and impossible historical exercise. Because of the nature and timing of its settlement, and the continuing importance of overseas connections, Australia — far from being or becoming a nation apart — was really one small part of an international urban, or suburban, culture, created by western civilisation. Metropolitanisation and the brief span of Australian history before 1900 gave the majority of the inhabitants of this continent insufficient time, opportunity or inclination to develop a truly distinct way of life. In fact, the major part of Australian effort was directed towards the precise opposite — an attempt to create provincial England in the Antipodes. This process was promoted by a continuous flow of people, capital, ideas and techniques from Britain. The urban areas which dominated Australian culture were most receptive to this inflow and made fewer concessions to the Australian environment. Inevitably, the inhabitants of Australia developed their own geographical, class, and — eventually — political loyalties, although not without much prompting. Whether or not these loyalties add up to "nationalism", and to what extent they were contrived, is a matter for debate. But social and economic historians might more usefully concern themselves with those factors which have given rise to the remarkable similarities — in popular culture, technology, social structure and way of life — not only between Australian cities, but between Australian, British, American and other cities of the western world.

Reading 15

Heaven and a Hills Hoist: Australian Critics on Suburbia

Tim Rowse

. . . It is commonplace now to remark on the urban nature of Australian society, to which many commentators have added "suburban". In 1964 Donald Horne evoked Australia's typicality:

> Australia may have been the first suburban nation: for several generations most of its men have been catching the 8.2, and messing about with their houses and gardens at the weekends. Australians have been getting used to the conformities of living in suburban streets longer than most people: mass secular education arrived in Australia before most other countries; Australia was one of the first nations to find part of the meaning of life in the purchase of consumer goods; the whole business of large-scale organised distribution of human beings in a modern suburban society is not new to Australians.[1]

It is precisely because Australian intellectuals have made this equation, between suburbia and Australia's "civilisation", that the word's uses are so rewarding to study. For the history of its uses condenses a number of themes in the history of our ideologies: in particular the question of an Australian experience as evident in the rural-urban conflict, and the fate of working class radicalism. There is no doubt that Australia is a profoundly conservative country, a stable place for capital investment where the basic political institutions are respected. Accordingly there is something undeniably authentic in any observation of Australia as suburbia; it probably *is* the most suburban nation in a strictly demographic sense. However, relying on "suburbia" as a summary image and in part as an explanation of Australia has entailed the unquestioning acceptance of a certain ideology of society . . . Firstly, the focus on and amplification of "suburbia" suggests a homogeneity in Australian society. Preoccupied by a search for the "average" Australian home and its life-style, commentators ignore important ethnic and class differences . . . Secondly, commentators have tended to see Australia as an ensemble of discrete individual house-holders, ignoring the less visible but more important relationships which connect individuals (in ways of which they may not be aware), relationships that make up social classes and political forces. For "suburbia" is a society without history or politics. Thirdly, though commentators have disagreed on whether suburbia constitutes a good or bad civilisation, they have all tended to pose the question of the good life in terms of what goes on inside the "spirit", or at least within one's suburban plot; hence apathy and isolation from politics have been idealised by some writers. In short, there has been a tendency to idealise people's apparent ability to escape the nemeses of the world "outside" suburbia: the world of work, industrial conflict, politics and collective action.

The distance between the rather abstract language of these last few sentences and the concrete and even colloquial discussion of everyday life and character that we find in our social critics is both a yardstick and a cause of the success, or the "convincingness" of the "suburbia" ideology.

Three periods can be discerned in its development. In the first period suburbia is portrayed as the antithesis of the fine place that a particular writer hopes Australia will be. In the second, the memory of this antithesis persists in an ironical acceptance of Australia's unquestionably suburban fate. In the third, the suburban home is reborn as a crucible of a more humane civilisation.

"The suburban home is a horror"

In 1945 Nettie Palmer wrote to her daughter of some mutual friends:

> She was answering one I wrote her some time ago asking her to tell me at her leisure why and how she found the life here unreal and unsatisfying . . . I felt the subject was really interesting and even important. She has answered carefully: but I think part of the explanation is unexpressed — it is latent but clear that here at home she mixes mostly with people who are suburban, and satisfied to be so; I don't mean merely that they live out of town, but they have the suburban outlook. In London — didn't live in the mental suburbs — there and in the US she lived among intellectuals and cosmopolitans. There are such here, perhaps not so easy to find: or perhaps the suburbans are too easy to find.[2]

The antithesis between the cosmopolitan and the suburban was not one that existed between nations, say Britain and Australia:

the struggle between them took place in every country. It was a contest between two attitudes to life: one whose intellectual horizons were broad, and which liked to look ahead and aspire to adventurous schemes of individual and social progress; and one that was narrow, self-satisfied, materialistic and parochial. This assured dichotomy was the property of a certain generation of Australian intellectuals which included the Palmers and their friends.

Louis Esson (1879-1943), a friend of Nettie and Vance Palmer, wrote into his play *The Time is Not Yet Ripe* (1912) a visionary protagonist and *alter ego*, Mr Sydney Barrett . . . The text of the play is followed by a small essay, "Our Institutions", which elaborates some of Barrett's aphorisms.

> The suburban home must be destroyed. It stands for all that is dull and cowardly and depressing in modern life. It endeavours to eliminate the element of danger in human affairs. But without dangers there can be no joy, no ecstasy, no spiritual adventures. The suburban home is a blasphemy. It denies life. Young men it would save from wine, and young women from love. But love and wine are eternal verities. They are moral. The suburban home is deplorably immoral.[3]

Esson's friend Vance Palmer shared similar hopes for an immanent Australian Socialism — a flowering of the best ethos of the Bush. By 1921, when it was clear that no such Utopia was going to eventuate, Palmer ruminated sadly on "Australia's Transformation". Whereas in fact this transformation hinged largely on the defeat of working class militancy, Palmer portrayed it as a becalming of the national spirit in a Sargasso Sea of "economic struggle".

> Today villadom and proletaria combine to fix the national life or cross swords in the struggle for economic power. *The Man From Snowy River* is deposed to make room for a sentimental "bloke" from the slums, and the life of the continent is held up by a quarrel between two classes of people on the seaboard.

The contrast between the Bloke and Paterson's "Man" is conducted at a number of levels . . . The "Man's" domain was the Bush, whereas Dennis sentimentalised the City. Palmer went on in this article to use the phrase "the dominance of villadom", and denounced modern productive life as being nothing more than the "supply of boots and chocolates to the suburbs". It is true, as David Walker has recently pointed out, that the socialist ferment of the decade 1910-20 is important in reaching an understanding of Vance Palmer;[4] but it must also be pointed out that Palmer never realistically related his socialist vision to the actual contemporary struggles of the working class: instead he saw them as tainted by their obsession with the material and indifferent to the "spiritual dimension". Suburbia and "villadom" for him evoked the pettiness of *all* parties to that "quarrel on the seaboard".

In his book *Australia* (1930), written in the midst of a serious crisis in the Australian economy, W.K. Hancock expressed concern that the ruling ethos in political life had permitted a soulless prosperity to grow up in the cities at the expense of primary producers' industries. The visitor to Australia

> has expected to see some evidence of the rigours and heroisms of pioneering, and such a stolid mass of commonplace urban prosperity heaped around the doors of an empty continent will appear to him unnatural, unseemly.[5]

In the late 1920s this familiar dichotomy had a new, urgent and conservative pertinence to the struggle between and within classes. In 1928 Hancock had written on "The Australian City" in the *New Statesman*. Starting with some sardonic cameos of the aesthetic innocence of the typical Australian home and the suburban wife's alleged hunger for social status, Hancock goes on to place these piquant vulgarities in the context of the political and spiritual dominance of the City over the Country. "Suburbia" in this article functions as a metonym in an argument (then emanating from the Country Party and representatives of British economic interests in Australia) for the scaling down of New Protection on the grounds that it gave the urban populace a standard of living which primary exporters could not afford to subsidise.[6]

But Hancock had a sense of the political ambiguity of the suburban spirit. "Conservatives may console themselves that, even in a so-called socialist community like Australia, this vast suburban mass is inevitably opposed to subversive change. There is no fear of its pulling down the comfortable house which it inhabits."[7] Frederic Eggleston drew the same comforting conclusion in his *State Socialism* (1932). The final chapter attempts to explain sociologically the intractable materialism that he saw as the leading trait of an electorate which voted for "state socialism" — an affluence underpinned by economically "unsound" government

policies. The political success of Labor had integrated the proletariat into capitalism; but their self-interested materialism was a
dead weight in the process of economic adjustment. The masses
lacked the civic virtue to renounce material wants for the sake of
threatened profit margins. Eggleston sketched a portrait of this
stubborn "self-contained man".

> The home of the "self-contained man" is in the suburbs; and in the
> highly developed suburbs of an Australian city, with good accommo-
> dation, a nice garden, a back yard, vegetables in his plot and fowls in
> the shed, a fence against intrusion, he has probably reached a higher
> pitch of development than anywhere else.[8]

Vance and Nettie Palmer, Esson, Hancock and Eggleston all
equated "suburbia" with a stifling materialism of outlook. But
whereas the first three intellectuals saw only the obliteration of
their hopes of a spiritually finer Australia, the latter two also
adopted a more pragmatic and political perspective. That spiritual
banality stood as a bulwark against Bolshevism. The question of
just how an individual suburbanite affirmed or denied
"civilisation" had started to become more complex.

No flies on the nature strip

The seeds of the more favourable evaluation of suburbia, found in
Eggleston and Hancock, have germinated since World War Two
in a more ironical appreciation of its strengths, particularly in the
writing of a younger generation of intellectuals who had never
known at first hand the earlier optimism about Australia's potential as a "socialist" Promised Land. By the early 1950s, when the
Keynesian welfare state seemed to have set mass material content-
ment on a firmer economic footing than in the interwar years, suburbia came to be seen in a more positive light — as an innocent
utopia. This seems to be the viewpoint controlling Robin Boyd's
classic evocation of suburbia in *Australia's Home* (1952). His
point was that while "factory, shop, office, theatre and restaurant
were not radically different the world over . . in the suburb was
experienced that essentially Australian part of town life which lay
between work and home."[9] Moreover, suburbia was coming to be
seen not so much as an aberration of the Australian spirit, but as
its abiding manifestation. The blurb on the Pelican edition of *The
Australian Ugliness* stated the relevance of Boyd's concerns:

"Looking at the face of Australia, Robin Boyd goes deeper, to analyse the character that gave it the expression it wears." As "suburbia" became accepted as an authentic image of the way ordinary Australians lived, the critical connotations of the term began to lose their force, giving way to a gentle irony and even to an aloof benediction. No-one did more to facilitate this shift than Barry Humphries.

At the time when the humorous Australian archetypes Dad and Dave, Ginger Mick and the Sentimental Bloke were losing their appeal, undercut by demographic changes and the political failure of Labor's "common Man" stereotype of the 1940s, Barry Humphries constructed new characters, notably Edna Everage and Sandy Stone. Neither inner urban larrikins nor bucolic yokels, they are truly "suburban". Everage apes but violates the conventions of taste, status and worldliness; Stone's life is a pathetic shell of would-be gentility and conformity. But the sense of their authenticity and familiarity has, over the years, come to undercut the critical edge of Humphries' satire: there has grown up an undeniable element of sentimental patriotism in the appreciation of Humphries' work. Edna and Sandy, understood as something indigenous, allow a cock-eyed pride in the uniqueness of Australian mores. The innocence was seen to be somehow admirable.

* * *

In *The Lucky Country* Donald Horne adamantly rejected the interwar snobbery about suburbia: it effectively dismissed the whole nation. Instead, he defended the vitality of the suburban lifestyle. "The profusion of life doesn't wither because people live in small brick houses with red roofs".[10] Moreover, it was the national lifestyle, a classless ethos: "The genteel have been vulgarised, the vulgar made more gentle. People now enjoy themselves more in the same kind of ways."[11]

But this commitment to suburbia is not sustained by Horne elsewhere. In a 1962 essay he defended Australian businessmen from their negative stereotype which he described as ". . . uneducated, provincially ignorant, suburban-minded, vulgar, anti-intellectual, reactionary, materialistic . . . more Babbitt than Babbitt".[12] More recently, in *The Australian People* (1972), the section called "The First Suburban Nation" is part of Chapter

Fourteen: "The End of Improvement: 1919-39" which traces, in the interwar period, the extinction of Australia's vital, progressive, nationalistic impulse. He pictures a period of philistine self-satisfaction in which life was privatised and domestic rather than open and communal, and in which "women developed the rituals of afternoon tea (dainty sandwiches and many varieties of sponge-cake) into a complex art".[13] . . . Horne's ambivalence towards suburbia is the inevitable result of an attempt to identify rhetorically with "the people", who are sound and happy but who deserve better government, and substantively with an emergent body of technocrats — those confident they could govern more effectively than the Coalition governments of the sixties.

Craig McGregor, presented by one publisher as a representative social critic of the young iconoclastic postwar generation, was more critical of Australian life than Horne was. But, like Horne, he also celebrated its vitality.

> There is a zestfulness about much of suburban life which is apparent in a thousand particulars from the sense of bustle and good humour in the thriving suburban shopping centres to the discotheques, sportscars, surfboards and juke boxes which help enliven the life of the younger suburbanites . . . Fairfield, probably Sydney's dullest suburb, also has the highest juvenile delinquency rate. Behind that facade, something is always happening.[14]

McGregor became a champion of "Alf" — the archetypal suburban house-holder. Yet in a subtle way this populist affirmation undercut his critique of Australia. He was more interested in evoking a "way of life" than in describing the structural features of Australian society which caused inequality and alienation in the first place. When he wrote approvingly that "for most people life begins at five o'clock on Friday arvo",[15] he was spelling out a theoretical emphasis, an implicit sociology. The Australia he described existed outside the workplace: the relations of home and hearth were held to be the locus of the "real" Australia, not the worlds of work and politics. He thus helped to support the apologetic image of Australia as an undifferentiated suburbia, composed of individual households standing free of class relations. McGregor was alert enough to see the dilemma raised by this perspective: if Australia was to change from being unequal and alienating, then each of its individual citizens would have to step away from the comfortable social anonymity of suburbia and become involved on one side or the other. Could McGregor endorse such involvement without shattering the image of suburban utopia?

> The man who becomes absorbed in his home is much less likely to become involved in public issues such as conscription or Vietnam or free enterprise, in the whole fabric of democratic activity. I think this is probably true but once again it has to be kept in perspective. There are some advantages in such a disengagement: the man who lives in a bung in Padstow is much freer, much less oppressed by community pressures and conformism, than Dublin terrace-dwellers or Naples proletarians: it is much easier for him to opt out of the church . . . mass prejudice and social authority and to choose his own allegiances. The Australian suburbanite is probably freer of the stifling pressure of social authoritarianism than any other city dweller in history.[16]

In this crucial passage, McGregor continues the ambivalent estimate of suburbia: Alf was apathetic about the Vietnam question and about poverty, but at least he was happy and free and able to escape the pressures of the world. McGregor offers to suburbanites the prospect of continuing to opt out of history, as it were — a choice less happily acknowledged by Eggleston in the Thirties. Thus McGregor's Alf is the son of Egglestone's self-contained man.

Green thumbs up

During the 1960s the Australian Labor Party developed a theory of reform which was quite coherent with McGregor's and Horne's emphasis on suburbia as the locus of Australian civilisation. ALP ideologues saw reform as the task of equalising different regions' access to community amenities. More equality between suburbs was to be achieved by siphoning off a greater proportion of the nation's wealth and spending it on better health services, housing, transport, sewerage. Suburbs of the major cities which had been denied these services by years of Coalition neglect were to benefit. Labor's perspective was that it represented not the aspirations of a working class constituted by its subordinate place in production, but the needs of disadvantaged householders, concentrated in regions. Just as the liberal-democratic notion of suffrage fragments social classes, by treating society as an ensemble of individual voters, so Labor's view fragmented the nation into privileged or disadvantaged households and neighbourhoods. As in Horne and

McGregor, its emphasis was on the social world outside the work-place, where the mobilisation of interests was much less saliently that of a class. After all, a class-oriented conception of the ALP constituency was inadmissible to these ideals precisely because the whole program was to be financed by the continued, privately-directed expropriation of working class labour — the fundamental source of all the inequalities being dealt with.

This schema of reform produced a truly formidable theorist in Hugh Stretton. No one has formulated such an articulate economic and philosophical case for the suburban way of life as he: where the Palmers condemned and Horne and McGregor hedged their celebration, Stretton praises without reservation. His words are simple and, at first, plausible:

> You don't have to be a mindless conformist to choose suburban life. Most of the best poets and painters and inventors and protestors choose it too. It reconciles access to work and city with private, adaptable, self-expressive living space at home. Plenty of adults love that living space, and subdivide it ingeniously. For children it really has no rivals. At home it can allow them space, freedom and community with their elders; they can still reach bush and beach in one direction and in the other, schools to educate them and cities to sophisticate them. About half the lives of most of us are spent growing up then bringing others up. Suburbs are good places to do it, precisely because they let the generations coexist, with some continuing independence for each.[17]

Stretton later turned his fire on a Left orthodoxy which he sees as being hostile to the development of private life and the private ownership of the things which really matter to people's daily lives. "Seeing the masses seduced by capitalism, 'hard' socialists respond by doubling their distrust of ownership. It does not occur to them that the house and garden and car turn people away from the party of equality chiefly because the party of equality officially despises the house and garden and car, and the life they allow."[18] The Left, says Stretton, forms an unholy alliance with the economic orthodoxy, which refuses to count in the National Product the useful things which people do for themselves at home, and so neglects to direct social investment into areas that will improve the domestic quality of life.

Stretton's argument is on the one hand a very eloquent plea for things which Australia needs badly: better housing, town planning and transport policies. But it is also a blueprint for the consolidation of modern capitalism's domestic annexe . . . For capitalism, the domestic sphere is both cheaply reproductive and privatised. Any attempt to upgrade community life that does not challenge the relationships of capitalist production would thus cut two ways. Life would be genuinely better, for some; but at the expense of leaving unquestioned the social division of labour, between workers and owners, and between men and women . . . Stretton's conservatism lies in his defence of the separation of the "private" world of consumption and sexual relations from the larger social processes, in work and in politics, in which this "privacy" is ultimately articulated. His enquiry into this crucial nexus is bracing — he has made a case against the Left which it must answer firmly — but ultimately he confirms it as a necessary separation. In Stretton, we find Alf's apotheosis.

Throughout the different uses discussed here, the term "suburbia" has developed in its idiomatic force its apparent authenticity as a description of the "Australian way of life". Beginning as an abstract . . . dismissal, it enjoyed a career as the metonym of a half-accepted civilisation — stolid electorate or satirical object. Recently it has passed into a much more accepting sociological usage, connecting to a program of reform which is sophisticated but fundamentally conservative of capitalist social relations. Inscribed in this career is the gradual acceptance by Australian intellectuals of their national civilisation as its urban and suburban self. The extent of this shift is marked strikingly at one point in Stretton's work:

> It is in private houses with storage space and some land around them that it is easiest to use more human energy in satisfying ways, and to manage with less powered commercial services . . . Environmental policies will always be determined chiefly by peoples' values; and urban houses and gardens are the nursery of most of the best environmental values. People who live in town but grow some foliage of their own, and keep a cat to deter mice, are the mainstay of all the movements which work to protect larger landscapes and eco-systems. Private residential land is both an environmental good which ought to be fairly shared, and a vital educator; a classroom for work-skills, play-skills, nature study and environmental values which an environmentally careful society could be mad to deny to any of its people.[19]

Palmer saw an unbridgeable antithesis between "villadom"

and "the Bush": Stretton sees in suburbia the nursery of a sentiment organic with the ecosystem.

But the continuities in the tradition of usage are stronger than this small upheaval in the geographical metaphors of Australian romanticism . . . Each writer has been seduced by the relatively high degree of sameness in the lives that we Australians live outside the place of work. As Hancock said, with a playful mixture of banality and insight: "There are no classes in Australia except in the economic sense". He was viewing Australian society through the wrong end of a Marxist telescope. His use of the word "except" trivialises the very processes which constitute ours as a class society, but it draws attention to the undeniably strong tendency for these divisions to be obscured in the forms of life led outside the workplace. Those who use "suburbia" as a defining image of Australian society lend their support to this obscuring emphasis.

Notes

Reading 1   Defining Australia (James Walter)

1. Raymond Williams, *Keywords: A Vocabulary of Culture and Society*, Fontana, London 1970, pp.178-9.
2. Benedict Anderson, *Imagined Communities: Reflections on the Origin and Spread of Nationalism*, Verso, London, 1983, p.15.
3. Williams, *Keywords*, pp.178-9.
4. Robert Pascoe, *The Manufacture of Australian History*, Oxford University Press, Melbourne, 1979, p.52.
5. John Colmer, "Australian Cultural Analysis: Some Principles and Problems", *Southerly*, 34, 3, 1978, p.246.
6. R.M. Crawford, "Australian National Character: Myth and Reality", *Journal of World History*, 2, 3, 1955, pp.704-27.
7. Vance Palmer, *The Legend of the Nineties*, Melbourne University Press, Melbourne, 1966, p.9. First published 1954.
8. Anderson, *Imagined Communities*, p.16.
9. Manning Clark, "A Letter to Tom Collins" (1943), in *Occasional Writings and Speeches*, Fontana, Melbourne, 1980, pp.91-3.
10. Manning Clark, "The Quest for Australian Identity" (1979), in Occasional Writings and Speeches, pp.215-33.
11. Judith Allen, "Mundane Men: Historians, Masculinity and Masculinism", *Historical Studies*, 22, 89, 1987, pp.617-28; Marilyn Lake, "The Politics of Respectability: Identifying the Masculinist Context", *Historical Studies*, 22, 86, 1986, pp.116-31.
12. Humphrey McQueen, "The Suckling Society", in *Australian Politics — A Third Reader*, H. Mayer and H. Nelson (eds), Cheshire, Melbourne, 1973, pp.5-13.
13. *Ibid.*, p.8.
14. *Ibid.*, p.5.
15. Richard White, *Inventing Australia: Images and Identity 1688-1980*, George Allen & Unwin, Sydney, 1987, p. viii.

Reading 2   Inventing Australia (Richard White)

1. R.H. Croll, *Smike to Bulldog: Letters from Sir Arthur Streeton to Tom Roberts*, London, 1946, p.128.
2. E.J. Hobsbawm, *Industry and Empire*, Penguin, Harmondsworth, 1969, p.157.
3. Charles Carrington, *Rudyard Kipling: His Life and Work*, London, 1955, p.212.
4. *Ibid.*, pp.166-7.
5. *Victorian Census*, 1891, 1901; *N.S.W. Census*, 1891, 1901; *Commonwealth Census*, 1911; Great Britain Central Statistical Office, *Annual Abstract of Statistics*, 1912. See also Graeme Davison, "Syd-

ney and the Bush: An Urban Context for the Australian Legend",
Historical Studies, 18, 71, October 1978, p.193.

6. John Steegman, *Victorian Taste: A Study of the Arts and Architecture from 1830 to 1870,* Nelson, London, 1970, pp.142-6, 282.

7. A.G. Stephens, *The Red Pagan*, Sydney, 1904, pp. 19-21.

8. Graeme Davison, "Sydney and the Bush", p.199; C.N. Connolly, "Class, Birthplace, Loyalty: Australian Attitudes to the Boer War", *Historical Studies*, 18, 71, October 1978, p.230.

9. Bernard Smith (ed.), *Documents on Art and Taste in Australia*, Oxford University Press, Melbourne, 1975, p.253.

10. Cited in Bernard Smith, *Australian Painting, 1788-1970*, Oxford University Press, Melbourne, 1971, p.104.

11. Randolph Bedford, *Naught to Thirty-Three,* Sydney, 1944, p.288.

12. David Denholm, *The Colonial Australians*, Penguin, Harmondsworth, 1979, pp.151-3.

13. J.H. Buckley, *The Victorian Temper: A Study in Literary Culture,* London, 1966, p.2.

14. Cited in Arthur W. Jose, *The Romantic Nineties*, Sydney, 1933, p.43.

15. *Ibid.*, p.52.

16. C.N. Connolly, "Class, Birthplace, Loyalty", pp.228-9.

17. Graeme Davison, "Sydney and the Bush", pp.192ff.

18. Victor Daley, "The Call of the City", in *Wine and Roses,* Sydney, 1911.

19. Cited in Bernard Smith, *Australian Painting*, p.88.

20. Cited in Graeme Davison, "Sydney and the Bush", p.208.

21. George A. Taylor, *Those Were the Days: Being Reminiscences of Australian Artists and Writers*, Sydney, 1918, pp.54-60.

22. Arthur W. Jose, *The Romantic Nineties*, pp.34-5.

23. *Ibid.*, p.40.

24. R.H. Croll (ed.), *Smike to Bulldog*, pp.21-3.

25. Victorian College of the Arts, *Von Guerard to Wheeler: The First Teachers at the National Gallery School 1870-1939,* Melbourne, 1978 (photos and prize lists); Janine Burke, *Australian Women Artists 1840-1940,* Greenhouse, Melbourne, 1980, pp.24-37.

26. Graeme Davison, "Sydney and the Bush", pp.207-9.

27. Ian Turner (ed.), *The Australian Dream*, Sun Books, Melbourne, 1968, pp.219, 225.

28. A.B. Paterson, "Clancy of the Overflow".

29. Arthur W. Jose, *The Romantic Nineties*, pp.19, 47.

30. Russel Ward, *The Australian Legend,* Oxford University Press, Melbourne, 1958, p.252.

31. Cited in C.M.H. Clark, *Select Documents in Australian History 1851-1900*, Angus & Robertson, Sydney, 1955, p.806.

32. Bernard Smith, *European Vision and the South Pacific 1768-1850*, Oxford University Press, Oxford, 1969, p.154.

33. Frank Wilkinson, *Australia at the Front*, p.68. See also L.M. Field, *The Forgotten War: Australian Involvement in the South African Conflict of 1899-1902,* Melbourne University Press, Melbourne, 1979, pp.135, 186.

34. Cited in Russel Ward, *A Nation for a Continent*, Heinemann, Melbourne, 1977, p.12.

35. For examples see John Barnes (ed.), *The Writer in Australia*, Oxford University Press, Melbourne, 1969, pp.3, 17, 38, 47-8, 57; Ken Levis, "The Role of the *Bulletin* in Indigenous Short-Story Writing during the Eighties and Nineties", in Chris Wallace-Crabbe (ed.), *The Australian Nationalists: Modern Critical Essays,* Oxford University Press, Melbourne, 1971, pp.49-52.

36. Leslie Stephen cited in James Laver, *The Age of Optimism*, Weidenfeld & Nicolson, London, 1966, p.176.

37. Ian Turner (ed.), *The Australian Dream,* pp.101-2. See also Bernard Smith (ed.), *Documents on Art and Taste in Australia*, pp.135-8.

38. John Barnes (ed.), *The Writer in Australia*, p.52.

39. Peter Coleman, *Obscenity, Blasphemy, Sedition: 100 Years of Censorship in Australia*, Angus & Robertson, Sydney, 1961, pp.105-6; Australian Writers' and Artists' Union, *Rules,* Sydney, 1910; Geoff Sparrow (ed.), *Crusade for Journalism: Official History of the Australian Journalists' Association*, Melbourne, 1960, pp.23-4; *Bookfellow*, June 1912, p.156.

40. Edwin J. Brady, *Australia Unlimited*, pp.123-24.

41. Photographed in *The Good Neighbour*, April 1954, p.1.

42. Richard White, "The Australian Way of Life", *Historical Studies*, 18, 3, October 1979, pp.528-9.

43. Elizabeth Webb, *Stet*, Brisbane, 1950, p.179.

44. George Caiger (ed.), *The Australian Way of Life*, Melbourne, 1953; W.V. Aughterson (ed), *Taking Stock: Aspects of Mid-Century Life in Australia*, Cheshire, Melbourne, 1953; Ian Bevan (ed.), *The Sunburnt Country: Profile of Australia*, London, 1953.

45. W.V. Aughterson (ed.), *Taking Stock,* p.i.

46. Oswald L. Ziegler (ed.), *Official Commemorative Book: Jubilee of the Commonwealth of Australia*, Sydney, 1951, p.40.

47. Institute of Public Affairs, *Report on the Activities of the I.P.A.,* Sydney, 1949.

48. Geoffrey Blainey, *The Tyranny of Distance: How Distance Shaped Australia's History*, Sun Books, Melbourne, 1966, p.334.

49. *The New Australian (Official Organ of the Big Brother Movement)*, 1, 1, February 1928, p.7.

50. Cited in W.D. Borrie *et al., A White Australia: Australia's Population Problem*, Sydney, 1947, p.151.

51. *The Good Neighbour,* August 1950, p.1.

52. "Nino Culotta" (John O'Grady), *They're a Weird Mob*, Ure Smith, Sydney, 1957, p.204.
53. Elizabeth Webb, *Stet*, p.49.
54. George Johnston, "Their Way of Life", in Ian Bevan (ed.), *The Sunburnt Country*, pp.151, 158.
55. W.E.H. Stanner, "The Australian Way of Life", in W.V. Aughterson (ed.), *Taking Stock*, pp.3-4.
56. Australian News and Information Bureau, *Australia: Portrait of a Nation,* Canberra, 1955.
57. George Caiger (ed.), *The Australian Way of Life,* p.6.
58. W.V. Aughterson (ed.), *Taking Stock*, p.8.
59. Brian Fitzpatrick, *The Australian Commonwealth: A Picture of the Community 1901-55*, Cheshire, Melbourne, 1956, p.15.
60. Roy Morgan, *Australian Public Opinion Polls,* February 1958, 1299-312.
61. Donald Horne, *The Lucky Country: Australia in the Sixties,* Penguin, Harmondsworth, 1966, pp.82-5.
62. Emery Barcs, "The Australian Way of Life", in Oswald L. Ziegler (ed.), *Official Commemorative Book: Jubilee of the Commonwealth of Australia*, p.40.
63. Henry Lawson, "The Spirit of Sydney".
64. Thomas Wood, *Cobbers*, London, 1934, p.168.
65. J.D. Pringle, *Australian Accent*, Chatto & Windus, London, 1958, p.18.
66. Peter Spearritt, *Sydney Since the Twenties*, Sydney, 1978, p.105.
67. *Commonwealth Year Book*, 1963, pp.217-20.
68. Alan Trengove, *What's Good for Australia . . .! The story of B.H.P.,* Sydney, 1975, p.191.
69. *Commonwealth Year Book,* 1963, pp.604-9.
70. *I.P.A. Review,* 3, 1, January-February 1949, p.14.
71. *Ibid.,* 18, 1, January-March 1964, pp.9-10.
72. David Kemp, "Political Parties and Australian Culture", *Quadrant*, 21, 2, December 1977, p.7.
73. *Argus Woman's Magazine,* 24 September 1947, pp.4-5.
74. *Commonwealth Year Book*, 1963, pp.195, 321.
75. George Johnston, *Clean Straw for Nothing. A Novel,* Collins, London, 1969, p.99.
76. Cited in National Capital Development Commission, *Tomorrow's Canberra*, Canberra, 1970, p.21.
77. Geoffrey Serle, *From Deserts the Prophets Come*, Heinemann, Melbourne, 1973, p.229.

Reading 3   Aborigines (John Rickard)

1. George Tinamin quoted in Phillip Toyne and Daniel Vachon, *Growing Up the Country,* Melbourne, 1984, p.5.
2. W.E.H. Stanner, *On Aboriginal Religion,* Sydney, no date, p.155.

3. Josephine Flood, *Archaeology of the Dreamtime,* Sydney, 1983, p.213.

4. Dampier quoted in C.M.H. Clarke (ed.), *Sources of Australian History,* Melbourne, 1957, p.25; Cook, pp.54-5.

Reading 4   Aboriginality as Civilisation (Colin Tatz)

1. *Jewish Encyclopaedia*, VI, p.330.

2. C.H. Cooley's sociological theory of the "looking-glass self", that is, the shaping of self-images according to the perception of how other people see us: *Human Nature and the Social Order,* New York, 1902, pp.183-4.

3. The range of "science" here is enormous: from Carl von Linnaeus (1707-1778) finding that Americans were reddish, choleric and erect; Europeans white, ruddy, muscular; Asiatics yellow, melancholic and inflexible; Africans black, phlegmatic and indulgent; then on to Georges Cuvier (1769-1832), Swiss founder of palaentology, who proposed a tripartite division of mankind based on Noah's three sons — Ham, Shem and Japheth; then to Guiseppe Sergi (1841-1936), the Italian psychologist, who divided mankind physically and mentally into Eurafricans and Eurasiatics: the long-heads and the round-heads.

4. See the essay "Population" by H. Sonnabend in *Handbook of Race Relations in South Africa*, Ellen Hellman (ed.), Oxford University Press, London, 1949, pp.7-9; see also *Population Registration Act*, No.30 of 1950.

5. *The Aborigines and Torres Strait Islanders' Affairs Act* 1965.

6. *Submission by the Northern Territory Government to House of Representatives Standing Committee on Aboriginal Affairs (Reference: Aboriginal Access to Legal Aid),* Darwin, 21 June 1979 (Official Hansard Report).

7. *Welfare Ordinance* No.16 of 1953, section 14.

8. "The Marriage of Mick and Gladys: A Discretion without an Appeal", Colin A. Hughes in *Decisions*, B.B. Schaffer and D.C. Corbett (eds), Cheshire, Melbourne, 1965, pp.302-21.

9. *Social Evolution*, Watts & Co., London, 1951, pp.1-16.

10. *Primitive Culture*, John Murray, London, 1903, 4th edn, p.1.

11. *Race Politics in Australia,* University of New England Publishing Unit, Armidale, 1979, p.86.

12. "Urbanising Aborigines: the Social Scientists' Great Deception," in *Social Alternatives*, 2, 2, August 1981, pp.16-22.

13. *Land Claim by Warlpiri and Kartangarurru-Kurintji,* Report by the Aboriginal Land Commissioner to the Minister for Aboriginal Affairs and to the Minister for the Northern Territory, AGPS, 1979, paras 206 to 223, especially 206, p.43.

14. I am indebted to Dick Kimber of Alice Springs for these pertinent examples.
15. *Land Claim by Alyawarra and Katitja,* Report by the Aboriginal Land Commissioner, Mr Justice Toohey, to the Minister for Aboriginal Affairs, AGPS, 1979, paras 98 and 106, especially pp.22-3.
16. *Lander Warlpiri Anmatjira Land Claim to Willowra Pastoral Lease Report*, Report by the Aboriginal Land Commissioner to the Minister for Aboriginal Affairs and to the Administrator of the Northern Territory, AGPS, 1980, para. 121, p.31.
17. *Op. cit.* (footnote 13), para. 222, p.46.
18. *NT News*, 21 July 1979.
19. Speech at Malmesbury, Cape Town, quoted in my *Shadow and Substance in South Africa*, Natal University Press, Pietermaritzburg, 1962, p. 40.
20. V. Gordon Childe, *Social Evolution*, Watts, London, 1951, pp.6-7.
21. *Ancient Society*, 1871.
22. "Plateau and Plain: Prehistoric Investigations in Arnhem Land, Northern Territory", unpublished PhD thesis, Australian National University, 1967.
23. *Preliminary Report on the Aboriginals of the Northern Territory*, Commonwealth of Australia, Parliamentary Papers, vol. III, 1913 — as part of the Report of the Administrator for the year 1912.
24. *Kalumburu: The Benedictine Mission and the Aborigines 1908-1975*, published by the Kalumburu Benedictine Mission, 1977: Preface by the Premier of Western Australia the Hon. Sir Charles Court OBE, MLA.
25. "East Kimberley Primitives", Fr Eugene Perez OSB, in *North of the 26th*, a collection of writings, paintings, drawings and photographs from the Kimberley, Pilbara and Gascoyne regions, Helen Weller (ed.), Artlook Books, Perth, 1979, pp. 346-8.
26. *Ibid.*, " 'Kalumburu': Considerations of the State (Difficulties, Possibilities and Dangers) of an Aboriginal Community", Eugene Perez, pp. 157-60.
27. *Sydney Morning Herald,* 5 October 1981.
28. *Dictionary of the History of Ideas*, Philip Wiener (ed.), vol.1, Charles Scribner & Sons, New York, 1973, p.614.
29. *Civilisation and Culture,* Sands & Co., London, 1916, pp.1-29.
30. *A Black Civilisation: A Social Study of an Australian Tribe,* 2nd edn, Harper Brothers, 1958.
31. "The Aboriginal Question", *Social Alternatives,* 2, 2, August 1981, pp.34-5.
32. "Family and Social Structure among Aborigines in Northern New South Wales", Yuriko Kitajoi, unpublished PhD thesis, Australian National University, 1976.
33. *Nationalism and History, Essays on Old and New Judaism,* Philadelphia, 1958, pp.41-60.

34. *Aboriginal Land Rights: A Handbook,* Nicolas Peterson (ed.), Australian Institute of Aboriginal Studies, Canberra, 1981.
35. *National Times,* 5-11 July 1981, p.24.
36. *The Bureaucratic Phenomenon,* University of Chicago Press, 1971, pp.195-208 in particular.

Reading 6   *Migrant Hands in a Distant Land (Jock Collins)*

1. Graeme Hugo, *Australia's Changing Population: Trends and Implications,* Oxford University Press, Melbourne, 1986, p.232.
2. Cited in R.T. Appleyard, *Immigration: Policy and Progress,* AIPS Monograph no.7, 1971, p.7.
3. First Report of the National Population Inquiry, *Population and Australia: A Demographic Analysis and Projection,* AGPS, Canberra, 1975, p.107.
4. Australian Bureau of Statistics, *Labour Force, Australia,* January 1987, no.62030, p.18.
5. While the English speaking (ES) and Non-English Speaking (NES) distinction is a generalisation that glosses over some important exceptions — particularly the Northern European experience — this distinction is used as convenient shorthand throughout the book. For a country with more than 100 birthplace groups, such generalisations clearly require complementary studies which reflect the unique experience of each birthplace group.
6. Department of Immigration and Ethnic Affairs, *Review of Activities '86,* AGPS, Canberra, 1986, p.116.
7. Geoffrey Blainey, *All for Australia*, Methuen Haynes, Sydney, 1984, p.100.
8. Andrew Jakubowicz, "Ethnicity, Multiculturalism and Neo-conservatism", in Gill Bottomley and Marie de Lepervanche (eds), *Ethnicity, Class and Gender in Australia,* Allen & Unwin, Sydney, 1984, p.28.
9. Cited in Janis Wilton and Richard Bosworth, *Old Worlds and New Australia*, Penguin, Ringwood, 1984, p.17.
10. *Ibid.*
11. Jean Martin, *The Migrant Presence*, Allen & Unwin, Sydney, 1978, pp.27-8.
12. Cited in Andrew Markus, "Labor and Immigration 1946-49: The Displaced Persons Programme", *Labour History,* no.47, November 1984, p.89.
13. Cited in Jean Martin, *The Migrant Presence*, p.89.
14. *Ibid.,* p.94.
15. *Ibid.,* p.31.
16. Jeannie Martin, "The Development of Multiculturalism", in The Committee of Review of the Australian Institute of Multicultural

Affairs (The Cass Report), *Report to the Minister for Immigration and Ethnic Affairs*, vol.11, AGPS, Canberra, 1983, p.133.

17. Michael Liffman, "The Origins of Multiculturalism", The Cass Report, vol. 11, p.77.

18. Al Grassby, *A Multi-Cultural Society for the Future*, Department of Immigration, AGPS, Canberra, 1973, p.4.

19. Jersey Zubrzycki, "Towards a Multicultural Society in Australia", in M. Bowen (ed.), *Australia 2000: The Ethnic Impact,* University of New England, Armidale, 1977, p.130-1.

20. The Australian Ethnic Affairs Council, *Australia as a Multicultural Society*, AGPS, Canberra, August 1977, p.16.

21. Australian Council on Population and Ethnic Affairs, *Multiculturalism for all Australians: our developing neighbourhood*, AGPS, Canberra, May 1982, p.2.

22. *Ibid.*, p.24.

23. Jean Martin, *The Migrant Presence*, p.71.

24. Review of Post Arrival Programs and Services (The Galbally Report), *Migrant Services and Programs,* AGPS, Canberra, May 1978, p.4.

25. Australian Institute of Multicultural Affairs (The AIMA Review), *Evaluation of Post-Arrival Programs and Services: A Summary,* Australian Institute of Multicultural Affairs, Melbourne, May 1982, pp.2-3.

26. Committee of Review of Migrant and Multicultural Programs and Services (The Jupp Report), *Don't Settle For Less,* Department of Immigration and Ethnic Affairs, AGPS, Canberra, 1986.

27. L.J.M. Cooray, "Multiculturalism in Australia: Who Needs It?", *Quadrant*, April 1986.

28. Frank Knopfelmacher, "Save Australia's British Culture", *Age*, 31 May 1984.

29. Des Keegan, "It's Time for the Silent Majority to Speak up", *Australian,* 17 December 1985.

30. Laksiri Jayasuriya, "Into the Mainstream", *Australian Society*, 1 March 1984, p.25.

31. Andrew Jakubowicz, "Ethnicity, Multiculturalism and Neoconservatism", p.43.

32. Marie de Lepervanche, "Immigrants and Ethnic Groups", in Sol Encel and Lois Bryson (eds), *Australian Society,* Longman Cheshire, Melbourne, 1984, p.184.

33. Andrew Jakubowicz, "State and Ethnicity: Multi-culturalism as Ideology", in James Jupp (ed.), *Ethnic Politics in Australia,* Allen & Unwin, Sydney, 1984, p.27.

34. *Ibid.*, p.24.

35. Joan Dugdale, *Radio Power: A History of 3ZZZ Access Radio,* Hyland House, Melbourne, 1979, p.88.

36. *Ibid.*, p. xi.

37. Marie de Lepervanche, "Immigrants and Ethnic Groups", p.189.
38. Andrew Jakubowicz, "The Politics of Ethnicity", paper delivered to the Australian Political Studies Association 22nd Annual Conference, Australian National University, 27-29 August 1980.
39. Review of Post Arrival Programs and Services (The Galbally Report), *Migrant Services and Programs,* p.5.
40. Stephen Castles, Mary Kalantzis and Bill Cope, "W(h)ither Multiculturalism?", *Australian Society,* October 1986, p.10.

Reading 7 Mistaken Identity (Stephen Castles, Mary Kalantzis, Bill Cope, Michael Morrissey)

1. Benedict Anderson, "Narrating the Nation", *Times Literary Supplement,* 13 June 1986.
2. Andrew Jakubowicz, "State and Ethnicity: Multiculturalism as Ideology", in James Jupp (ed.), *Ethnic Politics in Australia,* George Allen & Unwin, Sydney, 1984.
3. Richard White, *Inventing Australia*, George Allen & Unwin, Sydney, 1981, p.83.
4. Humphrey McQueen, *A New Britannia*, Penguin, Ringwood, 1970.
5. White, *Inventing Australia*, p.146.
6. See Tom Nairn, *The Break-up of Britain*, Verso, London, 1981.
7. Gellner, *Nations and Nationalism,* Basil Blackwell, Oxford, 1983, p.1.
8. Nira Yuval-Davis, "Ethnic/Racial Divisions and the Nation in Britain and Australia", *Capital and Class,* 28, 1986, p.92.
9. J. Lyng, *Non-Britishers in Australia*, p.1.
10. W.E.H. Stanner, "The Australian Way of Life", in W.V. Aughterson (ed.), *Taking Stock*, Cheshire, Melbourne, 1958, p.8.
11. White, *Inventing Australia*, ch.10.

Reading 8 Contesting Australia (Gail Reekie)

1. Not all of the historians cited have explicitly placed their work in the context of histories of the nation, and those who have referred to the contours of masculinist Australian history have typically done so in passing before rightly getting on with the job of simply writing women's history. This synthesis therefore turns the mirrors of the kaleidoscope to draw meanings and patterns from a multitude of random historical fragments.
2. Heather Goodall *et al., Labour History*, 54, 1988, pp. 114-9, Jill Julius Matthews, "A Female of All Things: Women and the Bicentenary", in *Making the Bicentenary*, Susan Janson and Stuart Macintyre (eds). Special issue of *Australian Historical Studies*, 91, 1988, pp.90-102.
3. For example, "Problems in Australian History", a course offered in

1989. Topics cover the white invasion, the penal colony, the "slave society", the environment, urbanisation, the "working man's paradise", imperialism, World War I and its effects, the depression, the Japanese advance, and World War II. The work of feminist historians (a bare handful of references compared to male historians) is only drawn on where it contributes to these debates. Discussion of issues such as the family, feminism, sexuality, reproduction, sexual violence, domestic labour or even "women" in Australian history is entirely absent. Feminist contributions to historical debate have been omitted in the listing of "diverse Australian historiographical traditions".

4. Benedict Anderson, *Reflections on the Origin and Spread of Nationalism,* Verso, London, 1982; Richard White, *Inventing Australia: Images and Identity 1688-1980,* George Allen & Unwin, Sydney, 1981.

5. White, *Inventing Australia*, pp.131-3.

6. Carole Pateman, "The Theoretical Subversiveness of Feminism", in *Feminist Challenges: Social and Political Theory*, Carole Pateman and Elizabeth Gross (eds), Allen & Unwin, Sydney, 1986, pp.1-10.

7. Pateman, "The Theoretical Subversiveness of Feminism", p.10.

8. Shirley Fitzgerald, *Rising Damp: Sydney 1870-1890,* Oxford University Press, Melbourne, 1987.

9. Beverley Kingston, *The Oxford History of Australia. Volume 3. 1860-1900. Glad, Confident Morning,* Oxford University Press, Melbourne, 1988, pp.115-21.

10. Heather Radi, "Feminist Histories", *Australian Feminist Studies,* 7/8, 1988, pp.231-4.

11. Penny Russell, "Family Life and Class Formation in Nineteenth Century Melbourne", *Lilith,* 5, 1988, p.115.

12. Kingston, *Glad, Confident Morning,* p.173.

13. Judith Godden, "A New Look at the Pioneer Woman", *Hecate,* 5, 1979, pp.7-20.

14. Marilyn Lake, "Building Themselves Up with Aspros: Pioneer Women Re-Assessed", *Hecate,* 8, 1981, pp.7-19.

15. Marilyn Lake, *The Limits of Hope: Soldier Settlement in Victoria 1915-1938,* Oxford University Press, Melbourne, 1987; "Helpmate, Slave and Housewife: Women in Rural Families 1870-1930", in *Families in Colonial Australia*, Patricia Grimshaw, Chris McConville and Ellen McEwan (eds), Allen & Unwin, Sydney, 1985, pp.173-85.

16. Carmel Shute, "Heroines and Heroes: Sexual Mythology in Australia 1914-1918", *Hecate,* 1, 1975, pp.7-22.

17. Kay Schaffer, *Women and the Bush: Forces of Desire in the Australian Cultural Tradition,* Cambridge University Press, Cambridge, 1988.

18. Rosemary Pringle, "Octavius Beale and the Ideology of the

Birthrate", *Refractory Girl,* 3, 1973, pp.19-27; Kieren Reiger, *The Disenchantment of the Home: Modernizing the Australian Family 1880-1940*, Oxford University Press, Melbourne, 1985.

19. Judith Allen, "From Women's History to a History of the Sexes", in *Australian Studies: A Survey*, James Walter (ed.), Oxford University Press, Melbourne, 1989.

20. Julia Kristeva, "Women's Time", *Signs,* 7, 1981, pp.13-35, Trans. Alice Jardine and Harry Blake.

21. Marilyn Lake, "The Politics of Respectability: Identifying the Masculinist Context", *Historical Studies,* 56, 1986, pp.116-31.

22. Genevieve Lloyd, "Selfhood, War and Masculinity", in *Feminist Challenges*, Pateman and Gross (eds) , pp.63-76.

23. Marilyn Frye, *The Politics of Reality: Essays in Feminist Theory,* Crossing Press, Trumansberg, NY, 1983.

Reading 9   The Politics of Respectability (Marilyn Lake)

1. Notable exceptions in Australian history are D. Walker, "The Getting of Manhood", and R. White, "The Importance of Being Man", in P. Spearritt and D. Walker (eds), *Australian Popular Culture,* Allen & Unwin, Sydney, 1979. In American history there is B. Ehrenreich's innovative, *The Hearts of Men*, New York, 1983; in New Zealand, J. Phillips, "Mummy's Boys: Pakeha Men and Male Culture in New Zealand", contained in a collection ironically entitled *Women in New Zealand Society*, P. Bunkle and B. Hughes (eds), Auckland, 1980.

2. "Contribution history" is Gerda Lerner's phrase, describing history which looks at women's contribution to "recognised social and political movements and categories"; G. Lerner, "Placing Women in History: a 1975 Perspective", in B.A. Carroll (ed.), *Liberating Women's History,* Urbana, Ill., 1976.

3. G. Davison, "Sydney and the bush: an Urban Context for the Australian Legend", *Historical Studies*, 18, 1978.

4. R. White, *Inventing Australia*, Allen & Unwin, Sydney, 1981, p.100.

5. A.W. Jose, *The Romantic Nineties*, Sydney, 1933, p.34; see also George Taylor's portrayal of the "Bohemian boys" in *Those Were the Days,* Sydney, 1918.

6. F. Adams, *The Australians*, London, 1982, p.144.

7. C. Hall, "The Early Formation of Victorian Domestic Ideology", in S. Burmann (ed.), *Fit Work for Women*, London, 1982.

8. *Ibid.*, p. 23.

9. M. Grellier, "The Family: Some Aspects of its Demography and Ideology in Mid-Nineteenth Century Western Australia", in C.T. Stannage (ed.), *A New History of Western Australia*, UWA Press, Nedlands, 1981, pp.498-9.

10. YMCA, First Annual Report: contained in *100th Annual Report,* McLaren Collection, Baillieu Library, University of Melbourne.

11. *Bulletin*, 3 November 1888.
12. R. Bedford, *Naught to Thirty-Three*, new edn, Melbourne University Press, Melbourne, 1976, p.73.
13. Adams, *op. cit.,* p.86.
14. R. Ward, *The Australian Legend,* Oxford Unversity Press, Melbourne, 1958, pp.97-100.
15. H. Reynolds, *The Other Side of the Frontier*, James Cook University, Townsville, 1981, p.58. It is clear that some European men established long-lasting relationships with Aboriginal women, but I think it is safe to assume that most frontiersmen abandoned the women and their "half-caste" children.
16. H. Lawson, "The Sliprails and the Spur", in *Winnowed Verse*, Sydney, new edn, 1944.
17. Ward, *op. cit.* p.199.
18. H. Lawson, "The Vagabond", in *Winnowed Verse.*
19. F. Adams, "The Men of the Nation", in *Songs of the Army of the Night*, Sydney, 1888.
20. W.G. Spence, *Australia's Awakening,* Sydney, 1909, and *Hammer*, 16 January 1892, quoted in N. Ebbels (ed.), *The Australian Labor Movement 1850-1907*, Sydney, 1960, pp.121, 166.
21. S. Lawson, *The Archibald Paradox,* Penguin, Ringwood, 1983, p.197.
22. P. McDonald, *Marriage in Australia*, Canberra, 1975, pp.113, 155.
23. Introduction to K. Daniels *et al.* (eds), *Women in Australia. An Annotated Guide to the Records,* AGPS, Canberra, 1977, p.xiii.
24. See, for example, the cartoon reprinted in J. Mackinolty and H. Radi (eds), *In Pursuit of Justice*, Hale & Iremonger, Sydney, 1979, p.106.
25. J.D. Bollen, *Protestantism and Social Reform in New South Wales 1890-1910,* Melbourne University Press, Melbourne, 1972, p.51.
26. *Bull-Ant,* 19 March 1891.
27. See M. Lake, "The Limits of Hope: Soldier Settlement in Victoria 1915-1938", Ph.D. thesis, Monash University, 1984, pp.66-7.
28. W. Lane, *The Workingman's Paradise,* Brisbane, 1892, p.45; advertisement from first paperbound edition, 1893.
29. Report of the Royal Commission on the Basic Wage, *Commonwealth Parliamentary Papers,* 1920-21, vol.4.
30. Lake, *op. cit.,* p.264.

Reading 11   The Australian Legend (Russel Ward)

1. B. Fitzpatrick, *The British Empire in Australia*, Macmillan, Melbourne, 1941, pp. 384-8; N.G. Butlin, "Company Ownership of New South Wales Pastoral Stations", *Historical Studies: Australia and New Zealand,* May 1950; and cp. "Times Special Correspondent", *Letters from Queensland*, London, 1893, pp.70-2.
2. H.W. Haygarth, *Recollections of Bush Life in Australia during a Residence of Eight Years in the Interior*, London, 1848, p.96ff.

3. *Gallops and Gossips in the Bush of Australia*, London, 1854, p.58.

4. B. Fitzpatrick, *op. cit.*, p.59; E.G. Shann, *Economic History of Australia*, Sydney, 1948, pp.207-11, 233.

5. John Henderson, Excursions and Adventures in New South Wales; with Pictures of Squatting Life in the Bush, etc., 2 vols., London, 1851, vol. 2, p.244; "Many most distressing cases came within my own knowledge; and when we hear of such things as of an old military officer reduced to the necessity of letting himself out to hire as a bullock driver; or of a shepherd suing his master for a year's wage . . . the pass at which things had arrived can be imagined."

6. "Tom Collins" (Joseph Furphy), *Such is Life*, Sydney, 1948 edn, p.205ff.

7. Vance Palmer, *Legend of the Nineties*, Melbourne University Press, Melbourne, 1954, p.109.

8. Percy F. Rowland, *The New Nation,* London, 1903, p.119 ff.

9. cp. F. Adams, *The Australians: A Social Sketch*, London 1893, pp.12-13; "In another hundred years the man of the Interior — the veritable 'bushman' — will be as far removed from the man of the sea-slope as the Northern Frenchman from the Southern, as the Castilian from the Andalusian . . .", and *passim*.

10. R.E.N. Twopeny, *Town Life in Australia*, London, 1883, p.99. Discussing larrikinism (in 1883) the author wonders, in vain, how it can be combated in "communities whose sympathies are so essentially democratic as those of Victoria and New South Wales — for in Adelaide the police has still the upper hand".

11. This version is from *The "Native Companion" Songster*, Brisbane, 1889.

12. G.F. Moore, *Diary of Ten Years' Eventful Life of an Early Settler in Western Australia*, etc., London, 1884, pp.91, 183-5, 196-7.

13. *Three Colonies of Australia*, etc., London, 1852, pp.307-8.

14. *First Report of South Australian Company*, London, 1837, 2nd Supplement, p.25.

15. E.W. Landor, *The Bushman: or, Life in a New Country,* London, 1847, p.263.

16. Anthony Trollope, *Australia and New Zealand*, Melbourne, 1876 p.69.

17. "An Emigrant Mechanic" (Alexander Harris), *Settlers and Convicts,* C.M.H. Clark (ed.) Melbourne, 1953 (first published 1847), p.24.

18. Trollope, *Australia and New Zealand,* p.202.

19. From about 1866 to 1885. See W.P. Webb, *The Great Plains,* Oxford, 1931, pp.205-7.

20. "An Emigrant Mechanic", *op.cit.,* p.26; Andrew Crombie, *After Sixty Years, or Recollections of an Australian Bushman*, Brisbane, 1927, pp.109-10.

Reading 12   *Sydney and the Bush (Graeme Davison)*

For more detailed footnoting the reader is referred to the original version of this chapter in *Historical Studies*, 18, 71, October 1978.

1. Lawson to G. Robertson, 21 January 1917 as quoted in Colin Roderick (ed.), *Henry Lawson, Collected Verse,* vol. 1, 1885-1950, Angus & Robertson, Sydney, 1967, p.423.

2. Russel Ward, *The Australian Legend,* Oxford University Press, Melbourne, 1958, *passim.*

3. N.D. Harper, "The Rural and Urban Frontiers", *Historical Studies*, 10, 40, May 1963, p.421; M. Roe, "The Australian Legend", *Meanjin*, 21, 1962, p.364.

4. Geoffrey Serle, *From Deserts the Prophets Come,* Heinemann, Melbourne, 1973, p.58.

5. "The Status of Literature in New South Wales II, How the Publishers Look at it", *Centennial Magazine*, 2, 2, September 1889, p.92.

6. Fred H. Bathurst, "Reporters and their Work", *ibid.*, 2, 7, February 1890, pp.498-502.

7. On the general characteristics of the "zone-in-transition" see E.W. Burgess, "The Growth of the City: An Introduction to a Research Project", R.E. Park, E.W. Burgess, and R.D. McKenzie (eds), *The City,* Chicago, 1925, pp.54-6.

8. "Titus Salt", "The Row in Our Boarding House", *Bulletin*, 19 December 1891.

9. "Faces in the Street", *Bulletin,* 28 July 1888 (my emphasis).

10. *Dawn,* 5 November 1889.

11. "Army of the Rear", *Bulletin,* 12 May 1888.

12. Sylvia Lawson, "J.F. Archibald", *Australian Dictionary of Biography*, vol.3, pp.43-8.

13. "With Dickens" (1900), *Collected Verse,* vol.1, p.389; J. le Gay Brereton, *Knocking Round,* Sydney, 1930, p.5.

14. G.R. Sims, *My Life. Sixty Years Recollections of Bohemian London,* London, 1917, pp.111, 135-7, 332; *Dagonet Ballads*, London, 1881; *Bulletin,* 12 February 1887, 6 July 1889.

15. James Thomson, *The City of Dreadful Night,* 2nd edn, London, 1894.

16. Henry Lawson, "Straight Talk", *Albany Observer*, 1890 in his *Autobiographical and Other Writings, 1887-1922*, p.11.

17. *Ibid.*, p.9. Compare C. Semmler, *The Banjo of the Bush,* 2nd edn, Sydney, 1974, ch.4-6.

18. "Clancy of the Overflow", 1889.

19. E.J. Brady, "Personalia", Brady Papers, M.L.

20. *Bull Ant,* 21 August 1890, *Rhymes from the Mines*, Sydney, 1896.

21. *Bulletin*, 1 June 1901, reprinted in *Downward?*, Sydney, 1903.

22. C. Mann (ed.), *The Stories of Henry Lawson,* First Series, Sydney, 1964, p.191.

23. A.G. Stephens, "Henry Lawson", *Art in Australia,* Sydney, 1922,

reprinted in C. Roderick (ed.), *Henry Lawson Criticism 1894-1971,* Angus & Robertson, Sydney, 1972, p.217.

24. "Borderland" (later re-titled "Up the Country"), *Bulletin*, 9 July 1892.
25. B. Nesbitt, "Literary Nationalism and the 1890s", *Australian Literary Studies,* 5, 1, May 1971, pp.3-17.
26. V. Palmer, *A.G. Stephens: His Life and Works,* Melbourne, 1941, pp.235-6.
27. W.D. Flinn to G. Black, 14 January 1892, Black Papers.
28. G.A. Taylor, *Those Were the Days,* Sydney, 1918, *Henry Lawson, by his Mates,* p.63.

Reading 13   The Pioneer Legend (J.B. Hirst)

1. Taken from *The Song of the Manly Man and other Verses,* London, 1908.
2. Robert Caldwell, *The Pioneers and other Poems,* Adelaide, 1898.
3. *Argus*, 2 September 1890.
4. *Mt Alexander Mail*, 20 March 1903.
5. This study is chiefly confined to these three colonies and states.
6. Old Colonists Association, *An Account of the Celebration of the Jubilee Year of South Australia* (1886), Adelaide, 1887; G. Serle, *The Rush to be Rich*, Melbourne University Press, Melbourne, 1971, p.236.
7. M. Aveling, "A History of the Australian Natives Association 1871-1900", Ph.D. thesis, Monash University, 1970, pp.103, 108; *National Australian*, March 1886, p.1, April 1886, pp.13, 17, July 1886, p.13, September 1886, pp.7-9; *Australian*, March 1887, p.10, March 1888, p.9.
8. 21 May 1898; 11 June 1898.
9. T.T. Reed (ed.), *The Poetical Works of Henry Kendall*, Adelaide, 1966, pp.198, 378, 438-9.
10. *The Collected Verse of A.B. Paterson,* Angus & Robertson,Sydney, 1921, pp.132-6. The poem first appeared in book form in *Rio Grande's Last Race and Other Verses*, Sydney, 1902.
11. Colin Roderick (ed.), *Henry Lawson, Autobiographical and Other Writing,* Sydney, 1972, p.6-8.
12. Colin Roderick (ed.), *Henry Lawson, Collected Verse,* vol.1, Angus & Robertson, Sydney, 1967, p.56.
13. Colin Roderick (ed.), *Henry Lawson, Short Stories and Sketches 1888-1922,* Angus & Robertson, Sydney, 1972, pp.24-5.
14. Lawson, *Collected Verse*, pp.361-3.
15. "Crime in the Bush", *Autobiographical and Other Writings,* pp.32-6.
16. *The Collected Verse of G. Essex Evans,* Sydney, 1928, pp.2-3, 89-91.
17. A.A. Phillips, *The Australian Tradition*, Cheshire, Melbourne, 1958, pp.43-8.

18. Lawson, *Collected Verse,* pp. 400-1.
19. Lawson, *Short Stories and Sketches*, p.544.
20. *Ibid.*, pp.107-9, 390, 731.
21. *Ibid.*, pp.431-2.
22. In his contrived contest with Paterson over the nature of bush life, Lawson mocked the view that "the bush was better in the 'good old droving days' ", *Collected Verse*, p.214, but he shared Paterson's romanticism more often than not.
23. *Collected Verse of A.B. Paterson,* pp.41-3.
24. *Empire*, 2, 4, May 1854; G. Serle, *The Golden Age,* Melbourne, 1963, p.133.
25. *Bulletin*, 21 January 1888, reprinted in Ian Turner, *The Australian Dream,* Sun Books, Melbourne, 1968, pp.226-34. Barry Andrews, *Price Warung* (William Astley), Boston, 1976, pp.99-101.
26. Lawson, *Collected Verse*, p.75.
27. *Age*, 16 August 1905.
28. Kay Daniels *et al.* (eds), *Women in Australia. An Annotated Guide to the Records*, AGPS, Canberra, 1977, pp.xxvii-xxviii.
29. *The Passionate Heart*, Sydney, 1918. See also Miles Franklin and Dymphna Cusack, *Pioneers on Parade,* Sydney, 1939, whose plot turns on the convict origins of a pioneer family.
30. *Argus*, 29 September 1909. Victorian Bush Nursing Association, *Report of the Central Council*, Melbourne, 1918, p.3.
31. *Collected Verse of G. Essex Evans*, pp.252-3.
32. *School Paper,* Grades III and IV, April 1924.
33. Victorian Education Department, *Education Gazette and Teachers' Aid*, 18 February 1916, p.30.
34. See B. Wannan (ed.), *Pioneers: Verse, Ballad, Picture,* Lansdowne, Melbourne, 1975.
35. *The Australasian Pioneers' Club Rules*, Sydney, 1910. The Club was founded following a meeting on 2 May 1910 convened by Mr Douglas Hope Johnstone, a direct descendant of Lieutenant George Johnstone who arrived with the First Fleet. Travers Burrows, *The Genesis of the Pioneers' Association of South Australia,* Adelaide, 1946.
36. Russel Ward, *The Australian Legend*, Oxford University Press, Melbourne, 1958, p.211.
37. Henry Lawson, *Short Stories and Sketches*, pp.41-2, 63, 103-4, 269, 275, 321-3, 417, 502, 507, 585; *Collected Verse,* pp.115-19.
38. "The Australian Legend", *Meanjin*, September 1962, pp.366-9.

Reading 14   *Urbanisation in Australian History (Sean Glynn)*

1. W.K. Hancock, *Australia*, Ernest Benn, London, 1930.
2. Russel Ward, *The Australian Legend*, Oxford University Press, Melbourne, 1958, pp.1-2.

3. R.W. Council, "Images of Australia", *Quadrant*, March 1968, p.18.

4. A. Birch and D.S. Macmillan (eds), *The Sydney Scene, 1788-1960*. Melbourne University Press, Melbourne, 1962, p.177.

5. For example J. Furphy, *Such is Life*, 1903; B. O'Dowd, *The Bush*, 1912; see later comment on C.J. Dennis.

6. Apart from *Bulletin* publications and the works of C.J. Dennis, the best known larrikin literature includes: Ambrose Pratt, *The King of the Rocks*, London, 1900 and *The Great 'Push' Experiment*, London; Louis Stone, *Jonah*, Sydney, 1911; Edward Dyson, Fac'ry 'ands, Sydney, 1912.

7. His works dealing with larrikin types included: *Songs of a Sentimental Bloke*, 1915; pocket ed, 1916; *The Moods of Ginger Mick*, 1916; pocket ed, 1916; *Doreen*, 1917; *Digger Smith*, 1918.

8. T.A. Coghlan, *General Report on the Eleventh Census of N.S.W.*, Sydney, 1894, p.181.

9. A group of late-nineteenth and early twentieth-century American writers who pointed out the evils of city life and government.

10. See Michael Cannon, *op.cit.*

11. Asa Briggs, *Victorian Cities*, Oldhams, London, 1963, p.302.

12. R.E.N. Twopeny, *Town Life in Australia*, Elliot Stock, London, 1883, p.2.

13. Asa Briggs, *op.cit.*, p.301.

14. J.D.B. Miller, *Australia*, Thames and Hudson, London, 1966, p.24.

15. Jeanne Mackenzie, *Australian Paradox*, Cheshire, Melbourne, 1961, p.125.

16. See H.N. Smith, *Virgin Land: The American West as Symbol and Myth*, Harvard University Press, Cambridge, Mass., 1950.

Reading 15   Australian Critics on Suburbia (Tim Rowse)

1. Donald Horne, *The Lucky Country*, Penguin, Ringwood, 1971, p.26.

2. Nettie to Ailsa Palmer, National Library of Australia MS 1174/1/6750, a reference given me by Humphrey McQueen.

3. Louis Esson, *The Time is Not Yet Ripe*, Philip Parsons (ed.), Currency/Methuen, Sydney, 1973, p.73.

4. "The Prophets Downcast: The Palmers and their Nationalism", *Meanjin Quarterly*, 2, 1976.

5. W.K. Hancock, *Australia*, 1961 edn, p.160.

6. "The Australian City", *New Statesman*, 21 January 1928, pp.454-6.

7. Hancock, 1928, *ibid.*, p.456.

8. Frederic Eggleston, *State Socialism*, P.S. King, London, 1932, p.331.

9. *Australia's Home*, Pelican, Ringwood, 1968, pp.12-14.

10. *The Lucky Country*, p.27.

11. *Ibid.*, p.29.

12. "Businessmen", in P. Coleman (ed.), *Australian Civilisation,* Cheshire, Melbourne, 1962, p.177.

13. *The Australian People,* Angus & Robertson, Sydney, 1972, p.193. The negative image of suburbia is often equally a negative image of women. A rough equation that seems to be employed is: women plus domesticity equals spiritual starvation. (Men plus wide open spaces plus achievement equals heroism of the Australian spirit.) The female influence in the "culture" is often taken to amount to an obsession with status and difference. Lady Macbeth has been written into this myth of mateship.

14. *Profile of Australia*, Hodder and Stoughton, 1966: Penguin, 1968. All references to Penguin edition; see pp.129-30.

15. *Ibid.*, p.131.

16. *People, Politics and Pop: Australians in the Sixties,* Ure Smith, Sydney, 1968, p.52.

17. Hugh Stretton, *Ideas for Australian Cities,* published by the author, North Adelaide, 1970, pp.20-1.

18. Hugh Stretton, *Capitalism, Socialism and the Environment,* Cambridge University Press, Cambridge, 1976, p.202.

19. *Ibid.*, p.192.

Sources

1. James Walter, from "Studying Australia: A Review of Approaches" and "Defining Australia: A Case Study" in James Walter, ed., *Australian Studies: A Survey*. Melbourne: Oxford University Press, 1989.

2. Richard White, *Inventing Australia: Images and Identity 1688-1980*. Sydney: George Allen & Unwin, 1981.

3. John Rickard, *Australia: A Cultural History*. London: Longman, 1988.

4. Colin Tatz, *Aborigines & Uranium and Other Essays*. Melbourne: Heinemann, 1982.

5. Ros Bowden, comp., "Raised to Think White" in *Being Aboriginal: Comments, Observations and Stories from Aboriginal Australians*. Sydney: Australian Broadcasting Corporation, 1990. From an ABC Radio program made by Ros Bowden and Bill Bunbury for the ABC's Social History Unit, with the voices of Coral Edwards, Lola, Joy, Robyn, Cherie and Kevin.

6. Jock Collins, *Migrant Hands in a Distant Land: Australia's Post-War Immigration*. Sydney: Pluto Press, 1991.

7. Stephen Castles, Mary Kalantzis, Bill Cope and Michael Morrissey, *Mistaken Identity: Multiculturalism and the Demise of Nationalism in Australia*. Sydney: Pluto Press, 1988.

8. Gail Reekie, "Contesting Australia: Feminism and Histories of the Nation". Previously unpublished paper.

9. Marilyn Lake, "The Politics of Respectability: Identifying the Masculinist Context". *Historical Studies* 22, no.86 (1986):116-131.

10. Barbara Jefferis, "The Drover's Wife" in Dale Spender, ed., *Heroines: A Contemporary Anthology of Australian Women Writers*. Ringwood: Penguin, 1991.

11. Russel Ward, *The Australian Legend*. Melbourne: Oxford University Press, 1958.

12. Graeme Davison, "Sydney and the Bush: An Urban Context for the Australian Legend" in *Intruders in the Bush: The Australian Quest for Identity,* ed. John Carroll. Melbourne: Oxford University Press, 1982 (repr. 1989).

13. J.B. Hirst, "The Pioneer Legend" in *Intruders in the Bush: The Australian Quest for Identity*, ed. John Carroll. Melbourne: Oxford University Press, 1982 (repr. 1989).

14. Sean Glynn, *Urbanisation in Australian History 1788-1900*. Melbourne: Nelson, 1975.

15. Tim Rowse, "Heaven and a Hills Hoist: Australian Critics on Suburbia". *Meanjin Quarterly* 37, no.1 (1978): 3-13.